Made in America
Regaining the Productive Edge

The MIT Commission on Industrial Productivity

Michael L. Dertouzos, Chairman
Robert M. Solow, Vice-Chairman
Richard K. Lester, Executive Director
Suzanne Berger
H. Kent Bowen
Don P. Clausing
Eugene E. Covert
John M. Deutch
Merton C. Flemings
Howard W. Johnson
Thomas A. Kochan
Daniel Roos
David H. Staelin
Lester C. Thurow
James Wei
Gerald L. Wilson

Made in America
Regaining the Productive Edge

Michael L. Dertouzos
Richard K. Lester
Robert M. Solow
and
The MIT Commission on Industrial Productivity

The MIT Press
Cambridge, Massachusetts
London, England

Fourth Printing, 1989

This book was set in New Baskerville by The MIT Press and printe
by Halliday Lithograph in the United States of America.

Library of Congress Cataloging-in-Publication Data

Made in America: regaining the productive edge
  Michael L. Dertouzos . . . [et al.].
    p. cm.
  Bibliography: p.
  Includes index.
  ISBN 0-262-04100-6
  1. Industrial productivity—United States. 2. Technological inn
Economic aspects—United States. 3. Research, Industrial—Uni
4. Competition, International.
  I. Dertouzos, Michael L.
  HC110.I52M34   1989
  338'.06'0973—dc19

Contents

Preface   ix
The Commission Staff   xi

1

Introduction   1

Semiconductors, Computers, and Copiers   9
Commercial Aircraft   11
Consumer Electronics   12
Steel   14
Chemicals   15
Textiles   16
Automobiles   18
Machine Tools   20
Education and Training   21

2

The United States in the World Economy   23

A Changing World   23
Productivity and Productivity Growth   26
Manufacturing Productivity   30
Productive Performance   32
Productive Performance and the Trade Deficit   33
Productive Performance and the Macroeconomic Environment   35
Why Manufacturing Matters   39
Diagnosing the Problem   42

3

Outdated Strategies   46

The Mass-Production System   47
Parochialism   49

4

Short Time Horizons   53

5

Technological Weaknesses in Development and Production   67

Designing for Manufacturability and Quality   69
Teamwork in the Product-Development Process   70
A Focus on the Manufacturing Process   72
Continuous Improvement   74
Who Is to Blame?   77

6

Neglect of Human Resources   81

Patterns of Education and Training   83
Formal Schooling   84
Training in the Firm   87
Education and Training Patterns   88
Retraining   90
Future Challenges   92

7

Failures of Cooperation   94

Cooperation within the Firm   95
Labor-Management Relations   98
Vertical Linkages   99
Horizontal Linkages and the Public Good   105

8

Government and Industry at Cross-Purposes   108

Too Much or Too Little?   108
Regulatory Policy   110

The Technological Infrastructure   112
National Defense   114

9

Emerging Patterns of Best Industrial Practice   117

Simultaneous Improvement in Quality, Cost, and Delivery   118
Staying Close to the Customer   119
Closer Relations with Suppliers   120
Using Technology for Strategic Advantage   121
Flatter and Less Compartmentalized Organizations   122
Innovative Human-Resource Policies   124
Obstacles to the Diffusion of Best Practices   126

10

Imperatives for a More Productive America   129

Long-Term Trends   129
Five Imperatives   131
Focusing on the New Fundamentals of Manufacturing   132
Cultivating a New Economic Citizenship in the Work Force   134
Blending Cooperation and Individualism   138
Learning to Live in the World Economy   141
Providing for the Future   143

11

Strategies for Industry, Labor, and Government   147

Strategies for Industry   148
Strategies for Labor   151
Strategies for Government   151

12

How Universities Should Change   156

Changes in the Engineering Curriculum   159
Changes in the Management Curriculum   160
Research   163
Awareness   165

13

Conclusion   166

INDUSTRY STUDIES

A
The Automobile Industry   171

B
The Chemical Industry   188

C
The Commercial-Aircraft Industry   201

D
The Consumer-Electronics Industry   217

E
The Machine-Tool Industry   232

F
The Semiconductor, Computer, and Copier Industries   248

G
The Steel Industry   278

H
The Textile Industry   288

Appendix I
Policy Recommendations Presented in Related Studies   303

Appendix II
The MIT Commission on Industrial Productivity   320

Notes   331
Index   341

Preface

Late in 1986 the Massachusetts Institute of Technology convened its first commission on a major national issue since World War II. We did this to address a decline in U.S. industrial performance perceived to be so serious as to threaten the nation's economic future.

Now, after two years of probing in detail into eight manufacturing industries, conducting hundreds of interviews and visits to firms spanning three continents, and hearing the testimony of chief executives and labor leaders, we have landed on what is to us a new and somewhat surprising territory: What seemed an impossibly messy undertaking at the beginning has acquired form and has revealed patterns. And the early dissonance caused by the different views inherent in our diverse professional specialties has yielded to a shared vision of a new industrial America, potentially more productive and a leader in tomorrow's world economy.

Our journey was stimulating and highly educational but not easy. In the mid-1980s the public discussion of competitiveness was brimming with conflicting and often visceral expert pronouncements. Countless proposed causes underlying America's plight were incongruously pitted against proud assertions of the nation's continued economic leadership. And anecdotes that could not be casually generalized were complemented by studies that were either designed narrowly to preserve disciplinary integrity or broadly to permit macroscopic analysis.

From the beginning we believed that our contributions would lie not so much in discovering something new, since so very much had already been said, but rather in separating the important and factual from the unimportant and conjectural on the basis of a detailed bottom-up study of specific industries. It is thus that we addressed MIT President Paul Gray's charge: to identify what happened to U.S. industrial performance and what we and others might do to help improve the situation. Accordingly, this book is authored by all the Commissioners. It was born out of our collective strength and would not have happened under the narrower focus of our technologists, our economists, or our management specialists.

In carrying out our task, one individual's contributions stand out: Richard K. Lester, the Executive Director of the Commission, spent almost his entire time on Commission business, directed our staff, which cumulatively comprised some thirty people, energetically contributed his creative ideas, and did most of the work in translating the Commission's work into this book.

Commissioner Suzanne Berger made extensive contributions to our work and to the writing of the book, particularly on matters concerning human resources; Commissioner Lester Thurow helped introduce the multiple dimensions of the problem; and Vice-Chairman Robert M. Solow steadily contributed his economic expertise to our meetings and to the book, notwithstanding a Nobel Prize diversion in the middle of the Commission's term. The Commission staff also gave much of their time and energy to help achieve our common goal.

Thanks also go to the thirty members of the MIT faculty who participated with the Commission in several of its study groups, and to the many other members of the MIT community who gave freely of their time and expertise. We would also like to thank the many experts in industry, government, and academia, too numerous to mention by name, whom we consulted and from whom we learned so much during the course of our work.

Finally, we are indebted to the Alfred P. Sloan and the William and Flora Hewlett Foundations for providing the funds that made this study possible.

Michael L. Dertouzos
Chairman, The MIT Commission on Industrial Productivity

The Commission Staff

A large team was involved in the work that led to this book, and none played a more valuable part than the Commission's staff. Deputy Staff Director Kirk Bozdogan and staff member Artemis March took leading roles in preparing the industry studies and helped to develop the Commission's research agenda. Staff members Charles Ferguson, Cathie Jo Martin, and Jim Womack also played important roles in the Commission's industry studies. Richard Kazis made valuable contributions to the Commission's work on education and training. Terry Hill was our able rapporteur. Robert Haavind carefully and patiently helped summarize the work of the Commission's industry-study groups. Over twenty talented graduate students also assisted the Commission's research; Stephen Filippone and Brian Sliker deserve special mention for their skill and hard work. Late in the process, the entire manuscript benefited from the skilled and diligent editorial review of Brian Hayes. Carol Robinson ably assisted in manuscript preparation. Last, but certainly not least, Ginny Sherbs served with distinction as the Commission's administrative coordinator; in circumstances that were never less than challenging, she kept the Commission running smoothly.

Made in America
Regaining the Productive Edge

1

Introduction

To live well, a nation must produce well. In recent years many observers have charged that American industry is not producing as well as it ought to produce, or as well as it used to produce, or as well as the industries of some other nations have learned to produce. If the charges are true and if the trend cannot be reversed, then sooner or later the American standard of living must pay the penalty.

The indictment of American industry has multiple counts. Products made in the United States are said to be inferior to foreign goods; this complaint extends both to consumer products, such as cars and clothing, and to industrial commodities, such as steel and semiconductor chips. American factories are accused of inefficiency; the work force is said to be indifferent and ill-trained; and managers are criticized for seeking quick profits rather than pursuing more-appropriate long-term goals. Designers, engineers, and the research community are also named in the indictment, on the grounds that America's best technology has been surpassed in many fields.

Some of the charges can be backed up by quantitative evidence. The United States buys far more overseas than it can sell in other countries, which has resulted in a huge current-account deficit: $161 billion in 1987. Most of this imbalance is generated by trade in manufactured goods. Growth in productivity, a crucial indicator of industrial performance, has been slower in the past 15 years than it was for at least two decades before; moreover, the rate of productivity improvement in the United States has fallen behind that in several Western European and Asian nations. Certain American industries that once dominated world commerce—automobiles and steel come immediately to mind—have lost much of their market share both at home and abroad; in a few industries, such as consumer electronics, the American presence in the market has all but disappeared.

These developments have provoked much anxiety in the United States. The fears of economic decline are surely linked to larger doubts about the nation's ability to retain its influence and standing in the world at large. (Indeed, it is widely acknowledged that political and military power depend ultimately on economic vitality.)

But there is also a defense of American industry. Recent economic news has been encouraging. The U.S. economy has been expanding at a healthy rate since the early 1980s, which makes this the longest peacetime expansion in the twentieth century. Inflation, which caused great unrest in the 1970s, was brought under control several years ago and remains fairly low. Unemployment is also down, and large numbers of new jobs have been created. A decline in the value of the dollar against other major currencies has contributed to a surge in exports of manufactured goods. There is also some evidence of a recent recovery in the rate of productivity growth for the manufacturing sector. In late 1988 America's factories were operating at close to full capacity, and there were signs that the trade deficit had finally begun to shrink.

Some observers conclude from these positive developments that there is nothing fundamentally wrong with American industry. The trade deficit and the other signs of apparent deterioration, according to this view, are results not of intrinsic deficiencies in industrial performance but rather of macroeconomic factors, such as international differences in rates of economic growth, fluctuations in currency-exchange prices, and the budget deficit of the U.S. government. A further argument on the side of the defense is that the rise and fall of industries is a natural part of economic evolution. At any given time a certain number of industries are sure to be in decline; thus, to make a fair assessment of the situation, one must be careful to avoid bias in the selection of industries.

Late in 1986 MIT established its Commission on Industrial Productivity to study the nation's industrial performance. The Commission sought first to weigh the evidence supporting the optimistic and the pessimistic views. We needed to find out whether there really are pervasive weaknesses in U.S. industrial practice. If weaknesses could be identified, we wanted to know their causes. We also looked at changes in the international economic system and considered how those changes might alter the requirements for successful industrial performance in the future. The ultimate aim was to formulate a set of recommendations that would help the nation to sustain strong growth in productivity.

As we undertook our studies, we knew we were not the first to explore this territory. Other groups and individuals were at work in the field, and many had already reported their findings. (A brief summary of these findings is presented in appendix I.) Still, we felt we could make a distinctive contribution. We are an academic body; the 16 Commissioners are all members of the MIT faculty. This circumstance gives us a special franchise to address one major factor in the equation that governs national productivity: education and the development of human resources.

We are also a highly interdisciplinary team. The Commission includes economists, technologists, and experts on organization, management, and political science. From the outset we drew on all of these perspectives in the belief that no single discipline could have a monopoly on wisdom in such a complex realm. It is also worth noting that members of the Commission have direct experience in industry through consulting and other work done outside the academic world.

The most important and most distinctive characteristic of our study was our determination to take a bottom-up approach. Our main focus was the nation's production system: the organizations, the plant, the equipment, and the people, from factory workers to senior executives, that combine to conceive, design, develop, produce, market, and deliver goods and services to the customer. Other examinations of U.S. competitiveness have concentrated on the wider business environment. Some have looked primarily at macroeconomic issues: at aggregate levels of income, spending, and employment and at the fiscal and monetary policies that affect these things. Others have emphasized laws and policies concerning international trade, taxes, antitrust, protection of the environment, rights to intellectual property, and so on.

In choosing to focus on the production system itself we did not underestimate the importance of macroeconomic issues and other factors that regulate the economy in the large; on the contrary, we return to them repeatedly in the course of this report. But we are convinced that high-level economic trends and policies alone cannot account for the current state of U.S. industry. To understand what has been happening to American productivity, one must know what has been happening on the shop floor, in the laboratory, in the boardroom, and in the classroom.

In order to gain the necessary microeconomic knowledge, we decided to start by examining specific firms and industries and to work up to more general conclusions and recommendations. Accordingly, we chose eight sectors of the economy for detailed study: automobiles; chemicals; commercial aircraft; the closely related industries of computers, semiconductors, and copiers; consumer electronics; machine tools; steel; and textiles. One reason for selecting these particular industries was that members of the Commission knew them well from their research and consulting. The choices were also motivated by our concern that the sample be sufficiently diverse. The industries chosen differ widely in age, size, and technological sophistication; there are winners and losers in international competition, sectors dominated by a few large firms and others that are highly fragmented, process industries and discrete-product industries. Figures 1.1, 1.2, 1.3, and 1.4 compare the selected industries with respect to imports and exports, employment, and balance of trade.

All of the selected industries are in manufacturing; no services are included, nor is agriculture, mining, or construction. The reasoning behind this decision is presented fully in chapter 2. For now it will suffice to say that we believe manufacturing is crucial to the nation's economic well-being and that our findings for manufacturing can be readily extended to other sectors of the economy. Table 1.1 shows the size of each selected industry as a fraction of all manufacturing.

To complete the industry studies, eight teams were formed from members of the MIT community. Each team, headed by a Commissioner, was asked to evaluate its industry with respect to efficiency, product quality, innovativeness, adaptability, and other aspects of performance. The teams compared American practices with those abroad and contrasted successful firms with failures. They visited more than 200 companies in the U.S., Europe, and Japan, including more than 150 plant sites. They interviewed almost 550 knowledgeable practitioners and analysts in industry, government, organized labor, and universities.

Early in the course of our investigation we initiated an additional study. This ninth study team was charged with looking into education and vocational training in various countries and examined the way companies cultivate and exploit their human resources.

The Commission's study teams returned with a large mass of detailed, diverse, and sometimes contradictory evidence. Drawing

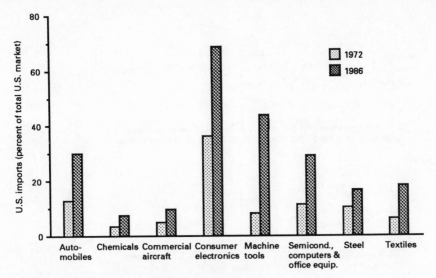

Figure 1.1 U.S. imports in industries studied
Sources: Based on data made available by the U.S. Department of Commerce, International Trade Administration, Office of Trade Information and Analysis, supplemented by data presented in U.S. Department of Commerce, International Trade Administration, *U.S. Industrial Outlook, 1988* (Washington, D.C.: U.S. Government Printing Office, 1988); and Organization for Economic Cooperation and Development, COMTAP Database.

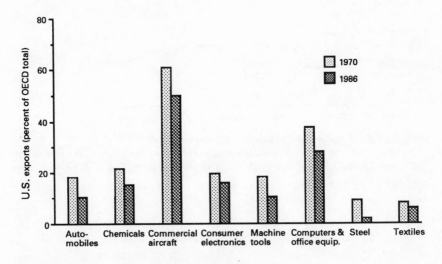

Figure 1.2 U.S. exports in industries studied
Sources: Based on data made available by the U.S. Department of Commerce, International Trade Administration, Office of Trade Information and Analysis, supplemented by data presented in U.S. Department of Commerce, International Trade Administration, *U.S. Industrial Outlook, 1988* (Washington, D.C.: U.S. Government Printing Office, 1988); and Organization for Economic Cooperation and Development, COMTAP Database.

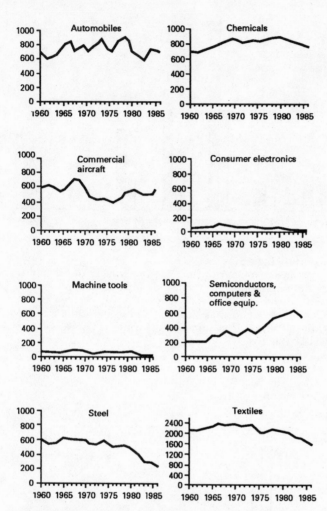

Figure 1.3   Employment trends in industries studied
Employment is in terms of thousands of employees. Source: U.S. Bureau of the Census, *Annual Survey of Manufactures, 1986* (Washington, D.C.: U.S. Government Printing Office, 1988).

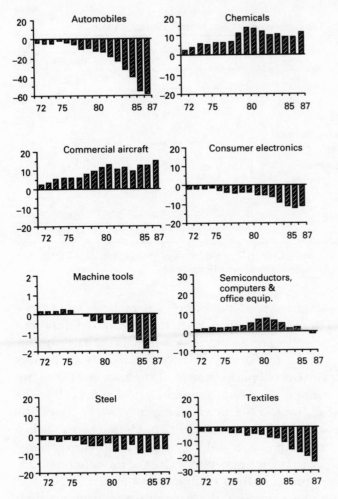

Figure 1.4   Trade balance in industries studied
Trade balances are in terms of billions of current U.S. dollars. Source: Data made available by the U.S. Department of Commerce, International Trade Administration, Office of Trade Information and Analysis.

Table 1.1

Industries studied as a percentage of U.S. manufacturing (1986)

Industry studied	Percent of U.S. manufacturing	
	Value added	Employment
Automobiles	5.7	4.3
Chemicals	9.7	4.7
Commercial aircraft	3.6	3.3
Computers, semiconductors & office equipment	3.7	3.1
Consumer electronics	0.3	0.7
Machine tools	0.3	0.3
Steel	1.5	1.5
Textiles & apparel	3.4	4.0
Total	28.2	21.9

Source: U.S. Bureau of the Census, *Annual Survey of Manufactures, 1986* (Washington, D.C.: U.S. Government Printing Office, 1988).

general conclusions from such evidence is necessarily an exercise in judgment. There is no algorithm that could take as input our mosaic of testimony, observation, cross-national comparisons, statistical analyses, and case histories and produce as output a number characterizing the overall performance of the national economy. We did not attempt to take such a mathematical approach to the problem. Instead, we worked much like a jury: we reviewed the evidence, assessed it, discussed it, and ultimately reached a verdict. The verdict is that American industry indeed shows worrisome signs of weakness. In many important sectors of the economy, U.S. firms are losing ground to their competitors abroad.

Determining the causes of these trends and gauging their significance also calls for human judgment. From our industry studies we have concluded that the setbacks many firms suffered are not merely random events or part of the normal process by which firms constantly come and go; they are symptoms of more systematic and pervasive ills. We believe the situation will not be remedied simply by trying harder to do the same things that have failed to work in the past. The international business environment has changed irrevocably, and the United States must adapt its practices to this new world.

On the other hand, there is certainly no cause for despair. In the course of its work the Commission discovered many American firms that are thriving in the new economic climate and indeed are leading the way in international competition. The success of those firms suggests a vision of a new industrial America, a nation equipped to exploit the best ideas and innovations from abroad as well as its own inherent strengths.

Almost all of the conclusions reached in this book can be traced back to the work of the study teams. Their observations will be referred to again and again in subsequent chapters. It therefore seems appropriate to present synopses of the eight industry studies before we proceed further; the findings of the education panel are also outlined here. More detailed summaries of the studies are given in the latter part of this book. Longer background papers prepared by the study teams during the course of their work are being published separately.[1]

Semiconductors, Computers, and Copiers

Microelectronics began as an American industry. All of the major scientific advances that created the industry—the transistor, the semiconductor chip, computers big and little—were American advances. Its firms—IBM, Digital Equipment, Intel, Apple, Xerox—are some of the leading lights of American industry.

Yet America's share of the microelectronics market is falling rapidly. In semiconductor production the U.S. portion has fallen from 60 percent to 40 percent in less than a decade. In the case of dynamic random-access memory chips, or DRAMs, the most widely used integrated circuit, Japanese companies hold 75 percent of the market. Today the three leading merchant semiconductor companies are all Japanese: NEC, Toshiba, and Hitachi. (A merchant company makes chips for sale to others; a captive producer, in contrast, manufactures chips to satisfy only its own needs.)

In the American semiconductor industry a flash-in-the-pan pattern has become all too familiar. First a high-tech start-up firm explodes into prominence with some brilliant initial products. The firm cannot repeat its successes, however; it does not grow into an IBM. The early products become obsolete, and internal funds needed to finance growth decline as sales fall off and markets become more competitive. Then employees begin to defect to newer firms in order to make their own entrepreneurial fortunes. Proprietary knowledge is sold (often to foreign firms) to raise funds; foreign competitors use this knowledge to push prices and profits down. Unable to make the rate of return on investment expected by shareholders, the American firm exits the market.

Both at home and abroad the companies that dominate the semiconductor business are vertically integrated firms. The only difference is that the Japanese firms produce more chips than they can use internally and sell the excess on the open market. American firms such as IBM and AT&T typically produce less than they need and rely on outside sources as buffer producers to smooth the swings in the market.

The process by which the American industry lost its dominant position is clear. Whenever demand fell, the small American firms had to forego investments in order to maintain their profit margin. The Japanese companies continued to build plant capacity, and on the next cyclical recovery only they were able to service customer demand promptly. American producers began building new capacity during the up-swing but when it came on line a year or two later, it was often too late. The new plants failed to earn enough profits to finance another generation of plants. The contest was between small, single-product, inexperienced, under-financed American start-ups and the heavyweights of Japanese industry. David did not defeat Goliath.

The United States is not used to designing national strategies for helping its industries catch up with dominant producers in the rest of the world. Sematech is an attempt to do so in semiconductors; it is a research consortium of chip makers and equipment manufacturers whose goal is to develop manufacturing technology for a new generation of chips. But the effort is being conducted under cover of national defense, rather than economic necessity, which handicaps it from the start. What the military often wants in a semiconductor chip (unsurpassed performance under conditions of conflict) is not what civilian industry needs (reliability and low cost).

In contrast to semiconductors, the computer market has remained more an American preserve. The United States runs a balance-of-trade surplus in computers, although it has declined from $7 billion in 1981 to $3 billion in 1987.

Two factors have helped to defend computer markets against foreign assaults. First is an enormous investment in existing computer software. No one wants to buy computers that become obsolete or require a disruptive changeover from one software system to another. This mechanism protects whichever company gets to the market first, and it could work in favor of the Japanese if they come to dominate the first widespread civilian applications of supercomputers.

The second factor is that the American computer industry is dominated by large, well-financed firms (IBM, Digital Equipment, Hewlett-Packard). They have staying power and the size needed to exert influence over the structure of their industry. IBM, for example, has joined the Sematech consortium with the aim of helping American equipment suppliers survive as leading-edge firms. IBM recognizes that its survival depends on the survival of the semiconductor-equipment industry.

Copiers tell yet another story. It is the story of a company that had a dominant position, lost it, but now seems to be regaining some of what it lost. Xerox invented the modern copier, but by 1979 its manufacturing costs were twice those in Japan, its product-development time was twice as long, and its product-development teams required twice as many people. The resurgence began with a close look at how its own subsidiary in Japan, Fuji Xerox, was operating. By adapting what the Japanese had done, Xerox was able to regain market share even at the low end, where price competition is most intense.

Commercial Aircraft

America's commercial-aircraft industry grew up in a symbiotic relationship with government. Military aircraft financed research and development on products and processes that could often be carried over into commercial products. (The Boeing 707 began as a military transport.) Regulated airlines were guaranteed fares high enough to pay for a large engineering staff and for rapid shifts to more sophisticated aircraft.

The American industry had other advantages as well. Most of the market for commercial aircraft was in the United States. Suppliers and users worked together much as if they were in the same industrial group. Technologically sophisticated users pushed technologically sophisticated suppliers, and technological leadership was the main arena of competition. The result was an industry totally dominated by American companies. Commercial aircraft became the nation's single most important export.

A company entering the commercial-aircraft market today must put up a huge investment (from $2 billion to $4 billion), must endure long periods of negative cash flow (from 5 to 6 years), and must wait even longer until costs are recovered (from 10 to 14 years). Under these conditions no private company could break into the market. The Europeans, however, were determined to break in, and so Britain, France, and Germany organized a government-owned commercial-aircraft manufacturer, Airbus Industrie. Years have passed; billions of dollars have been invested; profits are not yet in sight; but the Airbus has become a serious competitor. In 1986 its new orders exceeded those of McDonnell Douglas, and in 1987 it accounted for 23 percent of all new orders. Without government backing, Airbus could not have survived, but the Europeans can claim that they are only doing now what the American government did 25 years ago by other means.

While a partnership between government and business was creating a new commercial-aircraft manufacturer in Europe, that partnership in the United States was fraying. Deregulation, lower fares, and higher interest rates made cost more important than technological sophistication. The airlines reduced their engineering staffs and allowed financiers to make purchasing decisions. What had been a close working relationship between suppliers and customers became an arms-length negotiating relationship.

At the same time the connection between civilian-aircraft and military-aircraft technology became more tenuous. Boeing, the major American producer of commercial aircraft, has no military orders for fighters or bombers. Even if it had orders, military aircraft are now so different from commercial aircraft that technology-transfer would be difficult. Thus there is only a distant relationship between the American government and America's principal aircraft manufacturer.

Today Boeing is the world's technological leader in commercial-aircraft manufacturing, and it has the lowest production costs, but that does not guarantee it a single sale. Airbus can rely on the financial resources of three governments to offer inducements that Boeing cannot hope to match.

Consumer Electronics

The history of consumer electronics is a history of successive retreats by American firms, with the result that foreign manufacturers have won an entire market without ever having to fight a pitched battle. The American companies may never recover the lost ground.

Radios and other audio equipment were the first product category not to be contested. In 1955, 96 percent of all radios sold in the United States were also made in the United States; by 1965 the proportion was down to 30 percent, and by 1975 it was near zero.

Then television came under attack, and again American firms retreated. Television constitutes a huge market: $6 billion, or 22 percent of all consumer-electronics products sold. By 1987 the U.S. was down to one survivor, Zenith, with a 15 percent market share.

In the battle for the market in home video recorders, the United States surrendered without ever firing a single shot. Ampex, an American company, held the original patents and was active in the professional market, but it lacked the resources in engineering and manufacturing to bring costs down to a level where home systems could be sold. Today foreign producers are moving upscale and threatening its professional market.

The sequence of American retreats has followed a stylized pattern. The American firms set high goals for return on investments. Foreign firms select a market segment and by aggressive pricing force down the return on investment while building market share. Within a short period the American firms retreat from the market segment. The foreign firms then move on to set aggressive prices in some other segment, and the Americans once again retreat.

American demands for a high return on investment run counter to the realities of world trade. In a competitive world economy those willing to work for the least (on a quality-adjusted basis) set the standards for everyone else. This applies to capital as well as to labor. If Japanese or European capital will work for a 10 percent rate of return, American firms cannot earn 15 percent unless they are that much better than their Japanese and European competitors. In a world of approximate technological parity, they are unlikely to be consistently better.

For a time American firms can retreat to market segments that still offer a high return on investment, but eventually there will be no high-profit areas left. Further retreat then becomes impossible. This point has been reached in consumer electronics, and American firms have therefore withdrawn into other electronics sectors. These can be only temporary resting places, and the next targets for attack.

The loss of the consumer-electronics industry will have wider consequences. Autos and consumer electronics are places where companies learn mass manufacturing. They are, for example, the major customers for robots; without consumer electronics it is more difficult to have a successful robot industry. Consumer electronics also buys nearly half of all the semiconductors sold in Japan, a market not available to American producers.

Steel

The American steel industry was once the largest, most modern, and most efficient in the world.   From 1975 to 1985, however, it suffered declining demand for its products, loss of market share at home, falling production and employment, and low or negative earnings.

In the postwar decades the domestic integrated producers lost their technological lead. They failed to adopt quickly the newest technologies, such as the basic oxygen furnace, continuous casting, and computer controls, as these became available in other parts of the world.   And when the advantages of the new technologies became apparent, their adoption was delayed by financial commitments to existing plants and a shortage of investment capital. When cash did become available, other investments often proved more attractive.

Another part of the American industry, the minimills like Chaparral Steel, were technological leaders. They built new mills using electric furnaces and continuous casting; they pioneered new management techniques and built cooperative labor-management relations; they scoured the world for new technologies; and they sought close connections with their customers. Close cooperation with customers was particularly important to the success of the minimills.

The integrated producers, in contrast, missed opportunities to participate in joint R&D projects with the automakers (their major customers) on such tasks as improved steel stamping. The failure of many of the large steel firms to make needed technological changes was partly the result of inertia at the upper level of management.   The firms lacked an international perspective and were characterized by a mature, relatively inflexible organizational structure.

There were also other factors. The confrontation between President Kennedy and the U.S. Steel Company in 1962 established de facto price controls on steel for more than a decade. The industry was unable to raise prices during periods of high demand, and this constraint limited profits and hence the amount of capital available for modernization. Moreover, when investments were made in U.S. steel plants, the equipment frequently took longer to get into operation and tended to be more costly than in other countries. It takes four or five years to plan, design, and build a new blast furnace in the United States, compared with three years in Japan and two years in Korea. And in the United States construction costs average $1,700 per ton of finished capacity, whereas the range is from $700 to $1,500 in other countries.

Another major burden for the American steel industry has been the antagonistic tone of labor-management relations. Until 1982 labor unions won major concessions from the steel industry in wages, benefits, and work rules. The financial consequences of these concessions contributed to the erosion of U.S. competitiveness.

Where Americans are technological leaders, they have also retained economic leadership. An example is the argon-oxygen-decarburization process used to make stainless steel. There are other success stories. In 1986 Inland Steel was the world's lowest-cost producer of cold-rolled steel coils, and Armco Steel's new vacuum degassing system produces a superior product at a cost lower than that of any other steel supplier.

Chemicals

The chemical industry is one of the most successful American industries today. It exerts world leadership in technology, places a strong emphasis on research and education, and enjoys a healthy trade surplus. Its top management is research-oriented and views superior technology as a principal competitive asset, in the tradition of the nineteenth-century European chemical giants. It is one of the few industries in the United States in which technical people can rise to the top of the corporate hierarchy. And it is highly automated, so that labor costs play a smaller role than material costs in world competition.

High oil prices, fluctuations in foreign-exchange rates, environmental regulations, excess capacity, and a cyclical downturn in the economy in the early 1980s created a financial squeeze on American chemical firms. Part of their response was to retreat from markets in the rest of the world and to sell assets, but they also reduced R&D expenditures as a fraction of sales even as sales declined. They cut back on basic research to focus on near-term,

incremental product or process improvements to improve profitability. The firms survived the financial crisis, but in the long run no
company can compete in this industry unless it is competitive in the
science underlying the industry. This requires a commitment of
money and people.

The largest chemical companies in the world today are the Big
Three in Germany (Bayer, BASF, and Hoechst) and ICI in England. They are each 30 percent to 50 percent larger than the largest
U.S. firm (Du Pont). Germany's strength in the chemical industry
is rooted in its strong scientific and engineering tradition, maintained by an educational system in which the proportion of university graduates with degrees in engineering and science is almost
twice as great as it is in the United States.

About one quarter of the American chemical industry is owned
by foreign companies. America no longer has a feedstock-cost
advantage that helps the large-scale production of low-value-added
commodity chemicals. Many leading American chemical companies are increasingly turning to specialty chemicals, which are
small-volume, high-value-added, and research-driven items, as well
as to pharmaceuticals, biotechnology, and advanced materials.
The most successful firms have a long-term outlook, emphasize
research, stress quality, have a strong market orientation, and work
closely with potential customers.

Textiles

The history of the American textile industry is essentially a search
for low wages. The industry moved first from New England to the
Southeast and then went offshore, but the quest for cheap labor has
not brought success in the marketplace. Apparel imports have
gone from 2 percent in 1963 to 50 percent today.

The route to success in the modern garment trade is not low
wages. West Germany, for example, is the world's third largest
exporter of textiles in spite of wages that are now substantially
higher than those in the United States. Indeed, European producers have been successful with more handicaps than the Americans.
Unions are stronger in Europe, and labor legislation is more
constraining. In Italy and France, for example, layoffs and plant
closings are highly regulated.

The explanation of foreign success is not better government
protection of the industry. West Germany is the largest per capita

importer of textiles and apparel, importing four times as much as the United States. Yet Germany has successfully modernized and transformed its own textile sector. Productivity jumped 24 percent from 1980 to 1986. Exports have risen from 11 percent of total output in 1960 to 48 percent in 1984. To achieve these gains German firms have invested heavily in new technologies, labor-saving machinery, and new plants. German investment per employee more than doubled between 1970 and 1986, and the ratio of capital to labor is now more than 40 percent higher in textiles than it is in autos.

Both Italy and Germany operate in market niches in which they experience relatively little competition from low-cost producers. In these niches design, quality, responsiveness to fashion, and rapid adjustments are important. The Italians, for example, have developed close collaborations with well-known designers. U.S. producers, in contrast, have traditionally focused on long production runs of standard goods for mass markets. As incomes rise, however, the mass market increasingly becomes a series of niche markets.

Only now are American producers starting to organize themselves to serve these markets. Milliken, a major U.S. fabric producer, has reduced its average lot size from 20,000 yards a few years ago to 4,000 yards today. Jet dying allows it to dye lots of only 1,000 to 2,000 yards. Milliken now channels about 2 percent of sales into research and development. It builds many of its own machines to protect proprietary technology. New products, such as a soil release for polyester fiber, have been invented.

The American industry has a long way to go yet if it is going to adopt the successful strategies of other high-wage countries. Many American textile-mill managers have had few contacts with the apparel firms that purchase their fabrics. Close customer contacts are necessary in the German or Italian model. One needs to know what the customer will need tomorrow. U.S. firms have recently joined to launch the Quick Response Program, which was designed to integrate the different segments of the industry more closely, but not enough firms are yet involved in such projects.

And a different human-resource strategy is central. A good firm is not one that pays low wages; it is a firm that has the productivity to pay high wages, so that it can hire skilled individuals to operate sophisticated new machinery. The Commission heard from the manager of a high-fashion denim mill in Bergamo, Italy, who had visited a denim manufacturer in Texas. At the Texas plant the workers' faces were so blue from denim dust that they could not be identified. "I have no blue workers!" the Italian manager exclaimed. "The union wouldn't let me get away with it. I have had to invest in air-cleaning systems that remove all that dust. And it's far better for us that we've done this. We operate better in a cleaner plant. Most important, you can't hope to get real cooperation from 'blue men.' "

Automobiles

The mass-production of automobiles was invented in America and has become the nation's largest industry. It is also the major customer for many other industries, including alloy steel, aluminum, rubber, and machine tools. Yet imported cars have risen from less than 1 percent of sales in 1955 to more than 31 percent in 1987. In the 20 years since 1967 the United States has gone from an auto export surplus to an auto import deficit of $60 billion, the largest single element in the overall trade deficit.

In an industry where American production used to dwarf that of the rest of the world, Americans now stand third. Europe both buys and builds more cars than America, and Japan builds more. Foreign producers are squeezing the American companies from both ends of the price range. Korean and Japanese imports dominate the low end of the market, and European imports dominate the high end. The overwhelming advantage enjoyed by the American industry in the postwar years could not have been sustained indefinitely. But the erosion of U.S. dominance stems not only from the inevitable growth of overseas production but also from weaknesses in the domestic industry.

Many explanations have been offered. The American car companies did not foresee the oil crises of the 1970s and the resulting shift in demand to smaller cars; Detroit had little interest in producing small cars because profit margins were low. But this explanation can hardly account for foreign success with the most expensive models, which are also the most profitable.

Unions and managements have both been blamed. Managers were inward looking and shortsighted; unions stifled productivity and demanded wages that productivity could not support.

A lag in technology has been implicated. The last major innovation that was first installed in an American car was the automatic transmission in the 1940s. Four-wheel steering and four-wheel drive, turbocharging, and antilock braking systems were all first adopted on imported models. In 1985 the three leading Japanese producers recorded more than twice as many new patents in the United States as the three American producers.

But the roots of the problem go still deeper. A system of production and an accompanying market strategy were developed by the American auto industry in the 1920s and perfected over the next forty years. The American success was built on a few simple axioms. The American consumer wanted variety only as long as it did not cost very much. Labor was a commodity to be hired and fired as demand rose and fell. Designs were to last for years. Suppliers were treated in much the same way as the work force; they were both marginal elements of the production system, utilized in boom periods but jettisoned during the troughs. The system was to be robust so that no strike or supplier bottlenecks could bring it to a halt; hence large inventories were kept on hand. Minimum quality levels were maintained by checking and rework.

For 40 years it was a system that worked brilliantly, but it works no more. The Japanese have found a better way. The Japanese pioneered flexible manufacturing, in which a plant can shift in minutes from the production of one model to another. Die changes that took from 8 to 24 hours in American plants could be done in five minutes in Japanese plants. Perfect first-time quality was the goal. Waste of all kinds—inventories, defects, excess plant space, and unnecessary human effort—was eliminated. Continuous incremental improvements were every worker's major job. Because workers could not be laid off, human resources became a strategic asset. Above all, assemblers, workers, and suppliers were all on the same team.

These techniques allow the Japanese industry to work on a cycle of 7.5 years from initial conception until the last vehicle rolls off the assembly line. The American product cycle lasts from 13 to 15 years. As consumer preferences change, faster response becomes an overwhelming advantage.

There is also much to learn from the success of several European carmakers. The internal markets of the European carmakers are small and segmented. A car ideal for Italy is not suitable for Sweden. Consequently, the European builders could not adopt the American methods of mass production. Their products had to differ in more than cosmetic details, and they had to operate efficiently with much smaller runs of each model.

By copying foreign practices, American firms have lessened their disadvantages in time to market, productivity, and product quality, but they are still not yet at parity. The best American plants are not quite as good as the best Japanese plants, and the worst American plants are far worse than the worst Japanese plants. On average, American plants still require 40 percent more effort to accomplish the same amount of manufacturing as plants in Japan and produce cars with twice as many defects as their Japanese counterparts. Japanese plants in the United States have come close to the quality and productivity attained in the best plants in Japan. The most famous of these transplants is the NUMMI joint venture between General Motors and Toyota in California. It has demonstrated an ability to raise productivity and quality sharply using an existing plant and work force.

Machine Tools

It is not possible to have world-class manufacturing without world-class tools. It is not possible to have world-class tools if one has to import them all. Yet the American machine-tool industry is dissolving. In 1964 the United States was a net exporter; in 1986, 50 percent of its machine tools were imported. Production is now only half of what it was at the peak.

As in autos, the Japanese are pushing up from the low end and the Germans are pushing down from the high end. The Japanese success is based on a policy coordinated by the Ministry of International Trade and Industry (MITI). The industry standardized its products; firms were encouraged to specialize in one or two products; electronic controls all came from one firm (which ensured compatibility); and R&D support was provided for cooperative development of flexible manufacturing systems.

In Germany machine-tool builders are usually affiliated with a parent engineering group. Cooperative specialization on high-end niches is the basic strategy. Both builders' and users' work forces are technologically sophisticated. An infrastructure of apprenticeships, polytechnic schools, universities, and technical institutes produces manufacturing expertise on many levels: skilled shop-floor people, practical engineers, and more research-minded engineers.

The causes of failure in the American machine-tool industry are clear. The industry is fragmented, and its many small firms do not have an infrastructure of support from sophisticated users or government. As the industry converted from comparatively simple machines to the more elaborate, computer-controlled ones, the small American companies fell behind. Users in the United States were slow to adopt new technologies, but machine-tool builders were also laggards, even when it came to using their own products in their own shops.

To smooth production, American firms backlogged orders when times were good, but this led to long delays (sometimes years) before customers could get the products they wanted. These long order books could be "cherry-picked" by foreign firms that could offer quick delivery.

Most important, neither universities nor industry accorded high status to manufacturing engineers and process technologies. The best students were not drawn into manufacturing, let alone into what was perceived as the mature, conservative, grubby world of machine builders. Yet more-glamorous activities cannot survive without improvements in this grubby world.

Education and Training

It is no mere truism that the ultimate resource of an industrial economy is its people. One of the most disturbing ways in which the United States has lately fallen behind other nations is in developing and nurturing the skills of its people.

The problem has been well defined in recent years. American elementary and secondary students tend to fall near the bottom of any comparative international test. American universities turn out too few scientifically and technically trained people: 6 percent of American baccalaureates are in engineering versus 20 percent in Japan and 37 percent in Germany. The American system of on-the-job training is called "following Joe around," and it does not work. Both candidates in the recent presidential election cited the problem and promised to be the "education President."

Although everyone sees the need for a better-skilled work force, no one is willing to act alone to improve education. The individual does not know where he will be employed and does not want to invest time and money in acquiring skills that could become worthless. Firms feel that they cannot educate their workers, because they would go off to other employers who could pay higher wages because they did not have to incur training costs. Local governments are reluctant to raise taxes to pay for good schools, because firms could locate next door and get a well-educated work force free.

All of these parties are acting rationally according to their own narrowly defined interests, but the overall result is detrimental to all. Meanwhile, the federal government has come to see education more and more as an individual or local responsibility. Federal aid to education is one of the few places where government spending has actually been cut under the Reagan administration. This policy will not break the impasse.

2

The United States in the World Economy

Events inside individual factories, companies, and industries represent the ground truth of the national economy. The Commission has emphasized the importance of examining such events at close range, but views from a greater height are also revealing: they offer less detail but a broader perspective. Furthermore, looking at the entire economy in the aggregate makes it easier to interpret such quantitative measures of performance as productivity. This chapter is largely concerned with what can be learned from aggregate measures of American productivity and competitiveness.

The belief that there is something fundamentally wrong with American industrial performance is fueled by an awareness of decline relative to other industrialized nations. But this perception of ebbing economic power has to take account of the fact that the overwhelming superiority of the American economy in the years following World War II grew out of extraordinary circumstances that could not be sustained. The American lead was bound to erode as other countries recovered from the devastation of the war and rebuilt their industrial base.

A Changing World

The postwar American economic advantage rested on five pillars. First, the American market was eight times larger than the next-largest market. American industry enjoyed economies of scale that no one else could hope to achieve. Costs per unit of output in such industries as automobiles and steel were simply beyond the dreams of even the largest foreign producers.

Second, when it came to technology Americans were superior. World War II had destroyed the scientific establishments in much of the rest of the world, and Europe had given America some of its very best brains. American firms did not compete with foreign firms. They built products that foreigners could not build. The Boeing 707 flew; the British Comet suffered from metal fatigue and all too often did not fly.

Third, American workers were more skilled on average than those in other countries. America had invented mass public elementary and secondary education. After the war, when the GI bill was added to the land-grant college system, America was unmatched in mass higher education as well. Large proportions of the U.S. population were highly educated and capable of acquiring skills that were beyond reach in much of the rest of the world. Higher skills led to lower costs and an ability to employ technologies that would have outstripped the available human talent in any other country. No other industrial democracy could have even thought of putting a man on the moon in the 1960s, and the other country that tried, the Soviet Union, did not succeed.

Fourth, the United States was far richer than other nations. Americans could afford to do things that others could not. Because Americans had more discretionary income than others, the first mass market for almost everything was in the United States. This gave American firms an opportunity to move down the learning curve before anyone else could even get on it. America was not a high-saving, high-investment nation after World War II, but it was so rich that a modest proportion of its GNP devoted to investment still gave it much more capital per worker than other nations that were saving and investing a much higher proportion of their total income. If America's per capita income was eight times that of Japan—as it was in the 1950s—a Japanese family could save three times as much as an American family and total investment per worker would still be more than twice as high in the United States.

Finally, American managers were the best in the world. In America commerce and business management were the route to the top. Many of the most talented Americans had gone into management before the war, and afterward American industry could draw on a skilled cadre of middle- and upper-level managers. In prewar Europe, by contrast, talented individuals were more likely to be drawn to careers in military service or colonial administration.

Put a huge market together with superior technology, more capital, a better educated labor force, and more accomplished managers and the postwar economic primacy of the United States was assured.

But both inside and outside America changes were in progress that would vitiate these advantages. As other nations began to reconstruct their industries and as their income levels started to catch up with those in the United States, the relative size of the American market declined. Today it is not quite twice as large as the Japanese market. And in Europe the process of economic integration, underway since the 1950s, is fast approaching the milestone year of 1992, when the prospect is for a unified market of 320 million people with a per capita income not much different from that of the United States. In addition, developments in telecommunication, computer, and transportation technologies and the dismantling of many trade barriers since the war mean that the size of internal markets is less important than it used to be. The Japanese can produce and sell six times as many video recorders as they themselves buy.

Other countries also noticed the payoff from the American system of universal education and adapted and improved it. The American functional-illiteracy rate is now above that in the rest of the industrial world, and the rate of graduation from high school is below average. At the same time, technology has moved in directions that require a much better educated and skilled work force.

In terms of purchasing power Americans have peers in many other industrial countries; others can now afford to do anything that Americans can afford to do. With more discretionary income overseas and new products increasingly introduced there first, foreign firms can jump on the learning curve first, and Americans have to play catch up.

For managers, the lure of alternative career opportunities is in some ways the reverse of what it used to be, and managerial talent and experience is no longer clearly better in the United States than it is elsewhere. In Germany, Japan, Britain, and France, business management has replaced military and colonial service as the principal route to the top. In the United States, by contrast, the defense sector now provides many attractive opportunities for advancement and high earnings. And for the significant fraction of the nation's technical professionals who are engaged in it, defense work is perceived to offer technological challenges and excitement that most civilian products cannot match.

Many of these changes were inevitable. The recovery of war-damaged economies in Europe and the Far East was to be expected and should be welcomed. The question is whether there have also been pervasive weaknesses in U.S. industrial performance that have caused the American economy to lose ground.

Productivity and Productivity Growth

In view of all the turmoil over the apparently declining stature of American industry, it may come as a surprise that the United States still leads the world in productivity. Averaged over the economy as a whole, for each unit of input the United States produces more output than any other nation. With this evidence of economic efficiency, is there any reason for concern? There are at least two reasons. First, American productivity is not growing as fast as it used to, and productivity in the United States is not growing as fast as it is elsewhere, most notably in Japan. Second, other indicators of industrial performance that are less easily quantified than productivity but no less important tell a disquieting story. In such areas as product quality, service to customers, and speed of product development, American companies are no longer perceived as world leaders, even by American consumers. There is also evidence that technological innovations are being incorporated into practice more quickly abroad, and the pace of invention and discovery in the United States may be slowing.

In a vigorous economy, productivity must not only be high but should also be steadily increasing. It is the drop in the rate of productivity growth that has alarmed many observers of American industry. The decline has not been a steady or a gradual one; instead, a distinct reduction in the rate of productivity growth appeared sometime in the late 1960s or early 1970s.

One common measure of productivity, called labor productivity, is expressed in dollars of output (adjusted for inflation) per hour worked. In the two decades before the slowdown began, the labor productivity of the U.S. economy improved at an average rate of 3 percent per year. In the two decades since then, the rate of growth has been little more than 1 percent per year. Small differences in annual growth rate have a dramatic cumulative effect. If productivity had continued rising at 3 percent per year, the U.S. economy would now be almost 50 percent more productive than it is. Slower growth in output per hour worked sooner or later leads to slower growth in wages. After 1965 hourly compensation in the business sector increased at only half the rate of earlier years. Since

1973 real hourly wages have risen even more slowly, and by some measures they have actually declined.[1]

Another measure of productivity, multifactor productivity, is a composite measure of how efficiently an economy makes use of both labor and capital inputs. Growth in multifactor productivity reflects such factors as the introduction of new technology, improvements in the skill and motivation of the work force, and better techniques of management and organization. Multifactor productivity has followed a course similar to that of labor productivity. From 1948 to 1973 the annual growth rate averaged about 2 percent, but between 1973 and 1979 it dropped almost to zero. Since then there has been a slight improvement, but the current growth rate still remains far below that of the years before 1973. The trends in both labor productivity and multifactor productivity are summarized in figure 2.1. The slowdown in productivity growth has been felt throughout the economy, although by no means uniformly. Table 2.1 gives a breakdown by industry.

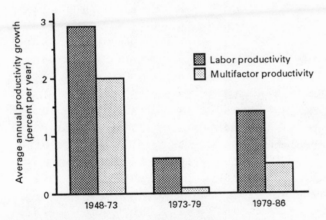

Figure 2.1   U.S. productivity trends
Labor productivity is in terms of output per hour. Multifactor productivity is in terms of output per unit of combined labor and capital input. The data are for all sectors of the U.S. economy except government. Source: U.S. Department of Labor, Bureau of Labor Statistics, *Monthly Labor Review*, May 1988.

Table 2.1

Multifactor productivity growth in major U.S. industries, 1948–85

Industry	Average annual percentage change				
	1948–85	1948–65	1965–73	1973–79	1979–85
Major aggregates					
Farming	3.4	3.4	2.8	1.8	5.6
Manufacturing	2.0	2.5	1.8	0.6	2.1
Nonfarm, nonmanufacturing	1.1	2.1	0.9	− 0.2	− 0.4
Manufacturing except					
nonelectrical machinery	1.9	2.6	1.9	0.6	1.1
Manufacturing industries					
Food	2.6	2.9	3.6	0.1	2.9
Tobacco	0.2	2.7	2.0	− 0.2	− 8.0
Textiles	3.9	4.6	2.0	5.7	2.6
Apparel	2.1	1.9	2.7	2.8	1.5
Lumber	2.4	3.8	1.0	1.5	1.3
Furniture	1.7	2.0	1.6	2.1	0.5
Paper	2.0	2.0	3.7	0.1	1.8
Printing and publishing	1.0	2.1	0.8	− 0.2	− 0.9
Chemicals	3.2	4.1	4.0	1.1	2.0
Petroleum	0.6	2.9	0.8	− 1.4	− 4.0
Rubber	1.9	2.2	1.7	− 0.8	4.0
Leather	0.8	1.1	1.8	0.2	− 0.6
Stone, clay, and glass	1.4	2.2	1.0	0.5	0.9
Primary metals	0.0	1.0	0.7	− 2.8	− 0.9
Fabricated metals	1.3	1.8	1.3	0.0	1.1
Nonelectrical machinery	2.5	1.4	1.5	0.4	9.1
Electrical machinery	3.4	4.2	2.7	3.5	1.9
Transportation equipment	2.0	3.5	1.2	0.1	0.6
Instruments	2.5	3.6	2.4	2.7	− 0.5
Miscellaneous manufactures	2.0	2.6	2.9	0.1	1.2
Nonmanufacturing industries					
Mining	0.6	3.1	2.0	− 6.0	− 1.5
Construction	− 0.2	2.9	− 3.9	− 2.2	− 2.0
Transportation	1.6	2.1	2.7	1.5	− 1.3
Railroad	2.7	4.1	1.8	1.3	1.4
Nonrail	0.7	0.5	2.7	1.3	− 2.0
Communications	3.9	5.6	3.4	2.4	1.3
Public utilities	3.5	5.8	3.0	− 0.6	1.7
Trade	1.9	2.6	2.4	0.4	0.8
Finance and insurance	0.3	1.3	0.6	− 0.7	− 2.0
Real estate	0.6	1.8	0.3	1.4	− 3.2
Services	0.7	0.4	1.4	0.4	0.8

Source: Baily and Chakrabarti, *Innovation and the Productivity Crisis* (Washington, D.C.: Brookings Institution, 1988).

The recent trends in productivity need to be understood in an international context. The change in growth rate observed around 1970 was not confined to the United States. On the contrary, every advanced industrial country, including Japan, experienced something similar at about the same time (see figure 2.2).[2] It follows that the causes of the slowdown are unlikely to be found in some specifically American event. There is some comfort for Americans in that knowledge, but not much. Since then the United States has trailed virtually all other industrial countries in productivity growth. The current rate of growth, a little more than 1 percent per year, is not enough to sustain a healthy rate of improvement in the nation's standard of living.

The historical factors presented earlier must be considered in interpreting the economic data: Following World War II, as other countries rebuilt their industrial base, expanded their economies, and invested in education, research, and development, it was only to be expected that they would show faster growth. They were merely catching up. This equalizing tendency was not only inevitable but also desirable, even from the narrow viewpoint of Ameri-

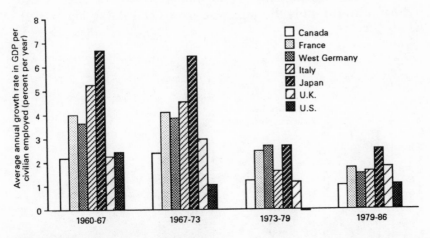

Figure 2.2 Output per employee
Gross domestic product (GDP) is the value of all final goods and services produced within the country. (Gross national product [GNP] is the value of all final goods and services produced by domestically owned factors of production. In recent years GNP has slightly exceeded GDP in the United States.) Sources: Calculated using data from OECD, *National Accounts, 1960–86*, vol. 1; OECD, *Labour Force Statistics, 1963–83*, table 6; OECD, *Labour Force Statistics, 1965–85*, table 6; OECD, *Quarterly Labour Force Statistics, 1987*, no. 2.

can self-interest. The resurgent economies of Europe and Asia were new markets as well as new competitors; furthermore, a world in which all products and ideas come from one country is a world that wastes the talents of most of its population, talents that hold the potential of enriching everyone.

The historical perspective can account in part for America's lost preeminence, but the explanation is not altogether reassuring. Although the U.S. economy is still the most productive overall, in certain sectors the best industrial practice is now to be found elsewhere in the world. In those fields other nations are no longer catching up; they have left the United States behind.

Manufacturing Productivity

There is at least one recent development that might be taken for a positive sign: the surge in U.S. manufacturing productivity since 1979. Growth rates for both labor and multifactor productivity have rebounded strongly from the post-1973 slump (see figure 2.3), and in recent years manufacturing productivity has been improving faster in the United States than almost anywhere else in the industrial world; only the Japanese have been doing better (see figure 2.4).

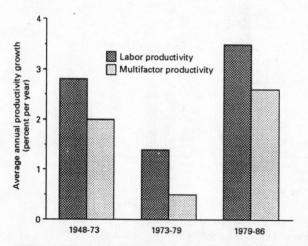

Figure 2.3   U.S. productivity trends in manufacturing
Labor productivity is in terms of output per hour. Multifactor productivity is in terms of output per unit of combined labor and capital input. Source: U.S. Department of Labor, Bureau of Labor Statistics, *Monthly Labor Review,* May 1988.

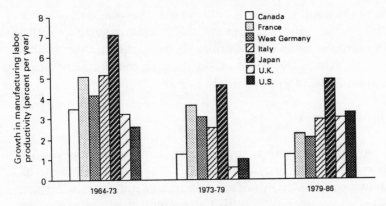

Figure 2.4　Manufacturing labor productivity
Labor productivity is the average annual growth rate of constant-price value added per person employed. Sources: Data from OECD sources, various years: *National Accounts*, vol. 2; *Labour Force Statistics*; and *Industrial Structure Statistics, 1985*; U.S. Bureau of Labor Statistics, "News," June 15, 1987, p. 12; and D. J. Roy, Central Electricity Generating Board (U.K.), personal communication, April 15, 1988.

There is a dark side to these developments, however. A significant fraction of the productivity gains in manufacturing were achieved by shutting down inefficient plants and by permanently laying off workers at others. Employment in U.S. manufacturing industry declined by 10 percent between 1979 and 1986, and that loss of jobs accounted for about 36 percent of the recorded improvement in labor productivity.[3] Another reason for caution is that the productivity recovery spanned a deep recession; productivity growth always accelerates following a recession as factories increase their output and take up the slack in the economy. These factors suggest that part of the recent improvement may turn out to be a one-time gain.

Moreover, the Department of Commerce, the key source of statistics on U.S. manufacturing output, recently acknowledged several flaws in its method of calculating these numbers.[4] The flaws may have led economists to overestimate growth in manufacturing productivity during the 1980s. The department is reviewing its data and methods, and it expects to revise the estimates downward, but by how much remains to be seen.

Much of the evidence we have gathered points to the manufacturing sector as the area where the American advantage in cost and quality has been most severely eroded. The problem is particularly evident because many U.S. manufacturers now compete directly with foreign rivals in both domestic and overseas markets. According to one estimate, about 70 percent of U.S. manufacturing output now faces direct foreign competition.[5] Indeed, the intensity of this competition is doubtless a factor contributing to the recent surge in U.S. manufacturing productivity.

Productive Performance

As our case studies illustrate, productivity is only one of the factors that affect the performance of a company. Success may depend as much or more on the quality of a firm's products and on the service it provides to its customers both before and after the sale. The firm's response time may be as important as the cost and quality of its products. Competitiveness may hinge on the speed at which new concepts are converted into manufacturable products and brought to market, on the flexibility with which the firm can shift from one product line to another in response to changing market conditions, or on the time it takes to deliver a product after the customer places an order. There is also the crucial question of how well the company has chosen its markets; all the efficiency, quality, and speed in the world will count for little unless the firm is producing goods that the customer wants.

In principle, productivity measurements should reflect these factors. Improvements in quality and service should increase the market value of the product, and the higher value, in turn, should automatically be factored into measures of productivity growth. In practice, however, the measurement process does this very ineffectively, and productivity trends do not tell the whole story of how well firms or industries are innovating, producing, and competing.

Hence, while trends in labor and multifactor productivity may be the best available indicators of how well the nation's production system is performing, they cannot be relied on exclusively for monitoring economic progress or for charting a future course. Unfortunately, there are no national indices of such important aspects of performance as quality or innovativeness or speed of product development. The best that can be done is to examine the situation in various industries on a case-by-case basis and to build up from specific observations to more general conclusions.

The synopses of the Commission's industry studies illustrate another important point. Certain industries play a crucial role in long-term national productivity growth and competitiveness because of their potential for generating technological spillovers or because other industries depend on them. These economically strategic sectors may have little effect on a country's present productivity statistics, but they may make a disproportionate contribution to long-term productivity growth. International comparisons that fail to take account of relative strengths in such strategic sectors and technologies may therefore be quite misleading.

To account for all of these important yet not conventionally measured factors, the Commission adopted the term *productive performance* as a broader measure of economic vitality. The productive performance of a firm or an industry is compounded of its productivity and of various other factors that tend to be ignored in most economic statistics, like quality, timeliness of service, flexibility, speed of innovation, and command of strategic technologies.

To sum up, the U.S. economy faces two serious productivity-related problems. One is the general productivity slowdown and the need to restore the economywide growth rate to something approaching the long-term historical average. This is a problem that every industrial nation shares to some degree. Second, America's longstanding productivity advantage over other nations is being eroded. Part of this equalization results from the growing economic strength of the other countries and is not unwelcome, but part too stems from weaknesses in U.S. industrial performance. It is primarily this latter issue that we address in this book.

Productive Performance and the Trade Deficit

The nation's productivity problems are tied up in popular discussion with the problem of imbalances in international trade, particularly trade in manufactured goods. Producers in Europe and Asia are winning a large share of the U.S. market at the same time that U.S. manufacturers are losing their export markets. There is, of course, a connection between productive performance and the trade balance. Other things unchanged, higher quality and lower cost in American industry would reduce imports and increase exports. But the two problems are not identical. It is entirely possible to solve the problem of foreign trade without mending the nation's deficiencies in productive performance.

There are at least three ways to improve the trade balance without making any drastic change in product quality or cost. The first is to depreciate the dollar against other currencies. A cheaper dollar reduces U.S. costs in terms of foreign currencies and thereby makes U.S. goods more competitive at home and abroad.

It should be kept in mind that the U.S. balance of trade for goods and services was in a small surplus as recently as 1981. The drastic deterioration in the U.S. trade position coincided with a sharp appreciation of the dollar in the early 1980s, brought on in large part by high interest rates that attracted foreign capital. Since 1985 the dollar has been depreciating, and the trade balance has already improved considerably; this has contributed to a strong revival of American manufacturing.

Symmetry is not to be expected here: the trade balance of 1980 will not be achieved if the dollar falls to its 1980 level. One reason that trade cannot bounce all the way back is that foreign industry has continued to gain in relative productivity. Another reason is that producers abroad are willing to accept lower profit margins rather than give up their foothold in the U.S. market, along with their investment in distribution networks, marketing arrangements, spare-parts supply, and so on. Nevertheless, depreciating the dollar is one way to balance the foreign trade account.

There is a second possibility: the U.S. trade balance improves when the American economy is depressed and the rest of the world is prosperous. An economy in recession buys less of everything, including imported goods. Moreover, weak markets at home free up productive capacity for exports and provide a motive to seek export markets. These mechanisms have been demonstrated in reverse by recent American experience. Part of the current U.S. trade deficit is the price of prosperity: the U.S. economy is now in the sixth year of an upswing, while much of Europe has been growing more slowly over that period. Even Japan had a relatively weak recovery, by its own remarkable standards, after the 1979 oil crisis. A recession in the United States, greater prosperity in Europe, or the resumption of economic growth in the paralyzed countries of Latin America would automatically improve the trade balance.

The trouble with these schemes is that currency depreciation or recession improve the trade balance by impoverishing the country. Depreciation increases exports by making Americans work for less in terms of foreign goods. Recession reduces imports by reducing incomes.

There is a third route to equilibrium in the balance of trade without changing product quality or cost: protection, in the form of tariffs, quotas, domestic-content requirements and the like. The disadvantages are well known. Other countries may retaliate, with the end result being a much-reduced volume of trade, to the disadvantage of all. Furthermore, protection releases the pressure on domestic industry to improve its efficiency, and domestic consumers pay the price. Protection merely accepts defeat. (There is, on the other hand, every reason for U.S. policy to be tough in insisting that other countries dismantle their own protectionist devices.)

All three of these approaches improve the trade balance at the expense of the standard of living. The recent American experience has been essentially the reverse: the standard of living has been raised by borrowing from overseas, thereby running a large external deficit. But the option of continued borrowing from overseas will almost certainly soon be exhausted.

There is only one way to improve the trade balance while simultaneously maintaining a high and rising standard of living at home. It is by improving the productive performance of the American economy. That is why this book is devoted entirely to productive performance as the route to enhanced U.S. international competitiveness.

Productive Performance and the Macroeconomic Environment

Although the Commission has concluded that macroeconomic manipulation alone cannot solve the nation's productive-performance problem, we also recognize that the problem cannot be solved without some improvement in the macroeconomic environment. The reason is that investment, in the broadest sense, is crucial for productivity, and the macroeconomic environment largely determines the level of investment. We shall consider these links in turn.

"Investment," as we must use the term, is more than business spending for plant and equipment, although that is a very important component. Investment is any use of current resources for the purpose of achieving a future return. Thus, investment includes not only a new plant or buying machinery but also, for example, the use of public resources to improve roads, airports, harbors, and the like. Some expenditures are harder to classify. Education is sometimes its own reward and should be counted as consumption, but much of ordinary schooling and essentially all of occupational training is investment. (We regard it as a most important form of investment, and one that has been dangerously neglected.) Finally, nearly all spending for research and development, whether conducted in universities, businesses, or government laboratories, is investment; indeed, basic research, which is most emphatically oriented to the future, may be the clearest case of all.

The productivity level achieved in a particular industry or in the economy as a whole depends on the skill, health, and motivation of its work force; on the quality of the materials they have to work with; on the speed, precision, and capacity of the capital equipment with which they work; and on the technological level of the production process itself. In almost every respect, then, today's level of productivity depends on the amount of investment made in the past. There is even the important possibility that sustained investment in new technology will raise not only productivity itself but also the rate of increase in productivity. Hence, the link between investment and productivity is likely to be strong.

The link between the macroeconomic environment and investment is created in several ways. Most investment decisions are made by profit-seeking business firms, which will spend resources now if they foresee adequate future profit stemming from the investment. In the first place, then, investment requires some feeling of optimism about the state of the national economy in the future. A depressed economy is never a beehive of investment activity. Second, an investing firm must acquire funds to spend, either by borrowing, by selling equity, or by accumulating its own retained earnings. No matter where the money comes from, there is a cost of capital, which represents a threshold that an investment must get over to be a viable competitor for funds. The higher this required rate of return, the fewer investments will qualify. In general, a society in which the supply of capital is scarce, as evidenced by a low national savings rate, will generate a high cost of capital and a low rate of investment. The high cost of capital may attract investment from abroad, but whatever investment is financed that way will be owned abroad.

This discussion suggests several ways in which the general macroeconomic environment can influence the rate of investment: through the effectiveness of macroeconomic policy in generating secure prosperity, through the interaction of fiscal and monetary policy in affecting interest rates, through the impact of the tax system on the relative advantages of saving and consumption, and through the size of the government budget deficit, which can be viewed as a form of negative saving. These issues have been much discussed in the technical literature of economics, in earlier studies of the competitiveness problem, and even in political campaigns.

Some analysts have concluded that macroeconomic factors are the dominant influence on the nation's productivity performance. For example, George N. Hatsopoulos, Paul R. Krugman, and Lawrence H. Summers have recently argued that the main reason for lagging U.S. productivity growth is the low rate of capital formation; this they attribute mostly to the high cost of capital to U.S. firms, which they blame on the low national savings rate.[6] These authors conclude that increasing the rate of savings and investment is the key to improving national industrial performance.

There are good reasons to think that the capital-formation problem in the United States may only be part of the story. Martin Baily and Alok Chakrabarti recently reviewed efforts to understand the causes of the U.S. slowdown in productivity growth.[7] They listed the various explanations that economists and others have proposed, and weighed the evidence in support of each one. A slackening in the rate of capital investment has consistently figured among the prime suspects. Baily and Chakrabarti found that the rate of capital investment did indeed decline after 1973, but they concluded that the decline could only explain a rather small part of the productivity slowdown.

When the focus shifts from the general picture to particular industries, further questions arise. Consider the automobile industry. A survey conducted by the International Motor Vehicle Program at MIT found that the number of defects reported in the first six months of use is almost twice as high for cars produced in American plants as in Japanese plants. The Commission's automobile study team also learned that American car builders take about 5 years to take a new design from the conceptual stage to commercial introduction, in contrast with 3.5 years for the Japanese; the American firms use about twice the amount of engineering effort besides. These deficiencies in quality and product development have seriously hurt the American companies in their efforts to compete with the Japanese, yet their relationship to the higher cost of capital and general macroeconomic environment in the United States seems tenuous at best.

Nor do macroeconomic factors determine the speed with which firms identify and respond to changes in the market and to new technological possibilities. To understand how a firm interacts with customers and suppliers, detects shifts in demand, and uncovers new opportunities, we need to know more than the prices the firm pays for its inputs and charges for its products. To evaluate the sources of flexibility in the firm's use and redeployment of human and capital resources, we need to consider a range of variables that cannot be deduced from a top-down perspective on the economy.

There is also the obvious point that some American industries have done much better than others both from a productivity perspective and in international competition, even though they are all operating in the same macroeconomic climate. At the least, this means that there must be particular circumstances influencing each industry's performance. And if nonmacroeconomic factors are playing an important role in specific industries, perhaps they are playing a more pervasive role in the overall determination of productive performance.

That is the thesis we advance in this book. Without disputing the importance of the macroeconomic environment, we believe that current international differences in productive performance, as well as changes in performance over time, have been powerfully affected by other things too. Specifically, we think that failures by American firms and industries to adapt to new conditions have also played an important role. Some of these shortcomings are deeply rooted in organizational structures and social attitudes, and they will be at least as difficult to put right as any macroeconomic problems.

Even if macroeconomic factors are not the primary cause of the nation's productivity-performance problems, some people argue that the main thing, still, is to get interest rates, exchange rates, the tax laws, and other aspects of the external environment right and then to let firms and industries shift for themselves. Those that survive will have met world standards. Those that cannot meet world standards should not survive, and trying to keep them alive will only make more trouble. This line of argument has quite a lot to commend it, but it also has a major flaw. If organizational and attitudinal deficiencies do indeed have an important bearing on American industrial performance, as our findings indicate, then a purely macroeconomic approach is insufficient. This is because there is no efficient market in which organizational forms and attitudinal complexes compete with one another. Only an extraordinary optimist could believe, for example, that the current wave of takeover activity is an efficient way to deal with the organizational deficiencies of American industries. In at least one respect, its tendency to favor short time horizons, we believe it is part of the problem, not part of the solution.

Why Manufacturing Matters

The Commission has concentrated much of its effort on identifying and prescribing cures for weaknesses in manufacturing performance. But how important is manufacturing? Its share of total employment, more than 30 percent not long after World War II, has been shrinking steadily and is now below 20 percent. Meanwhile, employment in the service sector has been increasing both in absolute terms and as a share of the total. By this measure, at least, manufacturing is less important than it was in the past. Indeed, some see a transition from manufacturing to services as an inevitable and desirable stage in the economic development of the nation, with the U.S. increasingly leaving manufacturing to other countries.

We think this idea is mistaken. A large continental economy like the United States will not be able to function primarily as a producer of services in the foreseeable future. One reason is that it would have to rely on exports of services to pay for its imports, and this does not seem realistic. In 1987 gross U.S. exports of services, excluding income from overseas investments and overseas sales of government services, were worth about $57 billion, whereas the total value of goods and services imported into the United States was about $550 billion. Trade in services is increasing, to be sure, and the United States is among the world's largest exporters of services. Imports as well as exports of services have been growing rapidly, however, and U.S. trade in services, excluding official transactions and investment income, is approximately in balance.

The notion that the United States could eventually become almost exclusively a producer of services is all the more implausible when it is recognized that all of the manufactured goods now produced domestically would have to be imported (and hence paid for with exports of services). In 1987 the total value of manufactured goods purchased in the United States was about $1 trillion, nearly 20 times the volume of services exported. Moreover, the

long-term trend in the United States is toward increased demand
for manufactured goods. Between 1960 and 1986 total spending on
manufactured goods other than food and fuel in the United States
increased threefold in real terms.[8] In short, it is unreasonable to
expect that the United States could achieve a trade surplus in
services large enough to satisfy its huge appetite for manufactured
goods, if all such goods had to be imported.

There is also reason to believe that if large sections of American
manufacturing industry were ceded to other countries, high-wage
nonmanufacturing industries would follow them, including many
of the service industries that provide inputs to manufacturing, such
as design and engineering, payroll, inventory and accounting,
finance and insurance, transportation, repair and maintenance of
plant and equipment, testing services, and the like. According to a
recent estimate by the Congressional Office of Technology Assessment, private service industries supplied 17 cents of inputs toward
each dollar of manufacturing output.[9]

The United States thus has no choice but to continue competing
in the world market for manufactures. The ultimate scale of
American manufacturing industry is not known, but it will not be
trivial. The important question is not whether the United States will
have a manufacturing industry but whether it will compete as a low-
wage manufacturer or as a high-productivity producer.

If labor and capital were perfectly mobile across national borders, there would be less need to worry about the viability of
American industry. Labor and capital resident in the United States
would earn what they could elsewhere, or they would go elsewhere.
But labor is far from mobile internationally, and capital, while
more mobile, is not perfectly mobile. Hence, the best way for
Americans to share in rising world prosperity is to retain on
American soil those industries that have high and rapidly rising
productivity. Manufacturing, and high-technology manufacturing in particular, belongs in this category.

A related fact is that manufacturing firms account for virtually all
of the research and development done by American industry. They
thus generate most of the technological innovations adopted both
inside and outside their own industry. High technology manufacturing industries account for about three-quarters of all funding
for research and development, and the other manufacturing
industries account for most of the rest.[10] The roots of much of the
technological progress responsible for long-term economic growth

can ultimately be traced to the nation's manufacturing base. Because of this connection, high-technology and high-value-added services as well as products depend on the presence of a healthy, technologically dynamic manufacturing sector.

Finally, even if all the economic arguments for the importance of manufacturing were somehow rendered moot, the nation's manufacturing base would still remain fundamentally important to national security. The Department of Defense has estimated that it purchases about 21 percent of the gross product of U.S. manufacturing industries and over a third of the output of high-technology manufacturing industries; it depends on virtually every sector of the manufacturing base for its matériel.[11] For the nation to become heavily dependent on foreign technology for its defense would be politically and militarily untenable.

These arguments for the importance of manufacturing still do not explain why it is the exclusive focus of the Commission's report. Manufacturing may be essential, but it accounts for less than a fourth of the GNP and for less than a fifth of all employment. Further, manufacturing is certainly not the only troubled sector of the economy; as shown in table 2.1, productivity growth in many nonmanufacturing industries has been significantly worse. Since these other segments now account for such a large part of the economy, progress in them is essential; the nation cannot sustain an overall improvement in its standard of living without them, no matter how well manufacturing performs.

Again, then, why did the Commission study only manufacturing? In part, we were choosing the segment of the economy with which MIT, an institution with technology at its core, has the closest ties; we chose it because we know it best. We should also acknowledge that the choice may have caused us to miss certain causes of productivity weakness or opportunities for productivity growth. We suspect that one such neglected area may be low productivity among white-collar workers, which is emerging as a particularly serious problem in the services sector and which deserves more careful attention than we have been able to give it.

For the most part, however, we believe that our findings in manufacturing apply equally well to nonmanufacturing industries in the private sector, or at least to that large and important part of the services economy that is technologically advanced. Our assessment of productive performance was designed to extend well beyond the factory floor to the entire system of production-related functions and skills: from product and process development and design to product distribution and customer service. Many of these functions are, of course, also central to service industries. In fact, the boundary between manufacturing and service industries is becoming increasingly blurred. Many manufacturing firms have always performed in-house such functions as accounting, market research, engineering, design, and maintenance, which, if performed externally, would be counted as services. These service-oriented functions are contributing more and more to overall production costs as automation reduces the number of workers on the production line. (For most manufacturers, direct labor costs now account for less than 10 percent of total costs.) Furthermore, products in many industries now combine hardware, software, and services. For example, builders of machine tools are beginning to supply integrated systems consisting of the machine tools themselves, electronic controls, information systems, and engineering software packages; they see themselves as selling "solutions" and developing processes, rather than as selling hardware.

Perhaps the ultimate justification for our exclusive focus on manufacturing is to be found in the results of our study. As things turned out, the weaknesses we discovered concern the way people cooperate, manage, and organize themselves, as well as the ways they use technology, learn a new job, and interact with government. These weaknesses are not at all unique to manufacturing.

Diagnosing the Problem

As we pointed out above, many previous studies of the productivity problem have implicated macroeconomic policies as the likeliest cause. There has been no shortage of other suspects, however. Many of these concern other aspects of the environment within which firms must operate. Other proposed causes have to do with the internal organization and management of firms.

Among factors often cited are a broad range of nonmacroeconomic government policies and practices. Some of these factors can be classified as regulatory policy (including environmental regulation), product-liability laws, occupational health and safety regulation, food and drug regulation, antitrust policy, and legislation regulating the labor market. Other policies are designed to provide a supportive environment for small businesses and emerging technologies or to support American industry in international competition. Tax laws have a pervasive effect on business costs and incentives. The nation's defense programs draw heavily on human, technological, and financial resources that might otherwise be used in civilian industries. A common complaint is that U.S. policies compare unfavorably with the policies of other governments in these areas, so that American firms competing internationally do not do so on a level playing field.

Another target of criticism is the short-sightedness of American investors. It is frequently asserted that American industry has been hampered by investors and financial institutions that are driven by short-term expectations and have little interest in, or understanding of, the long-term needs of the businesses they invest in.

Some critics of American industry argue that the single most important cause of deteriorating productivity is management failure. They charge that corporate managers, made complacent by decades of American dominance, were caught unprepared by the surge of foreign competition and were ill-equipped to raise their performance and the performance of their firms to match it. These critics assert that American managers focus too heavily on meeting short-term financial objectives, that they value too lightly knowledge of production and markets, and that they pay too little attention to foreign markets.

Another common contention is that the quality of the work force has declined relative to that in other countries, if not in absolute terms. The schools are widely perceived to be failing to teach the basic skills needed for the modern workplace. Some also question whether American workers at all levels of the work force are as willing to work as they used to be. Others blame unions, claiming that organized labor has been slow to recognize the new realities of international competition and that necessary corporate-restructuring efforts have been obstructed by inflexible, uncooperative unions.

The list of suspected causes of the nation's productive-performance problem is longer even than this. In reviewing the suggested causes we were struck by the lack of consensus on what matters most. We had no illusions that all ills could be attributed to a single factor—the problem is far too complex for that—but neither were we ready to accept that the problem consists of a very large number of different causes, each requiring separate treatment.

We were also struck by the top-down nature of much of the previous discussion. Most of the earlier studies treat the economy as a black box, which leads to a natural inclination to focus on macroeconomic explanations. Even where other factors are invoked, the explanations tend to take on an abstract quality that is difficult to connect with what is actually happening on the shop floor, in the office, or in the marketplace.

Some studies have approached the question from a less Olympian perspective but also from a narrower one, with the boundaries sometimes arbitrarily drawn. Often partisan interests are apparent: labor blames management; managers blame labor and the government; engineers criticize financial strategists and vice versa; and everyone blames foreign governments. We suspected from the outset that the problem has at least as much to do with the *interactions* of various factors as with any single factor. But this was again a hypothesis that could be tested only through close observation of individual industries and individual firms in those industries. Hence our eight case studies.

As the studies got under way, the immediate result seemed to be more confusion rather than less. Each industry team told a different story. Outcomes and explanations for outcomes at first seemed idiosyncratic. Among the struggling industries, the causes of difficulty and decline seemed different in each case. Likewise each success had a unique explanation.

As we began to compare our observations across teams and in more detail, however, recurring patterns of weakness in productivity performance began to emerge. Eventually, by working together and sifting the evidence from the team reports, the Commissioners discerned six interrelated patterns of behavior that best characterize the evidence. These patterns, which are central to the arguments developed in this book, are discussed in the next six chapters under the following headings:

• Outdated Strategies
• Short Time Horizons
• Technological Weaknesses in Development and Production
• Neglect of Human Resources
• Failures of Cooperation
• Government and Industry at Cross-Purposes

Each of the industry teams also found strong American firms, fully able to hold their own in world competition. On examination, the experiences and practices of these firms too fell into certain patterns, which are set forth in chapter 9.

The organizational patterns and attitudes that we believe are at the root of the productivity problem are notoriously hard to change, even once the need for change is recognized. For example, we have found many circumstances where greater teamwork and cooperation would be to the benefit of all, but employees have no incentive to form teams when their firms base promotion, pay, and other rewards entirely on individual performance. At a larger scale, firms cannot risk cooperating with one another without some change in the prevailing atmosphere of self-reliance and mistrust. Change, if it is to occur, will have to take place on a broad front involving firms, government, educational institutions, and organized labor. There is consequently every reason to open public discussion of these systemic rigidities and of ways to remedy them.

3

Outdated Strategies

The decline of the U.S. economy puzzles most Americans. The qualities and talents that gave rise to the dynamism of the postwar years must surely be present still in the national character, and yet American industry seems to have lost much of its vigor. In looking for ways to reverse the decline, it is only natural to turn to the methods that succeeded in the golden years of growth and innovation. Many business managers have adopted just this strategy. The results, unfortunately, are rather like those of a man who keeps striking the same match because it worked fine the first time.

In industry after industry the Commission's studies have found managers and workers so attached to the old way of doing things that they cannot understand the new economic environment. Challenged by stronger foreign competition and stagnant productivity, they respond by clinging more tenaciously to the patterns of production and organization they associate with the heyday of American economic primacy. To some extent, it is the very magnitude of past successes that has prevented adaptation to a new world.

The industry studies reveal two main elements of past practice that are impeding progress today. First is the reliance on mass production of standard commodity goods. Mass production was the driving force behind American postwar prosperity, but it is often no longer an appropriate model for managers and workers in the changed circumstances of today. The second major problem is parochialism. For decades American industry was able to thrive by producing mainly for its own markets and by drawing technical expertise mainly from its own factories and laboratories. The legacy of these years of self-sufficiency is an economy ill-equipped to compete for worldwide markets or to exploit foreign innovations.

The Mass-Production System

The great success of the American economy in the twentieth century was a system of mass production of standard products for a large domestic market. The system turned out a large volume of goods at low cost. It also provided jobs that paid well and were fairly stable, except for recurring economywide recessions. The success of mass production was most dramatic in the American automobile industry, which was once the envy of the world. As the Commission report on this industry describes, the mass-production model was a system of interdependent and mutually reinforcing elements. The automakers saw their target as a domestic mass market whose demands could most profitably be met by a flow of relatively inexpensive and undifferentiated products. The same cars, with only cosmetic differences, were produced year after year for everyone. The industry emphasized price competition and put less stress on improving product quality or design. In the workplace, management sought to maintain control through the simplification and specialization of jobs and by establishing steep hierarchical ladders. In line with these conceptions of the market and the workplace, technological innovation was oriented toward tooling and machinery suitable for long runs of standard designs. Suppliers and customers were kept at arm's length, and relations with them sometimes took on an adversarial aspect.

In its essential elements the system of mass production characterized most of American manufacturing. Indeed, within the United States the triumph of this system was so complete that other patterns of production were virtually wiped out. There was little room left in the economy for a craft tradition, with less-hierarchical work organizations and the direct participation of skilled workers in production decisions, or for other means of serving smaller segments of the market.

Craft methods also came under pressure in other industrial countries as they attempted to imitate the American example. Nevertheless, the alternative ways of organizing production did survive overseas. They formed the nucleus of the new approaches to manufacturing that have emerged since the 1970s. As Michael Piore and Charles Sabel describe in *The Second Industrial Divide*, the countries in which the alternatives to mass production remained strong—most notably West Germany, Japan, and Italy—have been the countries most successful in pioneering new forms of workplace organization, more-flexible technologies, and patterns of production that efficiently satisfy the demand of limited segments of the market.[1]

The success of the Japanese car industry is based on a system different in almost every feature from Detroit's mass-production system. The Japanese have succeeded by providing different products for each segment of the market. To do so efficiently and profitably, they have developed technologies, product-development methods, and patterns of workplace organization that allow them to reduce the volume of production and increase the speed with which new products are brought to market. This has required the creation of a highly skilled work force as well as the development of flexible automation. They have emphasized quality and service as well as cost. To target the needs of specific market segments, they have moved closer to customers; to reduce costs and improve quality, they have moved closer to suppliers. Collaborative relations with subcontractors are maintained even in hard times, whereas U.S. firms would typically respond to a contraction of demand by cutting off orders to their suppliers.

As the superiority of these patterns became clear to American car manufacturers, they attempted to copy them. At this point, however, the strengths of the earlier mass-production system became an obstacle to reorganizing the firm. Manufacturers were reluctant to abandon such features of the mass-production system as long runs of standard cars and the prerogative of laying off large numbers of workers. These attachments to the old ways can undermine the implementation of the new system.

U.S. firms have also had difficulty matching the product-development performance of the Japanese, who have responded to the fragmentation of markets and the increasing demands of customers by developing the capability to introduce large numbers of innovative new products and at the same time reduce the time to market.[2] (The main reasons for the impressively short Japanese product-development times are discussed in more detail in chapter 5.)

Textiles are another industry with a long tradition of mass production. Some American textile firms have now moved to shorter runs and more-flexible machinery, but they continue to rely on a low-cost, low-skill labor force. It seems doubtful that an undertrained work force can realize the possibilities of the new machinery. Rapid changeovers and diversity in the product line require workers who know how to readjust looms or dye-vat controls, reprogram cutting machines, and carry out many other adjustments and repairs. The legacy of past success thus blunts the thrust of reform in American industry.

Of course, there are examples of American firms that have developed organizations and strategies that enable them to compete successfully in world markets. The Commission has tried to understand why these examples are not more generally emulated and why changes do not diffuse more rapidly and broadly throughout American industry. The evidence from the industry studies points to the continuing influence of ways of thinking and operating that grew out of a mass-production model. Managers today often acknowledge that one or another feature of this model ought to be scrapped, and so, for example, they will set up quality circles or reduce batch sizes. But everything we have learned from our industry studies in the United States and abroad suggests that individual parts of the old patterns cannot be replaced piecemeal. It will not do to borrow pieces of the West German or the Japanese system and try to make them fit an American context. Rather, for any of the reforms to survive and flourish, the environment in which it is implanted must be transformed.

Parochialism

At the high tide of American economic expansion, American firms found a seemingly unlimited and uncontested outlet for their products in their own domestic market. The home market was large, unified, and familiar. Foreign markets were small, segmented, and protected not only by tariff barriers but also by impenetrable distribution systems. Above all, they were foreign: operating in them required linguistic and cultural skills that Americans did not have and did not wish to acquire. Hence, most foreign markets and foreign competitors were largely ignored.

In the first two decades after the war, when the major trading partners of the United States were still weak competitors and when foreign markets were still small, the costs of such parochialism were sustainable. Today the global business strategies of European and Asian firms have fundamentally changed the game. The sectoral studies show that foreign competitors have captured significant segments of the U.S. market and challenge American companies in all world markets. The nation is inextricably linked to the rest of the advanced industrial world. America must sell abroad to pay for the goods it buys abroad and for the money it has borrowed abroad. Hiding behind the protective walls of tariffs and quotas is not an option; it would impoverish the United States and put at risk the entire international economic order.

To sell abroad requires an understanding of foreign societies that Americans have not possessed. The issue is not simply that Americans cannot speak the languages of the countries in which they wish to do business, although linguistic handicaps are important. Even more damaging is the assumption that American tastes, American ways of doing business, and American products are universal (or ought to be). In an interview with the Commission's textile study group, a textile and garment manufacturer who has been very successful in the United States ruefully recalled a failed attempt at selling in European markets: "We thought we could just ship in our sweatshirts and they'd sell themselves." No one should be surprised that large gas-guzzling American cars have had little appeal to Europeans, who must cope with high gas prices and narrow city streets. Similarly, American manufacturers have had little success in selling gigantic computer-aided cutting machines to small, crowded European garment factories. (French and Spanish firms, in contrast, have designed equipment on a scale to fit the facilities of the average plant.)

Americans have not taken seriously the needs and preferences of other societies, at least in part because they simply have not perceived those needs and preferences. Many Americans pay scant attention to life beyond the nation's borders. The educational system, from kindergarten through graduate and professional schools, has reinforced this inward-looking bias and has failed to open windows onto the world. The principal economic rivals to the United States, on the other hand, have long understood that operating in a foreign society requires mastery of the language as a prerequisite, together with significant exposure to different cultures.

Parochialism has been an economic handicap, because it cripples efforts to sell in foreign markets. Equally important, it has made U.S. companies slow to see what their competitors were preparing for U.S. markets. In the 1950s and 1960s, for example, American steel producers underestimated the strength of emerging foreign competition. They lagged behind Japanese and European steelmakers in the adoption of new process technologies, like the basic oxygen furnace; later they were again slow to adopt continuous casters and such quality-enhancing technologies as vacuum degassing and oxygen injection. The critical error in these cases was not so much a failure to innovate as a failure to recognize the worth of someone else's innovation. The Commission's steel group contrasted the haphazard search for new process technology conducted by U.S. integrated steel firms with the much more intensive and systematic efforts of the Japanese, who visited foreign plants and scanned the international technical literature.

In the machine-tool industry the Commission study found that the narrow geographical horizons of U.S. firms helped Japanese companies to create an initial opening in the American market. Unlike the strongly export-oriented European and Japanese firms, few U.S. machine-tool builders thought of themselves as competing in international markets, as needing to export, or as needing to take into account what builders and users in other countries were doing. Foreign firms used their export markets to offset fluctuations in home-market demand. U.S. firms, with little export volume to fall back on, adopted a strategy of backlogging orders during periods of strong domestic demand so as to smooth out production and employment levels over the course of the business cycle. This policy left the American makers vulnerable to low-cost, high-quality imports that could be delivered quickly. Japanese machine tools, built to inventory and stockpiled at U.S. distribution points, were available immediately, while domestic producers had waiting lists of up to two years. As American buyers gained experience with the reliability of Japanese machines and the vendors' rapid and courteous service, they reordered and spread the word.

Parochialism has also blinded Americans to the growing strength of scientific and technological innovation abroad, and hence to the possibility of adapting the discoveries for use in the United States. The dominance of American science and technology in the early postwar decades was so great that companies could operate as if American laboratories were the only ones generating useful knowledge. American firms therefore failed to build up the networks of contacts abroad that underpin systematic attempts at technological scanning. They saw no need to translate technical publications and reports into English, as they assumed that anything of significance would soon enough make it into one of the journals they were accustomed to read. What's more, when foreign discoveries were brought to the attention of U.S. firms, they were frequently discounted. The story of process innovation in steel has already been cited; similar episodes are reported in other sectors as well. In textiles, for example, innovations with great potential for the industry were brought to the notice of American industry giants but were ignored. An example is the Kawabata measuring system.[3]

A number of firms have begun to recognize the need to scan globally for best practice and to transfer new ideas and methods across borders. The concept of "competitive benchmarking" is now becoming more widely accepted in American firms. At Xerox, for example, every department is expected to conduct a global survey to find the firm or organizational unit that performs its function the best. This performance level then becomes the target for the Xerox unit. Other companies have used the strategy of forming joint ventures with best-practice firms from other countries as a learning tool. Examples include the joint ventures of General Motors with Toyota, Ford with Mazda, Chrysler with Mitsubishi, and Armco with Kawasaki Steel. Still other companies are now beginning to include foreign experience as a critical part of their management-development programs. But the number of top American executives with extensive overseas experience is still rather small. Ensuring that the next generation of corporate executives has a broader international background is a task that must be taken up jointly by the universities that train managers and the firms that employ them. We will have more to say about this when we present our recommendations for education and for management practice.

4

Short Time Horizons

It is no great insight to say that successful business planners have to pay attention to both the long-term and the short-term consequences of their decisions. There are many cases where a firm has hung on too long or given up too soon. In this chapter, we investigate a tendency for American business to be preoccupied with short-term results.

We begin by describing a number of instances in which American firms have given ground to overseas competitors despite holding an early lead in technology or sales or both. In these instances it is reasonable to conclude that U.S. firms were less willing than their rivals to live through a period of heavy investment and meager returns in order to secure a foothold in a growing market. There may be cases in which the roles were reversed, but the evidence suggests that it is usually the Americans who are most concerned with near-term outcomes.

This is not to suggest that the decisions motivated by short-term concerns were necessarily wrong or that they would later be regretted or even that the whole economy, as distinct from the individual firm, would have been better off had they gone the other way. They may have been quite rational decisions. Indeed, we shall show that one important environmental factor, the higher cost of capital, pushes American companies irresistibly in the direction of a shorter time horizon. So long as U.S. firms must pay more for the use of capital, in their own self-interest they must seek quicker payoffs than their rivals.

Nevertheless, we believe that the disparity in time horizons is caused by more than a difference in interest rates and required dividend yields. There is evidence, difficult to quantify but ultimately convincing to us, that other forces also drive American business to excessive preoccupation with immediate profit, even to the sacrifice of longer-term opportunities. As is discussed later in the chapter, these problems stem in part from the practices of financial institutions and corporate managers and sometimes also from the risks perceived to be associated with the policies of the U.S. and other governments.

Our study of the consumer-electronics industry showed how the longer time horizons of the Japanese electronics companies helped them to dominate the market for videocassette recorders (VCRs). American firms were the first to introduce video-recording technology, but the early products were complex and expensive and suitable only for industrial and professional applications. Many years of further development were needed to create low-cost, highly reliable products suitable for the mass consumer market. Several Japanese manufacturers succeeded in perfecting the designs and the manufacturing processes, but no American firms did. The Japanese are now virtually unchallenged as makers of what has become the most important single product in the consumer-electronics market.

One key factor in the Japanese success was superior engineering, which will be further discussed in the next chapter. Another factor was the willingness of the Japanese firms to invest heavily in both product development and process development for more than two decades while cash returns were low and growing only very slowly. American industry proved much less ready to do this. Over the same period many U.S. firms were in fact retreating from consumer-electronics markets, progressively ceding products and functions to foreign competitors and diversifying into less-risky and more-profitable businesses, such as car rentals and financial services, completely unrelated to their original line of work.

The VCR case illustrates an important lesson that applies to all businesses in which products and production processes are technologically complex. Competitive success in such industries is rarely the result of overnight breakthroughs; rather, it is built on years of effort, years spent testing, adjusting, improving, refining, and in the process accumulating detailed technical knowledge of products and production techniques. Often progress also involves the parallel development and eventual synthesis of several different technologies. Surprises are inevitable, and they are not always pleasant ones. Firms engaged in such development must expect to enter technological culs-de-sac from time to time. The successful firms in these industries are those with the conviction and the stamina to stay the course in spite of risks and mishaps and the probable sacrifice of profits in the short term. In industry after industry, we observed an unwillingness on the part of U.S. firms to forgo these short-term returns and, as in the consumer-electronics case, an associated tendency to diversify into activities that are more profitable in the short run.

Diversification is not a bad thing in itself. Neither stockholders nor executives have or should have an unlimited appetite for risk. Nevertheless, we think that we have detected something approaching a systematic unwillingness or inability of U.S. companies to "stick to their knitting" and maintain technological leadership after the first big returns have been captured. They thereby allow longer-winded companies, most notably Japanese firms, to take over technological preeminence and market share. This is a particularly disturbing phenomenon, because it suggests a fundamental weakness in just those technologically dynamic industries, such as semiconductors and advanced materials, that provide the foundation for building and sustaining an economy characterized by high growth in productivity.

The U.S. preoccupation with short-term gains has manifested itself in other ways as well. In several of our industry studies we observed the following pattern. Japanese firms enter a new market at the low-cost end of the product range; American firms choose not to contest these market segments, often in spite of their high growth potential, because the immediate or near-term profit margins are lower; the Japanese then exploit their growing market presence and reputation and the effects of the learning curve to move up market and challenge the American producers directly. This pattern has repeated itself in a broad range of markets, including machine tools, copiers, consumer electronics, and semiconductors. In each case the Japanese firms enjoyed other advantages too—superior manufacturing techniques, lower labor costs, and sometimes direct support from the government—but in every case their longer time horizon was a key factor in their success.

The competitive advantage associated with longer time horizons is particularly strong in rapidly growing markets. Japanese firms have been willing to take on high levels of debt in order to invest in new production capacity and marketing infrastructure ahead of the growth in demand; in effect, they have been investing to grow demand. Thereafter they have priced their products aggressively and often far below costs in the early phases of a developing market. By these means the Japanese firms have been able to sustain higher growth rates than their American rivals. U.S. companies are usually reluctant to adopt such policies, because they entail a sacrifice of short-term profits and higher risks to shareholders. But in high-growth markets, aggressively pursuing market share and then defending it are keys to competitive success. Costs decline more rapidly as the manufacturer learns how to build the product more efficiently and as the growing production volume offers a larger base of units over which to spread fixed costs.

The Japanese market for medical-imaging equipment is a good example of this phenomenon. U.S. firms were the first to enter the market with the computer-aided tomography (CAT) scanner in the early 1970s.[1] They concentrated on the high end of the market, selling mostly to large hospitals and research institutions. The Japanese entered later, with lower-priced systems that typically had fewer features but that smaller hospitals could afford. They focused on building market share, sacrificing short-term profits in favor of cutting prices, expanding production capacity, and improving the product. Sales volume grew faster in the low end of the market, and progress down the learning curve was more rapid. Although prices were falling, the Japanese firms could commit funds from cash flow to expand their sales and service capabilities and also to upgrade their products. Meanwhile, under pressure from headquarters to increase profits, the American producers boosted prices and cut back on marketing and sales resources. The benefits were short-lived. By the late 1970s the performance of the Japanese products had risen to match that of the American equipment, but their costs remained lower. The U.S. firms quickly began to lose market share and profitability.

A postscript to the VCR case study tells a similar story. Ampex, the American company that first demonstrated practical video tape recording, failed to commercialize a consumer-oriented product and instead concentrated on sophisticated broadcast video equipment. Now Ampex is losing ground in this area too as the profits, technology, and scale economies achieved by Japanese manufacturers of consumer VCRs are brought to bear on higher-value-added market segments.

Our industry studies also revealed many instances in which a concern with short-term profitability undermined or inhibited cooperative relationships. We observed this on several levels, from interdepartmental interactions within firms divided into separate profit centers to the contractual relations between large corporations. We shall discuss the cooperative shortcomings of American industry later in more detail. Here we simply point out the connection between that problem and the problem of short time horizons.

In the realm of producer-supplier relations, for example, some dominant firms have forced their suppliers to cut costs in ways that ultimately proved imprudent. The lower prices may have benefited the more powerful firms in the short run, but the longer-term consequences were often unhelpful and were sometimes clearly injurious to all the firms dependent on the suppliers. Vendors were discouraged from investing to improve the goods or services they were supplying. In competitive markets it is unrealistic to expect companies to renounce entirely the coercive power that comes with superior market position in exchange for the potential benefits of collaboration with suppliers or clients. But our case studies revealed a greater willingness on the part of U.S. firms than their European and Japanese counterparts to sacrifice the advantages of long-term relationships for the benefit of a short-term gain.

The case-study evidence suggesting an American bias toward quick profits is reinforced by economywide trends in investment and in research and development. Figure 4.1 shows that the rate of

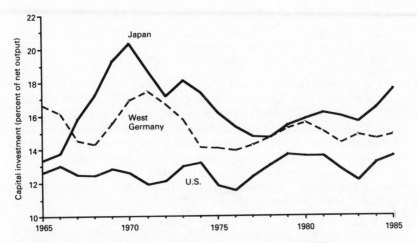

Figure 4.1   Business-sector capital investment in the U.S., Japan, and West Germany
Business-sector capital investment was taken to be gross fixed capital formation excluding dwellings and the nonmarket activities of the government. It was computed at constant, native-currency prices and is expressed as a percentage of net output in the private sector. Sources: Organization for Economic Cooperation and Development, *Flows and Stocks of Fixed Capital, 1960–1985* (Paris: OECD, 1987); Organization for Economic Cooperation and Development, *National Accounts of OECD Countries,* vol. 2, *Detailed Tables, 1964–1981* (Paris: OECD, 1983), table 2b; Organization for Economic Cooperation and Development, *National Accounts of OECD Countries,* vol. 2, *Detailed Tables, 1973–1985* (Paris: OECD, 1987), table 12.

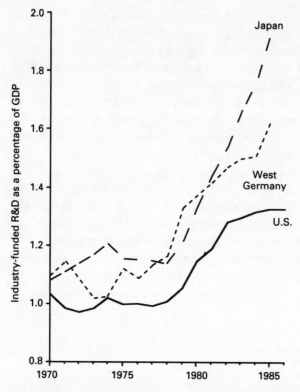

Figure 4.2   Industry-funded research and development
Sources: National Science Board, *Science and Engineering Indicators—1987* (Washington, D.C.: U.S. Government Printing Office, 1987), appendix table 6-1, p. 293; National Science Foundation, *National Patterns of Science and Technology Resources: 1986*, Surveys of Science Resources Series, NSF 88-305 (Washington D.C.: U.S. Government Printing Office, January 1988), table B-5, p. 46; Organization for Economic Cooperation and Development (OECD), *National Accounts of OECD Countries, 1960–1986*, vol. 1, *Main Aggregates* (Paris: OECD, 1988), tables for the United States, West Germany, and Japan.

business-sector capital investment in the United States has been significantly lower than in Japan and West Germany for two decades. Similarly, figure 4.2 shows that spending on research and development by U.S. firms, expressed as a fraction of total economic output, has grown much more slowly in recent years than the corresponding investment in Japan and West Germany. *Total* spending on research and development as a percentage of gross domestic product is about the same in the three countries, but a much larger share of the U.S. total comes from defense-related research and development funded by the government.

What accounts for the short-term bias in American industry? Is it that U.S. firms tend to be myopic—that they focus on the short term because they are somehow incapable of looking as far ahead as their overseas rivals? Or are they forced by external circumstances—the macroeconomic environment or a cultural bias in American society—to focus on the short term, even though they may realize that it is not in their own best interest to do so? Or might it be that a short-term focus *is* in the best interests of individual firms, but not of the U.S. economy as a whole? Were U.S. consumer-electronics manufacturers acting against the interests of their shareholders when they diversified into more-profitable markets instead of trying to weather the deluge of low-cost, high-quality imports from fiercely competitive Japanese suppliers? Were U.S. steel companies wrong to diversify into new markets rather than modernize their plant as competition from imports intensified during the 1970s? Or were these companies simply doing the rational thing in their immediate circumstances? We address these questions next.

One explanation that absolves firms from responsibility for the problem focuses on the cost of capital. The cost of capital is a measure of how much a business must pay to get the funds needed to finance an investment expenditure. If the money is borrowed on the open market, its cost is the interest paid; funds obtained from retained earnings or from the sale of equity also have a cost that can be measured. In practice, the effective cost of capital to business firms is much influenced by tax rules.

The importance of the cost of capital in determining the rational time horizon for decisions is easily illustrated. Imagine two corporations, *A* and *J*, similar except that the cost of capital to firm *A* is 10 percent per year, while *J* pays only 3 percent. If we assume that they will pay back the capital at the end of two years, *A* can profitably invest $100 now only if the investment will return $121, while *J* can profitably undertake any investment that will return more than $106 in two years. Clearly, there are investments that *J* will make and that *A* cannot. Moreover, the disparity is far greater for 20-year investments: *A* can afford to undertake only those investments that will yield more than $673, while *J* needs only a payoff greater than $181. Thus, *J* has a mild advantage even in short-term investment but an insurmountable one when it comes to investments requiring a long time to germinate. *A* is *forced* to be shortsighted.

If the world capital market were perfect, corporations of all nationalities would raise capital wherever it cost the least, and *A* and *J* would be on the same footing. But capital markets are not nearly perfect in this sense, partly for natural reasons and partly for artificial (legal or customary) ones. Hence, *J* will have a big advantage when it comes to long-term investment.

Most recent studies indicate that the cost of capital to American firms is a good deal higher than the cost in Japan. It is generally agreed that a key reason for the disparity is the low rate of private savings and the high rate of government deficits in the United States. Net U.S. savings averaged 3.6 percent of gross domestic product between 1981 and 1986, compared with 17.3 percent in Japan (see table 4.1). Other contributing factors include tax policies that are more favorable to long-term industrial investment in Japan than in the United States. Comparing the real cost of

Table 4.1

Net rates of savings in the United States and Japan (percent of GDP)

	Households and private, unincorporated enterprises		Corporate and quasi-corporate enterprises		Government (national, state, local, and social security)		All sectors	
	U.S.	Japan	U.S.	Japan	U.S.	Japan	U.S.	Japan
1981	6.56	13.07	1.19	1.75	− 1.32	3.06	6.43	17.88
1982	6.40	11.82	0.43	2.40	− 4.15	2.81	2.68	17.03
1983	5.40	11.69	1.77	2.05	− 4.95	2.33	2.22	16.07
1984	5.80	11.25	2.50	2.54	− 3.92	3.26	4.38	17.05
1985	4.59	11.04	2.57	2.59	− 4.01	4.32	3.15	17.95
1986	4.50	11.48	2.28	2.50	− 4.31	3.99	2.47	17.97
1981–86	5.54	11.73	1.79	2.30	− 3.78	3.29	3.56	17.32

Source: Organization for Economic Cooperation and Development, *National Accounts*, vol. 2, *Detailed Tables, 1974–86* (Paris: OECD, 1987), table 1, pp. 32, 60.

capital in the two countries is a complicated matter, and not everyone agrees on how big the difference is. A recent study estimates that U.S. firms pay 50 to 75 percent more for investment capital than Japanese companies do.[2]

Some observers argue that the difference in the cost of capital between the U.S. and Japan is the overriding reason for the different time horizons of firms in the two countries.[3] We agree that the cost of capital is an important factor, but we do not think it is the only one. Corporations usually base their investment decisions on the return expected from the investment, often expressed as an equivalent annual percentage rate. This return must generally exceed some corporate hurdle rate, which incorporates not only the simple cost of capital but also an allowance for various risk factors associated with the investment. For risky investments the hurdle rate can be several times greater than the cost of capital to the firm. Differences in the pressure for short-term results can therefore stem from differences in perceived risks, as well as in the cost of capital.

In addition to the usual business risks, firms sometimes must also consider the effects of uncertainties in government protection from dumping or other trade abuses, patent protection, environmental or other liabilities, exchange rates, and competitors' plans to expand market share at almost any cost. Small disadvantages in trade or regulatory conditions or in cross-subsidy effects can easily reduce or erase modest profit margins. We believe that such factors may have played a significant role in the investment-decision process in some U.S. industries. Conversely, the supportive role played by the Japanese government in expanding their national manufacturing base and exports has very likely had the effect of reducing the perceived risk element in investment decisions by Japanese firms.

Another explanation of the problem concerns the manner in which American companies are financed. According to this view, the cost of capital may be less important than the nature of the institutions and arrangements that influence its supply. Japanese and European firms tend to raise more capital from such financial institutions as banks and less through open-market sales of securities. Banks and insurance companies provide long-term finance for Japanese industrial firms in ways that they do not in the United States. Typically, they own equity and are represented on the board of directors of the companies to which they lend. It is also common for industrial firms with long-standing commercial ties to own each other's stock.[4]

In contrast, a large and growing share of the capital of U.S. firms is owned by mutual funds and pension funds, whose assets are in the form of a market basket of securities. The actual equity holders, the clients of the funds, are far removed from managerial decisions. Their agents, the fund managers, have no long-term loyalty to the companies in which they invest, and they have no representation on their boards. Although some fund managers invest for the long term, most turn over their stock holdings rapidly in an effort to maximize the current value of their investment portfolio, since this is the main criterion against which their own performance is judged.

Firms respond to this financial environment by maximizing their short-term profit in the belief that the market would penalize them for taking the long view. Much of the evidence for this analysis comes from business executives describing their own perceptions and behavior. They say they feel themselves pushed in the short-sighted direction, against their own better judgment, by the fear that development and investment policies oriented toward the long term will be undervalued by the market and leave their firm vulnerable to takeover. We are persuaded by the argument that the wave of hostile takeovers and leveraged buyouts has contributed to an exaggerated focus on short-term returns.

At the same time senior executives are also motivated to maintain steady growth in earnings by their own profit-related bonus plans and stock options. A chief executive whose compensation is a strong function of his company's financial performance in the current year is naturally going to stress short-term results. Indeed, some executive-compensation schemes may encourage managers to adopt an even shorter time horizon than the capital markets do. We have found no shortage of executive bonuses geared to yearly or even semiannual performance.

Executives in other countries tend to be less preoccupied with earnings, dividends, and share prices. Japanese and European firms hold that managers are not only responsible to shareholders but also have a commitment to the larger community of employees, customers, neighbors, and suppliers and to the continuity and growth of the firm itself. Table 4.2 shows the results of a survey comparing the corporate objectives of about 500 major U.S. and Japanese companies. For the U.S. executives, return on investment

Table 4.2

U.S. and Japanese ranking of corporate objectives (10 = most important)

	U.S.	Japan
Return on investment	8.1	4.1
Share-price increase	3.8	0.1
Market share	2.4	4.8
Improve product portfolio	1.7	2.3
Rationalization of production and distribution	1.5	2.4
Increase equity ratio	1.3	2.0
Ratio of new products	0.7	3.5
Improve company's image	0.2	0.7
Improve working conditions	0.1	0.3

Executives of 291 Japanese companies and 227 U.S. companies ranked factors from 10, for most important, to 1, for least important. Source: J. C. Abegglen and G. Stalk, Jr., *Kaisha: The Japanese Corporation* (New York: Basic Books, 1985), p. 177.

was clearly the highest priority, followed by share price increases and market share. New-product introductions ranked seventh out of nine objectives. For the Japanese firms, market share was the most important objective. Return on investment ranked second, and new-product introductions were third. Share price ranked last.

Structural differences having to do with the size and maturity of the company also have an important effect on time horizons in some industries. Consider, for example, the merchant producers of semiconductors, the companies that make chips for sale to others. In the U.S. almost all of these companies are young, relatively small, and highly entrepreneurial. Their Japanese competitors, on the other hand, are large, diversified, and vertically integrated companies like NEC, Toshiba, Hitachi, and Fujitsu. There are American companies of comparable scale that manufacture semiconductors—notably IBM, AT&T, and the Delco division of General Motors—but they produce mainly to satisfy their own needs and seldom enter the merchant market.

As the Commission's semiconductor industry group reported, a pattern of instability, high mobility, and new-venture formation has characterized the young American merchant industry in the past 20 years. New companies tended to be highly innovative at first, but then frequently fell behind the fast-moving technological frontier. Many lacked the financial strength to fund expensive product-development projects and to tide themselves over during the downturns in this cyclical business. Market leadership was transi-

tory. Employee turnover averaged 20 percent annually. The instability and the high turnover contributed to the short-term focus.
Long-term commitments to suppliers and customers were avoided.
There was little training of employees, and accumulated experience was often lost through defections and layoffs. Every effort was
made to cash in quickly on any technological advantage by licensing new technology to both domestic and foreign companies,
which often became competitors.

In contrast, the Japanese semiconductor industry was far more
stable. Independent venture formation and mass defections were
almost nonexistent. Corporate risks were also reduced by a government-coordinated strategic program that encouraged exports,
rewarded investment in future productivity growth, protected the
domestic market, subsidized research and development, and discouraged conflict between firms. The big Japanese companies
could afford to be much more patient than their competitors in the
U.S. merchant industry, and they surely would have been even in
the absence of cost-of-capital differences.

Explanations that cite the cost of capital, the sources of financing, or the size and maturity of companies all tend to depict
corporate managers as victims of circumstance, forced by external
conditions into a short-term decision framework. Yet another point
of view lays the blame at the door of the corporate executive suite.
In a much discussed article Robert Hayes and the late William
Abernathy of the Harvard Business School argued that what they
call the "new management orthodoxy" is responsible for a pervasive myopia in American industry.[5] Managers today, according to
Hayes and Abernathy, prefer analytic detachment to hands-on
experience, and they focus on short-term cost reduction rather
than long-term technological competitiveness. This creates a "false
and shallow concept of the professional manager—an individual
having no special expertise in any particular industry or technology
who nevertheless can step into an unfamiliar company and run it
successfully through strict application of financial controls, portfolio concepts, and a market-driven strategy." A growing gap separates those who do, the line managers, from those in the executive
suite who judge them.

Hayes and Abernathy argued that executive ranks have come to
be dominated by individuals with financial and legal skills who
know too little about their firm's products, markets, and production processes and who rely instead on quantifiable short-term

financial criteria. These modern executives are more likely to engage in financial restructuring to bolster profits than to take risks on technological innovation. Further, their greater mobility means that they are less likely to identify with the long-term survival of the firm than with its profitability during the years they happen to be associated with it.

Another analysis of corporate shortsightedness suggests that the problem is not that managers rely too heavily on financial data but rather that they often misinterpret those data. Stewart Myers points out that it is easy to misapply standard financial calculations in evaluating investment opportunities, and many of the common errors impose a bias in favor of short-term investments.[6] Perhaps the most important of these errors is the use of unrealistically high hurdle rates in inappropriate attempts to correct for start-up risk.

Even a nominally correct analysis, Myers continues, may have limitations that lean in the same direction. The common method of financial analysis based on discounted cash flows has difficulty expressing the "option value" of an investment: the present value of future opportunities that will be opened up if the investment is made. Because option value tends to be underestimated, Myers concludes that the discounted-cash-flow method "is less helpful in valuing businesses with substantial growth opportunities or intangible assets. [It] is no help at all for pure research and development. The value of R&D is almost all option value."

There is no necessary implication here that standard financial calculations are wrong in any simple mathematical sense (although Myers gives some reasons why they might be). A more subtle bias may be at work. Once a particular discount rate is assumed, a discounted-cash-flow analysis yields answers that appear to be precise and well founded, but in fact, the future cash flows to be discounted are mostly conjecture. When a company invests in a novel technology, the early cash flows are inevitably uncertain, precisely because the potential of the technology is not yet known. The later cash flows are even more uncertain, since everything about the distant future is chancy. If management has any impatient tendency to favor short-term gains over long-term gains, this unavoidable imprecision offers a standing opportunity to express it.

We believe that Myers's ideas can plausibly explain why corporations relying on close financial calculations should exhibit a short-term bias. The remedy, however, is not to abandon rational analysis of investment decisions in favor of intuitive leaps of faith. Instead, the goal should be to develop tools for financial evaluation suitable for use in growing, high-technology businesses. In the meantime the more fundamental problem of lowering the cost of capital must also be addressed.

It is encouraging to note that not all of the eight industries studied by the Commission showed the same preoccupation with short-term goals. Our chemical-industry team found that several large U.S. chemical firms had successfully pursued a long-term strategy of expanding from the mature chemical business into emerging markets that offered higher growth but also higher risk. They made this readjustment even though they face the same pressures for short-term results that had driven firms in other industries to diversify into unrelated businesses offering greater short-term rewards. The Commission has attributed this behavior to the rich technological tradition and commitment to innovation in the chemical industry, which has spawned a managerial culture in which detailed knowledge of processes, products, and markets has been valued more highly than it is elsewhere.

Similarly, the American commercial-aircraft industry dominated world markets in the postwar years partly because of the willingness of the leading U.S. firms to invest in efforts at long-term development and repeatedly risk their futures on new products. According to our aircraft-industry team, this willingness in turn had a lot to do with the fact that the senior executives of the companies "loved to build planes." Of course, the captive military market, technological edge, and economies of scale available to U.S builders were also helpful in this regard.

Risk-taking on that scale may well be more difficult in today's financial environment. But managers are not without the ability to influence investor perceptions. A number of thoughtful U.S. businessmen told us that American managers' oft-stated concern about short-term financial pressures could be much reduced if the managers themselves were more willing or able to develop a long-term vision for their companies and to communicate it effectively to their investors.

5

Technological Weaknesses in Development and Production

In the postwar years the United States invested heavily in research, and the investment paid off, sometimes in surprising ways. Basic research, undertaken for its own sake, often led to commercial applications that could not have been predicted at the outset. Likewise, research for defense needs generated innovations useful for the civilian economy. These experiences shaped current expectations for science and technology.

There are important truths embodied in these expectations. Investment in basic scientific and engineering research *is* essential for long-term economic growth. Defense research *can* bear commercial fruit. But the nation's technological strength depends on far more than the health of its research laboratories, important as that is. Prowess in research does not lead automatically to commercial success. New ideas must be converted into products that customers want, when they want them, and before competitors can provide them, and the products must be made efficiently and well. Ralph Gomory of IBM recently observed, "You do not have to be the science leader to be the best consumer of science; and you do not have to be the best consumer of science to be the best product manufacturer."[1]

The United States is still unarguably the leader in basic research. The scale of its scientific enterprise is unequaled, and it is second to none in making new discoveries. Yet U.S. companies increasingly find themselves lagging behind their foreign rivals in the commercial exploitation of inventions and discoveries. Transistor radios, color televisions, videocassette recorders, and numerically controlled machine tools are just a few examples of products now dominated by foreign manufacturers, even though the major enabling technological advances were first made in the United States.

There is irony in this situation. The industrial lead built up by the United States earlier in the century rested in no small part on its superior performance in exploiting inventions made elsewhere. Later, during the first two decades of the postwar era, American firms dominated the early stages of the product cycle in most industries. Because of the unrivaled strength of the nation's research base and the industrial weaknesses of other countries, U.S. firms were almost always first to market with new products. In many cases overseas rivals eventually did acquire the technology, and their lower labor costs sometimes enabled them to manufacture the products more cheaply. By then, however, the American firms had moved on to the next generation of new products.

Today the industrial nations of Europe and Asia have greatly expanded their technological capabilities. They can understand and rapidly capitalize on promising technological discoveries made anywhere in the world. They have also developed their own private and public research establishments. The emphasis of their research is somewhat different, however. They have focused on applied research and on product and process development. As a result, they have greatly shortened the time between discovery and commercialization.

In the United States, meanwhile, outstanding successes in basic science and in defense research have left the product-realization process a poor cousin. As firms in other countries have improved their capabilities in these downstream areas, shortcomings have become evident in the performance of American industry in developing new products, engineering them, and manufacturing them. Specifically, our industry studies have revealed several closely related deficiencies in this area. American companies evidently find it difficult to design simple, reliable, mass-producible products; they often fail to pay enough attention at the design stage to the likely quality of the manufactured product; their product-development times are excessively long; they pay insufficient attention to manufacturing processes; they take a reactive rather than a preventive approach to problem solving; and they tend to under-exploit the potential of continuous improvement in products and processes.

We shall illustrate these shortcomings with examples drawn from our industry studies. Many of the examples are by now well known. Individually, the problems appear straightforward and relatively easy to correct. Collectively, however, they are the result of what, in the Commission's view, has been a long-term devaluation of production-related functions and skills. Public policymakers and educators share responsibility for this devaluation with the nation's industrial enterprises.

Designing for Manufacturability and Quality

American design engineers have too often neglected manufacturability and quality in their product designs. One of the problem areas has been a lack of attention to simplifying designs. Reducing the part count in a product can yield cost savings that ripple through the entire production system, affecting manufacturing efficiency, materials purchasing and handling, and the quality, reliability, and serviceability of the product itself.

IBM's Proprinter project is an impressive example of what can be achieved in this way. A multidisciplinary team was charged with the task of designing a computer printer with a much lower part count than earlier models and no springs or screws (which increase assembly time and decrease reliability). The result was a printer much simpler and easier to assemble than its predecessor. The number of components was reduced from more than 160 to 63. Essential to the success of the project was the multidisciplinary composition of the design team: product designers were joined by manufacturing engineers and even scientists. Though hardly a startling organizational breakthrough, this was nonetheless a departure from standard practice among American manufacturers. In the traditional system a new product is designed for function, and then the completed design is "thrown over the wall" to the manufacturing department, which has responsibility for both process design and production operations. This arrangement frequently leads to serious problems. Product-design groups neglect manufacturing considerations in their design, and manufacturing managers are preoccupied with production operations; thus, process design tends to be an orphan. When a production crew runs into problems, they throw the project back over the wall to the designers, who may have since moved on to another assignment. The result is unnecessary delay.

So successful was the Proprinter project that an individual assembly worker could put the printer together in three and a half minutes, which largely obviated the need for the highly automated and expensive assembly plant that had already been built to manufacture the new device. The lesson to be learned here is not that automation is unnecessary—on the contrary, its labor-saving benefits have made it an imperative in a broad range of industries, including this one—but rather that comparable or even greater gains in efficiency can sometimes be obtained by taking a coordinated approach to product design and the manufacturing process at the outset.

Multifunctional design teams and an orientation toward simplicity and quality have been a fixture of Japanese industry for a good deal longer and have contributed to Japanese advantages in quality and productivity. The survey of automobile assembly plants conducted by MIT's International Motor Vehicle Program showed not only that cars designed by Japanese firms were of higher quality than U.S.-designed vehicles but also that this quality advantage remained even when the Japanese-designed cars were assembled in U.S. factories. In other words, the Japanese engineers had incorporated quality-enhancing features into the design itself.[2] Building quality in at the design stage is a lot more efficient than applying quality controls retroactively to the output of production plants, as is often the case in the United States.

Teamwork in the Product-Development Process

Better coordination of design and manufacturing also leads to faster product development. This is an important advantage in rapidly changing markets, making it easier both to predict changes in consumer requirements and to incorporate the latest technological developments into the new product.

One of the most careful studies of how new products are developed was done on the automobile industry by Kim Clark and his associates at the Harvard Business School.[3] They compared similar projects in Japan and the United States and found that the Japanese automobile manufacturers on average needed only about half as many hours of engineering work to take a new car from the conceptual stage to the point of market introduction, and they did it in two-thirds the elapsed time. The Japanese advantage was attributed mainly to three organizational factors: a "heavyweight" project manager; resolving conflicts about objectives and roles at the outset of product development; and the pursuit of multiple development activities simultaneously. American automakers have typically used a series of product-development teams and managers: one for the initial product-definition stage, another for the engineering stage, and still another for the process-engineering stage that leads up to actual production. Personnel assigned to the project change from one step to the next. Coordination between various functional areas like body engineering, drive-train engineering, and overall product planning has often been weak.

In the Japanese auto companies, each new product is assigned a program manager who acts as the product's champion, carries great authority within the firm, and along with his staff, stays with the product from conception until well past the production launch. A key task of the manager is to make sure that all disagreements are aired and resolved at the outset. Achieving consensus takes a great deal of time and effort, but by skillful management at this point it is possible to gain the full commitment of all members of the program team so that subsequent progress is very rapid. Once work is under way, it proceeds simultaneously on various aspects of the project. The Japanese firms are able to achieve almost complete overlap of product and process engineering, for example. To make this work, an enormous amount of information must flow between the product designer and the process designer. Much flexibility is needed as well, because of the inevitable changes on both sides as the design proceeds.

Clark and Takahiro Fujimoto have provided a detailed description of how the Japanese design process works in the case of the dies needed to stamp the steel panels of a car body.[4] The car designers and die makers work together closely as part of a product-development team, so that the broad outline of the dies can be communicated to the die makers early in the development process. The die makers have developed a number of techniques to start work on approximate dies before the final specifications are known. At each step the die maker and the product designer rely on knowledge of each other's needs to weigh the risk of fundamental changes (which might require that an expensive die be scrapped) against the savings in development time of starting early. The result of this process is that Japanese automakers develop production-ready dies in 12.1 months on the average, whereas American firms require 23.1 months.

The time needed for product development is affected by technical as well as organizational factors. Another cause of longer lead times in U.S. companies is the less-systematic attention given to quality in the design of products and processes. Neglect of quality in the early stages of the product-development process leads to an often confusing proliferation of prototypes that attempt to correct for earlier omissions.

A Focus on the Manufacturing Process

U.S. industrial performance has suffered not only from a failure to coordinate the design and manufacturing functions effectively but also from a lack of attention to the manufacturing process itself. Process design and production operations have been neglected by management and held in low esteem by the technical community. This is in sharp contrast to industrial practice in Japan and other countries, where production has far higher stature and attracts some of the most qualified and competent technical and managerial professionals.

In recent years a number of American industrial practitioners and analysts have drawn attention to the strategic importance of production.[5] They point out that the United States no longer dominates in research and development and that the efficiency, quality, and flexibility of production processes are often the keys to competitive success. The message is starting to be heard in many quarters, but old attitudes die hard. In a recent interview with members of the Commission, a senior executive of one of the biggest U.S. industrial corporations referred to his company's manufacturing department as "a place where you go and stay until you die" and wondered whether "smart people" were needed in manufacturing.

In a recent comparative study of industrial research and development in Japan and the United States, Edwin Mansfield found that U.S. firms are still devoting only a third of their R&D expenditures to the improvement of process technology; the other two-thirds is allocated to the development of new and improved products.[6] In Japan these proportions are reversed. Interestingly, Mansfield reports no change in the allocation of R&D expenditures between products and processes in the United States between 1976 and 1985, despite the criticism that U.S. firms have received on this point.

The importance of process and production expertise was apparent in several of our industry studies. It was one of the factors, for example, that allowed the Japanese to supplant American manufacturers in the market for videocassette recorders. As we pointed out in the preceding chapter, the greater financial staying power of the Japanese companies was a key element in their success, but so too was their manufacturing skill. The expensive and complex recording machinery developed by Ampex and other American manufacturers had to be converted into a practical consumer product, and this was largely a matter of process engineering and design for manufacturing. The Japanese efforts were characterized by close coordination of design and manufacturing and an intense and sustained effort to develop simplified designs for both the product and the process. In contrast, the three U.S. efforts to develop a consumer VCR ran into serious manufacturing problems, which were never overcome.

Another perspective on manufacturing weakness in American industry emerged from our study of the machine-tool sector. Many factors have contributed to the decline of the U.S. machine-tool industry, but among the most important was a widespread neglect of production technology by users of machine tools throughout American industry. In the years following World War II, while other countries were rebuilding their industrial plant, American manufacturers grew complacent and allowed their installed base of machinery to age. When manufacturers did invest in new production equipment, they tended to choose proven technologies rather than new processes. With industrial managers under pressure for short-term results, this was a less-costly and lower-risk alternative. Moreover, manufacturing engineers and production managers, who were frequently recruited from the shop floor, had little grounding in engineering fundamentals and lacked breadth of technical knowledge. Many were uncomfortable with the newer technologies, particularly those based on electronics, and they saw no role for these developments in a competitive manufacturing strategy. Thus, users did not demand the best from the machine-tool builders, and the latter, who were already inclined toward technological inertia, never experienced a strong user pull that might have jolted them out of their torpor.

Machine-tool users in some other advanced industrial countries have exhibited a much greater degree of technical sophistication. German users, for example, have typically insisted on high performance, and they have translated their requirements into far more detailed and demanding specifications than those set by American users. Major German users have also been deeply involved in the development of new machine-tool products. The

German approach has not only stimulated process innovation but has also facilitated more-rapid diffusion of new processes and methods.

Continuous Improvement

Another area in which U.S. firms have often lagged behind their overseas competitors is in exploiting the potential for continuous improvement in the quality and reliability of their products and processes. The cumulative effect of successive incremental improvements and modifications to established products and processes can be very large and may outpace efforts to achieve technological breakthroughs.

The VCR is again a case in point. As our consumer-electronics group learned, Japanese manufacturers of VCRs made a continuing stream of improvements after the commercial introduction of the first recorders. One result was that a newer "breakthrough" technology, the videodisc, was never able to capture a substantial market share. The videodisc was an intrinsically lower-cost technology than the VCR, but it was capable of playback only, not recording. RCA, the principal backer of the videodisc, regarded it as a means of bypassing the severe manufacturing problems RCA had encountered in trying to develop a VCR product. But the videodisc project experienced delays, while VCR sales expanded, and the Japanese producers continued their progress down the learning curve. VCR prices dropped to levels that fatally undercut the videodisc market.

In the longer run, technological progress rests on a foundation of both incremental improvements and radical breakthroughs, and finding the right balance between them is a constant challenge. Lewis Branscomb has suggested that Japanese firms have been more effective in combining the two approaches. To illustrate the point, Branscomb describes the way Japanese engineers go about developing new consumer-electronics products:

After carefully assessing the functional requirements and the permissive cost of a new product for consumer markets, the engineering team (which will include manufacturing engineers) will work on a sequence of designs, incrementally approaching the cost target, testing for consumer acceptance. The initial design will very likely incorporate technical processes of a most sophisticated nature, taken from the best publications in science. But they will be used in an exceedingly conservative application. With this strategy they work their way down a pre-production learning curve before full-scale market introduction. When the product is introduced it already incorporates leading edge technologies with a high degree of extendability, but with little of the risk associated with pushing the limits of the technology too soon. American engineers faced with the same problem would spend much more time and money pushing the scientific level of the technology to a design point where it is clearly superior to proven alternatives before introducing it to their colleagues in manufacturing engineering. In all likelihood, their costs will be higher and risk of program slippage greater than the Japanese approach. And the technology in the product, when introduced, will be more difficult to extend incrementally.[7]

An important feature of the Japanese approach is the greater role of customer feedback in guiding incremental improvements to the product after it has been introduced into the marketplace. The Japanese company "gets the product out fast, finds out what is wrong with it, and rapidly adjusts; this differs from the U.S. method of having a long development cycle aimed at a carefully researched market that may, in fact, not be there."[8]

Branscomb's assertion that American engineers put more emphasis on breakthrough strategies is supported by Edwin Mansfield's comparative survey of research and development. Mansfield found that almost half of the R&D expenditures by U.S. industry go to projects aimed at entirely new products and processes, whereas only about a third of Japanese spending is for this purpose, with the balance presumably allocated to improving existing technologies.[9]

The Commission's comparison of technical problem-solving practices at integrated steel plants in the United States and Japan provides further evidence that U.S. industry has often lagged in the area of continuous improvement. In the American companies, technical specialists were deployed at a central location from which they were called in to deal with problems at plant sites. At the plants themselves the production workers and their supervisors, who mostly had only rudimentary training, often did not know enough about the technical details to solve problems on their own. If the problem was small, it might be ignored. Only in the more serious cases did upper management become aware of the problem and decide to call in a troubleshooting team. In such cases, several weeks might elapse from the time the problem was first identified until corrective action was taken.

In Japanese companies, on the other hand, each plant had an R&D and production group, and each member of the group had a background in both metallurgy and manufacturing. The Japanese had concluded that there were enough differences between plants to make this scheme more efficient than dispatching a central troubleshooting team. Rather than functioning in a reactive, firefighting capacity, the in-plant groups continually identified ways in which the production process could be improved. The Japanese firms maintained that if routine problems were quickly and efficiently addressed, and process improvements were continuously implemented, severe problems would be much less likely to arise.

In recent years a number of American integrated steel companies have formed joint ventures with Japanese firms. At National Steel, which is partly owned by Japan's NKK, the Japanese partner has set up technical teams of its own people and put them in National's plants even though both firms have their own research centers. These groups handle research, engineering, and production planning for each plant, so that the traveling troubleshooting team is no longer needed. This policy is at least partly responsible for the recent turnaround at National. The company's steelmaking productivity has increased by 40 percent, downtime has decreased by 50 percent, and the production of prime product is up 20 percent.

In a study comparing the use of flexible manufacturing systems in the United States and Japan, Ramchandran Jaikumar found similar differences in behavior.[10] Whereas U.S. managers tended to discourage workers from making changes to the system once it was working, adopting as a working principle, "If it ain't broke, don't fix it," Japanese managers were willing to continue tinkering with and improving their installations.

Our industry studies found that the lax attitude toward process improvement is widespread in U.S. companies but not universal. A notable exception is Chaparral Steel, one of the nation's leading minimill operators. Chaparral has achieved tremendous improvements in productivity by making a myriad of small changes on a continuing basis. Now the world's lowest-cost producer in its market segment, Chaparral reached this position by scouring the world for good ideas, experimenting with those ideas in the operating furnace, implementing those that worked well, and generally encouraging everyone involved in the enterprise, including production and maintenance workers and foremen, as well as engineers, to keep their eyes open for ways to make the process run faster and better. According to Chaparral spokesmen, the company's willingness to use its plant as an R&D facility—there are, in fact, no separate R&D laboratories—has been a key ingredient in its success.

Who Is to Blame?

The persistent failures of American industry to convert technologies into products have several root causes. In earlier chapters of this book industrial managers and executives have already been accorded a generous share of the blame. In the immediate postwar years they were complacent; they held stubbornly to an outmoded mass-production model; they set inappropriate financial goals; they relegated product realization and production engineering to second-class status; and they failed to make the investments in plant, equipment, and skills necessary for timely product development and efficient manufacturing.

But managers are not the only responsible parties; another detrimental influence has been the apparent indifference of government. Whereas the governments of most other industrial nations have actively and explicitly promoted research and technology for economic development, U.S. policy for science and technology has traditionally focused on basic research and paid much less attention to the commercial development and application of new technologies. The latter has been seen as the responsibility of the private sector. The Department of Defense, NASA, and other government agencies have invested heavily in technology development, but usually with specific missions in mind; commercial spinoffs are sometimes cited by those promoting the programs, but little is done to foster commercial exploitation. Recently, as concern about the nation's competitiveness has grown, the government has begun to assume a more active role in supporting the commercialization of technology. In the main, though, these efforts have focused on the commercialization of new products. Only very recently (in programs such as Sematech, the National Center for Manufacturing Sciences, and the Industrial Base Initiative, sponsored by the Department of Defense) has the federal government paid much attention to questions of manufacturability and process technology.

To all this must be added the effects of an American system of engineering education that has progressively deemphasized product realization and process and production engineering since World War II. The retreat from these activities has its origins partly in the wartime experience itself and especially in the dominant role played by physicists and other natural scientists in the development of nuclear weapons, radar, and other major wartime innovations. The physicists, whose education had stressed basic physical principles and experimentation, turned out to be better equipped to lead the way in these extraordinary new developments than the engineering profession, whose educational background had emphasized knowledge of the technological state of the art. In the postwar years that lesson stimulated a major reevaluation of engineering education, in which MIT played a leading role. The result was to place much greater emphasis on the fundamental principles of engineering and correspondingly less on familiarity with industrial technology. There was a pronounced trend away from industrial practice in the engineering curriculum.

This trend gained momentum in the postwar decades as the prodigious progress of science transformed virtually every field of technology. Advances in traditional industrial technologies, which had once been largely empirical, were increasingly fueled by new theoretical and experimental developments in related fields of science. At the same time scientific developments were spawning whole new industries, from semiconductors to satellites. As technology became increasingly based on science, the engineering curriculum evolved in the same direction. The trend was further promoted by the increasing importance of government funding for research at the nation's leading engineering schools, much of it provided by the military. The governmental sponsors were primarily interested in basic and applied scientific research. Although they sometimes funded research on specific product innovations, they rarely supported work on production processes and productivity-enhancing technologies.

As a result of these and related influences, applied science came to dominate the nation's leading engineering schools. Excellence in engineering science became the principal criterion for faculty tenure and promotion. At the same time the design of manufacturing processes and production operations acquired a reputation as lowbrow activities and largely disappeared from the curriculum. Apart from the field of chemical engineering, which in large measure *is* process engineering, university engineering schools have contributed little to the engineering of industrial-production processes.

The postwar evolution of the engineering curriculum in the direction of engineering science was both inevitable and desirable; theory and practice are each essential components of modern engineering education. But by now the pendulum has probably swung too far from real-world problem solving, especially as it relates to industrial production. Indeed, even product design has been deemphasized. Engineering students are taught to analyze systems but not really to design them. Many faculty members have little or no industrial experience, and few of those who do have such experience have worked directly in production-related positions. Engineering graduates of the nation's leading universities thus typically enter industry with little knowledge of manufacturing. Their education has prepared them primarily for careers in research and development.

In industry too the most prestigious engineering positions have been in research and development. Jobs in the high-technology sector have been especially sought after by graduating engineers. Here their lack of knowledge of production processes has been seen as less of a disadvantage, since for many of these companies survival and prosperity have hinged mainly on the ability to devise innovative products. Production capabilities are valued less highly. Often, in fact, new products are simply licensed to other firms for manufacture, or the principals of a new venture may sell their interest at an early stage in the product life cycle, before they have to face difficult production decisions, and move on to another start-up venture. Representatives of several high-technology companies commented on the not-invented-here attitude within their engineering staffs and the tendency to favor brand-new approaches over the modification of existing ones, even when the latter course would clearly have been preferable.

In American culture creativity and individualism are highly valued, and so it is not surprising that the job of reducing others' ideas to practice should be less attractive to young engineers than the opportunity to be creative in research and new-product development. But there is reason to believe that the professional norms of the engineering community have unhelpfully reinforced these tendencies by undervaluing such essential downstream engineering functions as verification and testing of design, manufacturing, and product and process improvements. The universities are not solely to blame for this; industrial management has been sending clear signals of its own. Even in some of the nation's most progressive manufacturing firms, where the manufacturing function commands much greater attention, both pay and promotion scales have long favored design over process and manufacturing engineers, and they have only very recently been equalized. And for every one of these companies there may still be many others whose managers would echo the sentiments of the executive who wondered about the need for "smart people" in manufacturing.

6

Neglect of Human Resources

Have Americans lost the work ethic? What has happened to the energy, mechanical genius, inventiveness, and willingness to work hard that drove American economic progress in the past? The idea that workers and managers are to blame for the trends in U.S. productivity is widespread today. Many people believe that America produces less well than the Japanese or the West Germans because American workers have become too affluent, lazy, and secure.

Our research on productivity and the quality of the work force suggests a very different explanation. We think the origins of the problem lie not in the disappearance or weakening of basic American values and capabilities but in the institutions that educate Americans for work. We have concluded that without major changes in the ways schools and firms train workers over the course of a lifetime, no amount of macroeconomic fine-tuning or technological innovation will be able to produce significantly improved economic performance and a rising standard of living.

The notion that the root of the problem is a loss of the work ethic is at odds with a simple observation: In some companies Americans produce as well and as much as any workers anywhere in the world. Even in the automobile industry, in which the Japanese are by most measures beating the Americans, American workers are able to produce as much and as well as Japanese workers when the Americans are in plants set up and managed by Japanese (such as the General Motors–Toyota NUMMI plant). In other industries, workers in plants owned and managed by American companies are as productive as any in the world, but these are companies with human-resource systems that incorporate many of the best practices of Japanese and German firms. An example is Chaparral Steel. This suggests that something in organization and management and not in intrinsic worker motivation explains the differences in productivity.

The failure to nurture human resources is evident long before Americans enter the workplace. Cross-national research on educational achievement shows young Americans falling behind children in other societies in mathematics, science, and language attainments at early ages and falling further behind as they progress through the school years.[1] The weaknesses of primary and secondary schools in the United States are reflected in high rates of functional illiteracy, even among workers with high school diplomas.

Yet another body of evidence argues for rebuilding the institutions that educate workers and managers instead of blaming them for laziness or complacency. This evidence comes from the record of firms as learning institutions. As we began interviewing managers across the country about their workers' skills and about the impact of new technologies on skill requirements, we were struck by how often we heard the same claim. The manager would say, "We have no training problem here. My workers are so ingenious they can pick up or figure out whatever they need to do the job. They don't need any special courses." In Italy we observed highly trained loom operators working together with fabric designers to exploit the technical possibilities of the loom and to dream up new products. In the United States we heard a prominent textile manufacturer boast that only the top manager in the plant knew how to set up the new looms and that the operators, "guys down from the hills who are good at fixing cars," did not need any special training to work on them.

Attitudes and beliefs like these, which we found in many industrial settings, reveal the problem in another light. The issue is not mainly what workers *will* do when motivated but rather what they *can* do, given their weaker basic education and the kind of work experiences provided by companies that have low regard for training and few institutional resources to provide it. There seems to be a systematic undervaluation in this country of how much difference it can make when people are well educated and when their skills are continuously developed and challenged. This underestimation of human resources becomes a self-fulfilling prophecy, for it translates into a pattern of training for work that turns out badly educated workers with skills that are narrow and hence vulnerable to rapid obsolescence.

The kinds of training that produce narrowly skilled workers may appear today as part of the productivity problem, but in the heyday of American prosperity they were an integral part of what seemed to be a winning model. As we noted in chapter 3, the mass production system in the United States was so successful that few questioned its basic assumptions. Key among those assumptions was the simplification of tasks through a division and redivision of labor that broke each task into its smallest elements. In firms organized according to the logic of mass production, workers are treated as replaceable parts. By defining jobs narrowly and making each job relatively easy to learn, American industry pursued flexibility through the interchangeability of workers with limited skills and experience rather than the cultivation of multiskilled workers. Employees could be hired and fired with the ups and downs of the business cycle without much loss of efficiency. The result was a progressive narrowing of worker responsibility and input and the tendency for management to treat workers as a cost to be controlled, not as an asset to be developed.

Patterns of Education and Training

What is the relationship between education and industrial productivity? Do the different patterns of education and training in the United States and in its principal economic competitors show up in differences in productivity in the firm and at the national level? The evidence we gathered suggests that they do.

To explore these issues, the Commission looked at the routes from schools to jobs in two sets of countries. In one group, including the United States, Sweden, and Britain, formal educational institutions provide most of the specialized skills that are used in work, and on-the-job training provides little beyond quick task-related instruction. We call these countries pattern *A* countries. In contrast, in pattern *B* countries, such as Japan and West Germany, on-the-job training is heavily relied on to develop general as well as specialized skills.

Consider the educational and training route from primary and secondary schools to work, with branching points in each country that channel off streams of the population into vocational education, apprenticeships, different forms of postsecondary education, and then jobs. The question we asked was whether different paths make a difference for productivity. We concluded that in the present period of industrial restructuring, pattern *B* countries find it easier to produce workers with the flexibility and skills needed to respond to rapid and unpredictable changes in technology and markets. Even among pattern *A* countries, however, there are considerable variations in the contribution schools make to a flexible, well-educated work force. The Swedish example demonstrates how much more the United States could achieve even if it were to remain a society in which firms do relatively little broad education of the work force and schools continue to shoulder the principal responsibility for vocational training. All of this is discussed in more detail below.

Formal Schooling

The starting point in all advanced nations is a common pattern of primary and secondary schooling until age 15 or 16. But there are major differences in the quality of educational inputs and outcomes. In the most recent study comparing science achievement, American 10-year-olds placed 8th out of 15 countries surveyed. American 13- and 17-year-olds placed even lower.[2] Preliminary results from mathematics studies rank American students from 8th through 18th.[3] Fewer than half of all American high school students take a mathematics or science course after 10th grade. Fewer than one-third of American 17-year-olds can solve mathematics problems requiring several steps. According to one estimate, three-fourths of all high school graduates lack the preparation to take a college engineering course.[4]

The failure of the educational system to retain and teach students from the poorest groups in society is even more acute. In some New York City schools, four out of five entering freshmen drop out without receiving high school diplomas. Even some who stay in school fail to acquire a basic level of proficiency in skills needed for daily life. For example, in a recent international survey sponsored by *National Geographic*, 45 percent of Americans did not know where Central America is located, only one-third could find Vietnam on a map, and fewer than half of those tested found the United Kingdom, France, South Africa, or Japan. Americans between 18 and 24 scored lower than their counterparts in the eight other countries surveyed.[5]

American and foreign students differ not only in their average scores on standardized tests but also in the dispersion of those scores around the mean. The Japanese aim at bringing all students to a high common level of competence, and they are largely successful. Most test scores cluster within a comparatively narrow range around the mean; in contrast to Americans, few Japanese receive very low scores. As a result of this high common level of competence, new entrants to the Japanese work force are generally literate, numerate, and prepared to learn. In the U.S. work force, in contrast, employers have discovered high rates of illiteracy and difficulty with basic mathematics and reading in workers with high school diplomas.

Beyond secondary school there are major differences in how young people are educated for work. In the United States and other pattern *A* countries, schools are the main institutions for teaching skills. Here the record is extremely uneven, with both achievements and failures. Though high school vocational education in the United States has been supported by the federal government for over 70 years and enrolls about five million students annually, it has a very disappointing performance and is not generally viewed as a viable preemployment training system. Employers do not see vocational high school programs as a prime source of skilled or even trainable workers. Indeed, often the fact of having participated in a vocational program stigmatizes workers in the eyes of employers.

With vocational education of limited effectiveness and few apprenticeships outside the construction trades, there is no systematic path to training for the non-college-bound. This lack of a structured transition from secondary schools to work results in weaker skills than those of European and Japanese workers. In this area American workers and firms are at a serious competitive disadvantage.

At the level of colleges and universities, in contrast, U.S. institutions are the envy of the world. At the mass-education end of the spectrum, community and technical colleges are flexible and responsive to the needs of working people and minorities and to the needs of local communities. About half of the community-college student population comes from the lowest socioeconomic quarter, in comparison with only 23 percent in four-year institutions. In many ways community colleges have taken over where secondary schools have failed. They often provide the reading, writing, and communications skills that many high school graduates lack. They offer preemployment training for a variety of technical and professional specialities. The community college system does have problems. Quality is uneven, and teachers and administrators may be uninspired. But the combination of relatively tight links with local employers and flexible policies on program cost, content, and delivery make community colleges quite effective in preparing people for employment.

At the highest level of the university system, graduate education, U.S. institutions are clearly superior. The best indication is the number of foreign students who come to the United States for advanced training. According to recent studies by both the Carnegie Foundation for the Advancement of Teaching and the Office of Technology Assessment, the U.S. system of research-oriented universities remains the most effective in the world, particularly in training people for basic research.[6] Four-year undergraduate education is also highly rated.

Young Americans receive most of their job skills in institutions of formal learning, and what they pick up on the job is usually of a limited nature, gathered from watching a colleague. Even in firms with organized training programs, in-plant training is usually short and highly focused on transmitting specific, narrow skills that are immediately put into service. When more general training or complex skills are involved, employers are likely to encourage employees to go back to school—community colleges, universities, or proprietary schools—and often provide tuition assistance for this.

A pattern of education for work that relies mainly on schools and only secondarily on training on the shop floor need not produce badly educated or narrowly skilled workers, as it generally has in the United States. Sweden is an example of a pattern A country that has successfully used schools to provide training and retraining throughout working life. About 90 percent of all Swedes remain in school after compulsory education ends at age 16. Those in vocational *gymnasiums* spend some time in firms, but with the schools supervising work experience. A survey of Swedish workers asked whether they had participated in any form of education in the previous year.[7] Over half of all skilled and white-collar workers answered yes, as did 43 percent of unskilled workers. The government also invests heavily in training centers that provide new skills for those working in declining industries. These continuing-education programs are largely responsible for low unemployment rates, even in regions experiencing industrial restructuring. Labor productivity in Sweden is high, and per capita GNP is among the highest in the world.

Training in the Firm

In contrast to the path from schools to work in pattern *A* countries like the United States and Sweden, pattern *B* countries like Japan and West Germany use on-the-job training to develop general, transferable skills as well as specialized capabilities. In West Germany, for example, young people move from schools into jobs along a route that involves a mix of education within firms and special vocational courses.[8] The majority of German 16-year-olds enter apprenticeships on leaving school. Apprenticeships are offered in 400 occupations. For each of these a training curriculum has been negotiated by officials from government, employers' associations, and trade unions. These curricula are regularly revised to keep pace with technological change. The apprentice spends an average of three years working in a firm under the supervision of a trained instructor, with about one day a week outside the company taking classes at a vocational school. National examinations certify the successful completion of an apprenticeship. Further promotions in a career require specific job experiences, further schooling, and certification by additional examinations.

In Japan education and training for specific jobs and for promotion within a career are planned and provided by individual firms and are not organized by national programs. Large companies give training and personnel planning high priority. Typically, division managers are responsible for designing the work experience and for training their subordinates, and these responsibilities are considered crucial for a manager's success. An engineer's or a manager's skill as a teacher also has great weight in promotion decisions.

There are four main components in the training provided by Japanese firms. Most important are the general skills acquired primarily by rotation through various departments. All new engineers hired at Sanyo, for example, must spend some time in sales and in rotations between research and manufacturing.[9] Workers rotate among assignments within the shop and also between shops.

The second component of training is off the job, usually in special centers the company organizes. For example, 10,000 of Sanyo's 30,000 employees pass through the Sanyo Corporate Educational Training Center each year, with each person spending at least three days at the center. Few engineers or managers ever return to external educational institutions for further training.

Third, Japanese firms encourage workers to develop skills through correspondence courses, whose costs the employer often reimburses on completion of the program. Finally, participation in quality circles and in other group activities focused on improving the firm's performance results in an upgrading of general capabilities. Japanese firms believe the educational effects of these activities are as important as their direct impact on production. Indeed, much of the substance of quality-circle activities is chosen precisely in order to improve general skills.

In sum, workers in pattern B countries acquire general and specific skills through a combination of highly structured workplace assignments, training, and some schooling. Employers see skill acquisition as a way of developing human capabilities over the long term. Only secondarily do they see training as a way of preparing employees for specific assignments. Indeed, firms in these countries often rotate specialized personnel out of activities for which they have been specially prepared and into new activities. The costs of these rotations must be high, for they involve heavy commitments to teaching on the part of all supervisory personnel. Moreover, at any one time many employees are operating as beginners. But such rotations are seen as crucial to developing a labor force with specific qualities: broad experience and capabilities and hence the capacity to deal flexibly with a varied set of production tasks, with unpredictable problems, and with changing technologies.

Education and Training Patterns

Comparative research on the contributions of education and training to productivity is only beginning. There are already many indications, however, that the on-the-job educational and training systems of pattern B countries like Japan and West Germany have advantages in producing a skilled and flexible work force. Such comparisons are very difficult, and the deficiencies in the basic schooling of U.S. workers would make rigorous comparisons of school-trained Americans with company-trained Germans and Japanese impossible under any circumstances. But even if American schools were to be improved, there are reasons to believe that learning work skills on the job might be preferable to learning them in schools.

The case for the superiority of the pattern B approach depends on a claim that the skills it develops are both broader and more relevant to the present and future needs of the company. A West German researcher, Wolfgang Streeck, concludes from his studies that in West Germany and Japan skills are broader because education is divided up between schools and firms in ways less functionally differentiated. Moreover, workplace training makes it more likely that workers will come to understand the big picture: how context shapes the task and how contingent factors must be integrated into performance. Broader skills enable workers to make larger contributions to the productivity of the firm and also to go on through life acquiring new skills. Streeck argues, "What firms need today is not just skills but broad and unspecific skills; not just 'functional' skills dedicated to a specific purpose, as they can be created by instant 'refresher courses' or the replacement of one subject in a curriculum by another, but skills as a *generalized, polyvalent resource* that can be put to many different and, most importantly, *as yet unknown* future uses."[10]

There is evidence that breadth of skills and greater flexibility do have an impact on industrial performance. In a study of matched pairs of manufacturing plants in West Germany and Britain, Arndt Sorge and Malcolm Warner concluded that broader training in German plants increased the flexibility of employees and thus reduced coordination costs and improved labor productivity.[11] Research by Ramchandran Jaikumar on the use of flexible manufacturing systems in Japan and the United States came to similar conclusions.[12] Japanese workers were able to exploit the systems more fully and produce a greater diversity of parts (by a factor of nearly 10), while achieving higher reliability with smaller crews. One of the principal explanations of the differences is the technological literacy of the Japanese workers and the breadth and generality of their skills.

Broad skills improve productivity not only through their direct effects on worker performance but also through their effects on workplace organization. Firms with workers who have been educated along a pattern *B* route typically have fewer layers of hierarchy, because workers are better able to coordinate their activities without the intervention of supervisors and are more likely to be able to repair, maintain, and change over the equipment on which they work without bringing in technicians.[13] This capacity for responding to breakdowns and new situations on the shop floor is one of the factors contributing to greater flexibility in production (including the ability to produce a greater diversity of products within the same shop), to higher rates of utilization of equipment, and to a lower rate of defects in products. The more egalitarian organizational structure of these firms is also given credit for a higher rate of innovations proposed at the level of the shop floor.

The difference that company-based training makes in job performance can be observed not only in blue-collar workers but also in technicians and engineers. Eleanor Westney and Kiyonori Sakakibara suggest that the Japanese competitive advantage in moving rapidly from development to the market derives from the close linkages between design and manufacturing.[14] These connections are ensured by the rotation of engineers from research and development into manufacturing; indeed, the engineer moves along with the product he has developed from one department to the next. A newly graduated American engineer may well arrive at his first job with a more extensive college engineering preparation than a Japanese engineering graduate, but these educational advantages are apparently counterbalanced after a few years by on-the-job training and rotations in Japan that produce engineers excelling in product development and manufacturing.

Retraining

The advantages of company-based training show up in another area as well: the retraining of the work force at all levels. Two kinds of retraining are needed. First, production workers, engineers, technicians, and managers may need to learn new skills as their companies undergo technological and economic transformation. Second, the unemployed need new training and jobs. Neither of these two issues is handled well in the United States today.

How will workers acquire the new skills that technological change, new tastes, and market shifts make necessary? Many observers of the American labor market believe that employers will have to hire new workers with just the skills required for the job and get rid of workers whose skills are obsolescent.[15] Some explain this trend by the characteristics of the new skills, which they claim cannot be learned in the firm. Others say that the mobility of workers makes it irrational for a firm to invest in extensive training, since the employee might take the newly acquired skills to another company. Still others point to the failure of programs for life-long continuing education to diffuse generally through the population, with the result that many in the work force have outdated educations.

Whatever the explanation of the trend, analysts generally agree on its consequences. As firms turn to external labor markets for workers with the new skills, even more of the education of the work force will be carried out in formal educational institutions, and even less in the plant. Pattern *A* will become further entrenched. Unless some new policies or practices intervene to commit them to the retraining of their existing workers, U.S. firms seem to be heading toward a mode of operation in which they periodically replace their work force. Older workers will be fired (or not rehired) to make way for new ones with the requisite skills.

In contrast, in Japan and West Germany, patterns of in-plant training and rotations provide continuous retraining for workers at all levels. Rotations create a multiskilled, flexible work force prepared for change by creating a mind-set for learning. Ronald Dore and Mari Sako note that in Japan "frequent retraining is seen as a necessary part of a normal career."[16] As a result, during severe economic dislocations it has been much easier to train workers for new jobs. Nippon Steel, for example, was able to rely on the prior computer experience it had provided to its steel-production workers in placing them in jobs in new businesses the company set up as it moved out of steel. In Nippon's new electronics and communications companies, 2,000 out of 2,500 new employees will be former Nippon Steel workers. Blue-collar production workers are being hired as programmers. As the personnel managers pointed out, all of these workers had been good high school graduates and had on average 30 hours a year of special in-house training courses. The ambitious ones had taken correspondence courses. Engineers as well are being moved out of steelmaking into new materials work and biotechnology. Rui Hara, president of Seiko Instruments, told a similar story of moving former watchmakers into robotics, computer graphics, and new consumer products.

On the second retraining issue, that of unemployed workers, U.S. experience is a dismal record of failure. Except for a few promising initiatives at the state level, the retraining of American workers dislocated in the past decade's dramatic economic restructuring has been modestly funded and minimally successful. The contrasting case is Sweden, where retraining of dislocated workers is a centerpiece of a national employment and training system focused on assisting workers in the core of the economy. The innovative effort to retrain and reemploy shipyard workers slated to lose jobs in the planned phaseout of Sweden's shipbuilding industry enabled the Uddevalla region and its work force to make a smooth transition. There the government has coordinated external training programs and matched employer needs with worker skills.

Future Challenges

There are a number of American firms that see maintaining and upgrading skills as central to their competitive strategy. The human-resource policies of companies like IBM, Digital Equipment, and Chaparral Steel go far toward overcoming the limitations we have identified. The problem is that the best practices of these leading firms are not diffusing widely or rapidly through the economy. Why? Many small and medium-size firms simply cannot afford the institutional resources for training that an IBM can marshal. Other companies are concerned that if they train workers, they will lose their investment when workers move on to other employers.

It is true that rates of worker mobility are higher in the United States than in Japan and West Germany, at least in the early years of employment.[17] But we doubt that the difference is enough to explain the differences in educational and training practices. In West Germany only a minority of apprentices stay on with the employer who trained them, and the value of the work carried out by apprentices is estimated to cover less than half of the training costs.[18] Yet German firms continue to invest heavily in apprenticeships, for they are convinced that a large pool of educated manpower is essential to economic prosperity. This conviction is institutionally buttressed by the system of tripartite bargaining among employers, government, and unions, which brings pressure to bear on individual firms.

In the United States individualism and distant or hostile relations between unions, employers, and government work against a consensus on company investment in training. Americans consider education to be good, but primarily because it contributes to individual mobility and enrichment and only secondarily for its contribution to common purposes. At certain historical moments—after the launching of the first Sputnik, for example—there is a surge of interest in what education means for the nation. Deep concern today over America's declining economic role in the world might provide another opportunity to emphasize the centrality of education to national objectives. But this would require a kind of national political leadership that has not yet appeared. While there are a few positive signs that emerging patterns of labor-management bargaining may focus on training, they do not seem sufficient to overcome the legacy of long neglect. Because of the widespread reluctance on the part of firms to invest more substantially in training and to reorganize the workplace in ways that would promote continuous learning, we believe that the natural diffusion of best practices will not work broadly or rapidly enough to produce the kind of educational effort that is needed.

These handicaps for the American economy are likely to become even more serious as the composition of the labor force changes in the coming decades. A majority of new entrants to the labor force will be drawn from groups that have historically been disadvantaged. White males will constitute only 15 percent of the new entrants to the labor market over the next decade. Three-fifths of the new workers will be female. Minority and immigrant workers will constitute larger proportions of the work force. These changes on the supply side of the labor force, when coupled with changes on the demand side for more and different skills, constitute a formidable set of challenges.

7

Failures of Cooperation

Underdeveloped cooperative relationships between individuals and between organizations stand out in our industry studies as obstacles to technological innovation and the improvement of industrial performance. Several examples were presented in previous chapters but always in the context of other weaknesses. Here we address the problem of cooperation in its own right.

Our studies have shown a lack of cooperation at several levels. The relationships affected include those between individuals and groups within firms, between firms and their suppliers or their customers, among firms in the same industry segment, and between firms and government. Then too there are the relations between management and labor.

Cooperation and competition are opposite sides of the same coin. Individual enterprise and competition are the foundations on which market economies are built, and anything that might undermine them tends to be viewed with suspicion. But cooperation and the pursuit of collective goals are essential too. A balance must be sought between the two poles. As the environment changes, sometimes so too must the balance.

The Commission's studies revealed many important cases in which outcomes have been adversely affected by an unwillingness to cooperate or in some cases by an inability to find ways to cooperate effectively. In situations involving the government the obstacles have sometimes been ideological, but in other cases the main culprit has been a lack of suitable institutional mechanisms. Sustained labor-management cooperation has been limited by the deep-seated antiunion attitudes of many American managers and a corresponding distrust on the part of many American union leaders of new forms of employee participation and work organization. Within firms, coordination has often been blocked by excessive specialization and compartmentalization of functions and by multiple layers of bureaucracy. Cooperation between firms has been inhibited by a preference for transactions at arm's length and narrowly conceived ideas of self-interest. In still other cases the behavior of companies or individuals could not be criticized; they were acting rationally in the circumstances they faced. Nevertheless, the sum of these individually rational actions fell short of what could have been achieved with greater cooperation.

Cooperation within the Firm

Within firms, human and organizational walls often seem to separate various functions. There is a slow or inadequate flow of information from marketing to research and development and from the latter to production. Professionals have difficulty working in teams with specialists in other disciplines. Decisions that should be integrated are instead made sequentially. Tasks are subdivided by discipline, and artificial boundaries are set up.

In an organization plagued by such failures to cooperate, work done within each specialized segment may be very competently performed, and yet the overall outcome may still be inefficient and wasteful. The organization of new-product development in the automobile industry, described in chapter 5, is a case in point. Another example is provided by high-bay warehouse systems for automated storage and retrieval of inventory. Developed by specialists in materials management, they offer elegant, sophisticated solutions to the problem of inventory storage and retrieval. Nevertheless, they are intrinsically less efficient than the just-in-time (JIT) production system, in which the need for large inventories is eliminated altogether. The tendency of American companies to favor these computerized inventory systems over JIT production again suggests a tendency for specialists to pursue the optimization of individual components and functions while losing sight of the larger objective of optimizing the entire system. As Robert Hayes and Kim Clark have observed:

The American mentality has also kept us from exploring the impact of changing the basic structure of problems. If one is confronted with a highly complex factory environment—lots of production stages, lots of products, lots of flow patterns, lots of inventory locations, and so forth—one can deal with it in one of two ways. One can either attempt to develop a highly sophisticated (and usually computerized) information and control system to manage all this complexity, or one can set about reducing the complexity. . . . We have spent over a decade and millions of dollars developing elegant Materials Requirements Planning systems, while the Japanese were spending their time simplifying their factories to the point where materials control can be managed manually with a handful of Kanban cards.[1]

An MIT study of a U.S. aerospace firm found an inefficient pattern of serial decision making in the development of new process technologies. Typically, the engineering and testing of a new technology was completed before organizational specialists and union representatives were consulted on key human-resource issues. As a result, conflicts often developed over training, wages, job classifications, and union contract issues that had been unanticipated or ignored by the engineering designers. Moreover, opportunities for organizational change or alternative ideas for solving technical problems were sometimes missed because the human and technical issues were considered in sequence rather than in parallel.[2]

Internal barriers to communication can also muffle the all-important voice of the customer in product selection and design decisions. Conversely, companies in which there is good communication between sales and service on the one hand and product development and production on the other can reap substantial benefits, as the recent experience of the British Steel Corporation attests. One of the world's largest integrated steel companies, British Steel has recently become the most profitable. It has attained this status by combining major improvements in efficiency in its commodity steel-producing business with a drive into new, higher-value-added product areas. A recent report suggests that a corporate reorganization in 1980, which followed years of heavy losses, is the best explanation for the company's transformation:

In that year [the company's new management] stopped dividing the company by skill and divided it by product instead. So, instead of all the salesmen being in one group and all the production managers in another, everyone concerned with making a particular product worked together. At the same time, dozens of plants were closed and consolidated into five main production centers.

The results have raised the status of the sales force and decentralized decision making. Managers can now concentrate on making decisions about new products. When the company had 32 plants, the whole operation had to be scrutinized from the center, and most of the management's

time was taken up avoiding bottlenecks (and the company's many atten-
dant union problems). Products took second place.

Now, with five plants, the operational problems are fewer and managers
can spend their time deciding which of 5000 different kinds of painted or
coated steel it would be most profitable to make this month. Without the
simplification of the operation, it would not have been possible to make
such marketing decisions. And without the enhanced role of the sales
force, managers would not know what would be most profitable. Because
the salesmen now work alongside the production engineers, British Steel
knows, in a way that it used not to, both what its customers want and what
its competitors are offering.[3]

The Commission learned that Chaparral Steel, one of a successful
group of American minimill companies, has taken this organizational approach a step further. With less than 1,000 employees (in
comparison with British Steel's 50,000), it has eliminated sales as a
separate function altogether and routinely sends its production
personnel on sales calls. The company believes that this increases
its responsiveness to changes in the market as well as its customers'
confidence that their needs will be met.

What accounts for the poor communication and coordination
among functions and departments found in many U.S. firms?
Organizational structure is clearly a key factor. In contrast with
their Japanese competitors, American firms have several extra
layers of hierarchy arranged as an organizational tree. To communicate with one another, people working in different departments
often have to go up the tree to their lowest-level common superior
and then back down. In Japanese firms the hierarchy has fewer
levels and it is layered rather than strictly treelike: people in one
layer generally know and can easily communicate with people in
the next-higher and next-lower layers, regardless of departmental
boundaries.

Vittorio Ghidella, former president of Fiat, observed in a talk to
the Commission that integrating research, development, design,
and manufacturing is a problem not only of organizational design
but also of attitudes. Much of the efficiency of modern organizations derives from their functional specialization. But specialization creates different ways of thinking and different approaches to
solving problems. If these barriers to communication are allowed
to persist, organizations become rigid and cannot cope with change.
Avoiding this requires both educational efforts and a rethinking of
incentives within the organization. Specialists must learn that what
they need to do cannot be determined without extensive input

from other functional areas. Rewards must be based on contributions to the multifunctional group, not just on individual or departmental achievements. Reporting by function must be replaced by reporting by group.

In the United States, functional and disciplinary divisions among technological and managerial professionals have, if anything, become more pronounced. In the university, technical disciplines have become narrower and more specialized. In interviews with the Commission several corporate executives expressed the opinion that technical professionals have little understanding of the total production system and often seem more dedicated to advancement within their discipline than to furthering the goals of their firm. Some of these executives further suggested that the universities bear a good deal of the responsibility for this situation.

Similarly, management graduates expect to specialize early on in a particular functional area like finance or marketing. According to our industrial interviewees, many management graduates have little idea how to work together or to manage small groups of employees. Many companies have abandoned management training that involves rotation through different departments. The practice has become unattractive to graduates, who are typically anxious to advance in their specialty, and probably also to the firms themselves, which may have concluded that the relatively high salaries paid to recently graduated M.B.A.s makes it difficult to justify the cost of yet another training program.

In Japan and Germany, training by rotation is still widely seen as an essential broadening experience. As engineering and business professionals in these countries move into management posts, their rotation through assignments in marketing, production, research, finance, and new-product and new-process development gives them a broad knowledge of the firm's technical and manufacturing capabilities. This experience also acts as a unifying influence when potentially divisive business decisions involving several corporate departments must be made.

Labor-Management Relations

While Germany, Japan, and most other highly industrialized nations competing with the United States have overcome conflicts over the rights of workers to unionize and to participate in enterprise decision making, U.S. firms and unions continue to expend valuable resources and energies battling over union organizing and the role of labor in society. This legacy of conflict has produced an adversarial pattern of industrial relations, one characterized by much conflict and little trust between workers and their employers. Research conducted at MIT over the past decade has shown that this traditional pattern of industrial relations produces low levels of productivity and product quality in industries as diverse as autos, office products, and paper.[4]

Yet this same research has documented the emergence of new forms of industrial relations in a number of leading union and nonunion firms in the United States. This new system is based on employee participation in shop-floor problem solving and in flexible teams that do away with the traditional narrow job descriptions inherited from the past. Equally important, as Haruo Shimada and John Paul MacDuffie have shown in their studies of Japanese auto plants operating in the United States, these flexible and participatory practices are tightly integrated with manufacturing processes and technology strategies. They use the term "humanware" to describe this integration and contrast this with the more traditional U.S. engineering strategy of separating hardware design from the design and management of systems of industrial relations.[5]

Finally, long-term trust and cooperation at the workplace is reinforced by a broader consultative role for union leaders in strategic managerial decisions involving new plant design, major investments in new technology, or a major retrofit of an existing facility. For this to work, union leaders must accept this new model and must commit their support to a more cooperative and flexible labor-management relationship. Boeing, for example, is working jointly with the International Association of Machinists to design two new production plants and to introduce state of the art sociotechnical design principles into a new facility for fabricating sheet metal. Xerox has done the same thing with the Amalgamated Clothing and Textile Workers, the union that represents all of its blue-collar employees. Early consultation is now accepted as a standard practice in the auto industry and is the policy of preference espoused by the leadership of the United Steelworkers.

Vertical Linkages

The vertical linkages in an economy, which connect a firm with its suppliers below and its customers above, can be conduits not only for incoming materials and finished products but also for technological innovations and other developments that enhance productivity. Know-how can move up and down the value-added chain. Many foreign companies are adept at capturing the benefits of this technology transfer. Our industry studies showed that by maintaining arm's-length relations with suppliers and customers, U.S. firms often miss opportunities for useful vertical interaction.

The instructive case of the machine-tool industry has already been mentioned. Relations between builders and users of machine tools are far stronger abroad than they are in the United States. Our machine-tool study group concluded that the lack of user demand for innovative products has been a key contributor to the decline of the U.S. machine-tool industry, as well as to the users' own lack of competitiveness in international markets.

Our study of the automobile industry found a similar contrast. U.S. assemblers have generally kept their suppliers at arm's length, whereas the Japanese industry cultivates carefully planned, dynamic linkages designed to ensure continuity, quality control, and flexibility. The traditional American approach to the organization of component supply has been for the assembler firm to design parts in house and then send out drawings to many suppliers for bids. The contracts offered have typically been for relatively short periods, and assemblers have not hesitated to shift orders to a lower-cost supplier on short notice or to terminate supply relationships during periods of weak demand. Suppliers have therefore had little incentive to invest their own capital in product innovations.

In the Japanese approach, by contrast, the assembler selects a small number of first-tier suppliers to design and deliver whole vehicle systems. The assembler deals primarily with these first-tier suppliers, who then deal with a second tier of suppliers, and so on. The web of relationships is close knit and durable, which allows the carmakers to spread their risks, since the suppliers are able and willing to be partners in the product-development process.

Japanese and American carmakers also differ in their attitudes about the quality of parts bought from suppliers. In the United States defective supplier parts have typically been treated as a kind of random error and discarded without any effort to learn from them. U.S. assemblers and large component suppliers have traditionally taken a casual attitude toward improving the manufacturing practices of their suppliers and subsuppliers. In turn, U.S. suppliers have taken the position that "how my factory operates is my business."

The Japanese assembler, on the other hand, insists on total conformity to standards. Every defective part is subjected to a detailed investigation in which the problem is traced back through the supplier system to its ultimate cause and a solution is developed. All of the Japanese assemblers and the first-tier component suppliers periodically audit the manufacturing practices of their suppliers and subsuppliers and take it as their right to make suggestions and demand improvements. Moreover, the assemblers and the first-tier suppliers organize their suppliers and subsuppliers into study groups for the explicit purpose of encouraging them to share knowledge of improved techniques. The result is that new techniques pioneered by one firm diffuse very quickly across an assembler's entire supplier base.

The American car manufacturers are making efforts to strengthen their supplier relations, but there is still a long way to go. At an MIT seminar in early 1988 a senior executive with one of the Big Three compared the recent experience of his firm with that of a leading Japanese manufacturer. Under severe competitive pressure, each company had embarked on a major effort to get their suppliers to cut costs. The U.S. firm managed to persuade its suppliers to agree to a 1/4 percent cost reduction; the Japanese firm achieved a 6 percent reduction. The American executive attributed much of the difference to the long-term relationships between the Japanese firm and its suppliers. Each had helped the other out in the past, and in the future it would probably be the suppliers that would need the help.

Our study of the textile industry showed how Japanese textile firms have taken advantage of close interfirm linkages to reduce inventory, cut down on order time, provide feedback about consumer preferences, and introduce new product and process technologies. In Germany and Italy, too, informal and contractual relationships between firms at different points in the textile complex have been a key source of competitive advantage.

Vertical linkages between U.S. textile firms have traditionally been much weaker. The flow of information about markets and technology has often been hindered by proprietary concerns and by attitudes of mutual suspicion. The procurement strategy of one major U.S. apparel manufacturer entailed approaching the weakest fabric producer, forcing its prices down, and then using that price to work down the prices of the others. The firm kept its predictions of its annual requirements confidential, lest its suppliers use this information to plan and stabilize their own operations. This pattern of relations has recently been transformed, to the benefit of both parties. The apparel manufacturer now negotiates longer-term contracts with its fabric suppliers. In exchange for the greater security, the suppliers now load up their trucks by cut and shade so that the apparel maker can work right out of them, thus greatly reducing the need for inventories and warehousing.

Today some of the most successful firms in the American textile industry are paying more attention to the productivity gains that can be achieved through closer vertical linkages. Fiber, textile, apparel, and retailing companies have recently joined to launch the Quick Response Program, designed to improve information flow, standardize recording systems, and improve turnaround time throughout the system. The advocates of the program hope it can cut the 66-week cycle from fiber to retail in the United States to 21 weeks, thereby lowering costs and making many imports less appealing.

Close producer-customer linkages often encourage innovation, since in many industries users are at least as important as the manufacturers themselves as originators of ideas for product improvement. Eric von Hippel of the Sloan School of Management at MIT has estimated that 75 percent of recent innovations in scientific instruments have come from users and that semiconductor chip manufacturers have accounted for two-thirds of recent advances in the equipment used to make the chips.[6] In such cases it is incumbent on producers not only to try to identify their customers' needs but also to pay close attention to improvements that customers themselves have made or are suggesting. This requires good working relationships at the technical level between producer and user. Once again, our studies have revealed that American industry lags in this respect.

The relationships between the steel companies and their capital-equipment suppliers during the introduction of the basic oxygen furnace are a case in point. The basic oxygen furnace requires special refractory brick for its lining. Refractory makers in the United States were mostly small firms with insufficient R&D capacity to develop the new refractories on their own. For the most part, the big steel companies refused to share information on their steelmaking techniques with them. In Japan, by contrast, MITI led an effort to upgrade the quality of the refractories and the facilities needed to produce them, and the major steel firms worked closely with these suppliers to develop and produce superior products.

Similar problems have arisen downstream in the steel industry. Although many U.S. minimill and specialty steel companies have developed close working relationships with their customers, technical linkages between *integrated* steel producers and their customers have traditionally been much weaker. Efforts are now being made to remedy this situation, particularly with the automobile industry, the largest consumer of steel.

Tenuous links between U.S. steelmakers and auto producers have been instrumental in making stamping costs higher in the United States than in Japan. Japanese dies cost less and can be changed much more quickly. And U.S. automakers have not been able to optimize the use of coatings on steel sheet or to achieve high efficiency in stamping or in part or tool design for high-strength, low-alloy steels. After years of providing little technical support to the auto companies, American steelmakers are beginning to invest in the improvement of steel stamping processes and tool design, and they have initiated several research projects under the leadership of the American Iron and Steel Institute. The steel suppliers have also organized Product Application Centers to help auto companies in prototyping new parts, and the automakers have agreed to buy steel from firms providing such support.

Lack of standardized tests and marking systems have hindered progress in user-supplier relations. For example, although the auto firms agreed on the need for machine-readable bar codes for inventory, they could not agree on one standard. The problem of standardization has also been evident in the corrosion tests used by the three U.S. auto firms and the largest integrated steel suppliers. The steel companies complain that the auto companies do not have effective supplier-rating systems that would help them know where they stand relative to their competitors or what the quantifiable problems with their materials are. Just-in-time delivery systems have also proved difficult to implement. According to the steel firms, one reason is that American auto companies vacillate in their demands, even after a model is in production, whereas Japanese engineers are reported to freeze a design months before production begins.[7]

As the Japanese auto producers establish production facilities in North America, they are taking the lead in redefining auto-steel company linkages. The relationship between Inland Steel and Honda, which recently opened two assembly plants in Ohio, is an illuminating example. Inland works with Honda on problems with production and quality, and Honda management visits the Inland plant to run sessions with Inland workers on quality improvement. In turn, Inland personnel suggest improvements in the auto part-stamping process. Inland's shipment rejection rate to Honda has decreased from 50 percent to 5 percent. As the Commission's steel industry report points out, the two firms have benefited by taking the time to become educated in each other's technology.

Another result of Edwin Mansfield's comparative survey of research and development spending in the United States and Japan, discussed in chapter 5, is that Japanese firms seem to give users a greater role in shaping their R&D programs than do American companies. According to Mansfield's data on 100 firms, one-third of the Japanese R&D projects in the sample were based on suggestions either from external customers or from the firm's own production personnel (also users), whereas only one-sixth of U.S. projects were suggested by these sources.[8]

Our industry studies revealed important exceptions to this general picture. For example, we found that the commercial aircraft industry in the United States has been characterized by strong working relationships between the airplane manufacturers and the airlines. Strong customer demand for technological advances was a key factor underlying the long-term risk-taking attitude of the aircraft manufacturers. Commercial customers wanted advances in speed, payload, and range because these translated into higher airline productivity and profits. Manufacturers were encouraged to apply advances in airfoil design, structures, and new materials. More recently commercial customers have emphasized fuel efficiency and lower operating costs, and manufacturers have responded with high-bypass-ratio engines, wide bodies, and many other technologies.

Major airlines have typically had large, strong engineering staffs that worked closely with manufacturers and played a leading role in fleet-purchase decisions and design details. It has been common for airline engineers to spend thousands of hours evaluating alternative designs from the same or competing suppliers, and making a case for alternatives that best fit the airline's needs. In the past several years this pattern has changed, and what was a strength is becoming a weakness. With the advent of deregulation, the airlines have reduced or eliminated their engineering staff to cut costs. The cost pressures are also leading the airlines to try to shift more of the risk of developing new aircraft to the builders. Stimulated by changes in the tax law, leasing companies have moved in to assume some of these risks. The result could be to further isolate the users from the builders at the technical level.

Horizontal Linkages and the Public Good

Cooperative relationships between firms in the same industry segment have often been more highly developed elsewhere than in the United States. The problem of such horizontal interfirm linkages is closely related to the broader issue of relations between industry and government. This is partly because interfirm cooperation in the United States has often, though not always, been inhibited by government antitrust regulation and also because where such cooperation has been successful, government has often played an important facilitating role. The general question of business-government relations is discussed in the next chapter. Suffice it to say here that our industry studies revealed several important instances in which the absence of horizontal cooperation in the United States led to the underprovision of such collective goods as joint research and development, standardization, and education and training, which were instrumental in promoting technological innovation and productivity growth in those same industries in Europe and Japan.

An example drawn from the machine-tool study illustrates the point. One of the most important obstacles to the development in the United States of a strong industry for numerically controlled (NC) machine tools was the proliferation of vendors producing the numerical controls themselves (as distinct from the lathes, milling machines, and other devices being controlled). No interface standards were developed, and as a result, incompatibility of controls became a major problem. Users hesitated about what products to buy, because today's purchase might not be able to communicate with tomorrow's. The fear of antitrust action held the machine-tool builders back from trying to standardize the interface.

In Japan, by contrast, the design and manufacturing of the control part of the NC tools was concentrated in one company, FANUC, with the active encouragement of MITI. This not only led to economies of scale but also avoided the incompatibilities that plagued American machine-tool users. Machine-tool builders were relieved of the burden of developing their own controls, and FANUC's concentration on the electronic side of electromechanical products reduced direct competition between itself and the builders. FANUC gained 80 to 90 percent of the Japanese market for controls during the 1970s and 40 to 50 percent of the world market by the early 1980s.

More generally, machine-tool firms have been encouraged to specialize in specific product lines in both Japan and West Germany to a degree unknown in the United States. In Japan, MITI has played a key role. In Germany, the federal and state governments, although highly supportive, assumed a secondary role, with the main initiative coming from powerful trade associations. Association members were encouraged to develop excellence in a limited range of products, thereby reducing overlap and direct competition. This pattern of cooperative specialization has facilitated exporting, by permitting trading companies and manufacturers' agents to represent a whole set of noncompeting companies overseas. Within each sector, however, a small number of firms compete fiercely on the basis of technical excellence and product innovation.

German machine-tool builders have also been nourished by close links with the strong infrastructure of apprenticeships, polytechnic schools, universities, and technical institutes. This system provides multilevel manufacturing expertise, including skilled shop-floor workers, practical engineers who can make things work and solve problems, and more research-minded engineers who push the limits of process technology. There is also a dense and intricate communications network among industry, trade associations, unions, and government, which widely diffuses ideas and helps to build consensus in such areas as collaborative research priorities.

As a rule, linkages and cooperative arrangements of these kinds have been far less well developed in the United States. Tight antitrust restrictions, although appropriate in many cases, have certainly been a deterrent in others, suggesting that a further selective relaxation of legal restraints may be in order. A significant step was taken in 1984, when Congress passed the National Cooperative Research Act, which gave industry an antitrust exemption for joint research and development projects. By late 1988 more than 200 applications to engage in cooperative R&D activities had been registered with the Department of Justice under the new act. Joint manufacturing and marketing consortia are not exempted, however, and further legislation may be needed to overcome the fear of litigation of companies contemplating such consortia.

In many cases, legal measures can go only so far in addressing this issue, which is at least as much a problem of custom and attitude as it is a problem of law. The contrast between the American and the Japanese efforts in the new field of higher-temperature superconductors is symptomatic of this. Although the key scientific discoveries were made only two years ago, a superconductor consortium of 44 Japanese firms organized by industry and government is already at work.[9] In the United States the need for a coordinated effort has also been recognized. But although several committees have studied the issue and submitted their reports, little if anything had been implemented by late 1988. A recent report by the Congressional Office of Technology Assessment suggested that the United States may be falling behind the Japanese in this field.[10]

A similar situation is developing in the field of X-ray lithography, a new technology that will very likely play a vital role in the manufacture of future generations of faster, more powerful semiconductors. This technology will be extremely costly to develop, in part because of the expense of developing a suitable X-ray source, and it is not likely that any company will be able to afford to develop it alone. In Japan a coordinated program involving industry and government was set up several years ago to develop the new technology. Toshiba, Fujitsu, Hitachi, NEC, and NTT are among the major companies participating in the program. As much as $700 million has already been spent. In the United States, by contrast, no such program yet exists, and development efforts are on a much smaller scale. IBM is the only American company that is making a serious commitment to the new technology, but even that giant company is showing signs of reluctance to proceed further on its own.[11] Other U.S. electronics firms opted out earlier because of the great expense involved. IBM has begun looking for development partners in government and industry, but as of late 1988 there were still no firm plans for collaboration.

Computer networking is another area where American companies have had difficulty cooperating. The need here is to establish common communication standards. Instead, each company tries to have its own solutions accepted as a national standard, with the result that U.S. standards organizations are compelled to accept a large number of such "standards." In Europe, by contrast, the centralized postal, telephone, and telegraph authorities have already agreed on data communication protocols not only for each country but also among several EEC countries.[12]

8

Government and Industry
at Cross-Purposes

The first five of the weaknesses identified by the Commission arise from strategic choices made within individual firms. Yet these choices can also be viewed as responses to an environment that rewards certain economic decisions and penalizes others. Firms operate in an environment shaped by federal macroeconomic policy and by a variety of other government policies concerning such matters as education and training, research and development, national security, economic and social regulation, and the nation's economic infrastructure. In this chapter we consider the incentives and constraints created by these various governmental actions outside the macroeconomic sphere.

Too Much or Too Little?

Our industry reports provide abundant evidence of the impact of government on industrial strategies and outcomes. The collapse of the U.S. consumer-electronics industry was affected in part by tariffs, quotas, antidumping and antitrust laws, and the way those laws were implemented. Similarly, in the textile industry differences in quota categories between American and European tariff regimes explain at least some of the differences in the ways this industry has rebuilt itself in the United States and Western Europe in the face of stiff third-world competition. Many other instances could be cited: environmental and health and safety regulations influence the profitability of the automobile industry; the lengthy approval procedures of the U.S. Food and Drug Administration delay the marketing of new drugs; antitrust legislation has been an obstacle to cooperative research in the machine-tool and semiconductor industries.

On the other hand, several of the industry studies contrasted the comparatively aloof policies of the U.S. government with the more supportive policies of foreign governments toward industry. Even aside from the controversial issue of whether certain American industries would have been strengthened by a higher degree of protection, the sectoral studies lead to no simple conclusions about the optimal role for government in the economy. Would the machine-tool industry have done better if the U.S. government (like MITI in Japan) had steered manufacturers toward a range of products with greater general utility in small- and medium-scale firms? Would the U.S. commercial-aircraft industry have been stronger if the government had hovered over its development, as European governments did for Airbus and the Concorde? Would the textile industry's research on automated sewing have had greater impact on the industry if, as in Japan, the government had parceled out research tasks and implemented a diffusion strategy? In short, is the problem too much government or too little?

The sectoral studies do not suggest that the American economy *as a whole* would be substantially different or stronger if the government had promoted particular firms and sectors, as governments in Japan and Western Europe are claimed to do. Indeed, there are reasons to question whether state initiative and support have played as significant a role abroad as is often supposed. Even in Japan and France, countries where the state is reputed to shape the industrial structure in accordance with some national strategic vision, some of the most recent research is far more skeptical about the actual influence of state policy and more inclined to emphasize the role of private-sector actors.[1]

Particular decisions in which, say, the Japanese government actively promoted a given course of action may well have been superior to the strategic decisions of American private firms. In particular cases the government's support, subsidy, and protection may have made the difference. What is open to serious question, however, is to what extent states have shaped objectives different from those that private industry would have pursued anyway. Did Japanese firms behave very differently than they would have without state pressure and initiatives? In other words, did industrial policy matter? And to the extent that it did, were there better outcomes across the whole economy, and not just for particular firms or sectors, than would have been likely without industrial policy?

Neither the scholarly literature on these controversial points nor the Commission's own research in our eight selected industries provides firm ground for concluding that there was too little government intervention in the U.S. economy.

Regulatory Policy

The evidence is also mixed regarding the charge of too much governmental regulation. It will always be possible to cite instances in which regulatory requirements raise costs and put a domestic industry at a competitive disadvantage or reduce its productivity. But in each such case regulation is intended to serve other purposes; when the enabling legislation was passed, the purpose was evidently thought to be worthwhile. No general principle can be stated here. It must be recognized that social goals sometimes conflict with one another. The political process has to decide how much of the cake to eat and how much to have. The most that can be asked is that regulations be framed and implemented in such a way as to produce minimal interference with productivity, consistent with the legislative purpose, in other words, that *inefficient* regulation be avoided. Environmental, health, safety, and other goals should be achieved at the smallest feasible cost in productivity.

In balancing economic costs against other social goals, it should be kept in mind that simple output per hour worked is an incomplete measure of productivity. Factories produce salable product *and* waste material; coal-burning power plants produce electricity *and* stack gases. In such calculations "productivity" must take into account both economic output and environmental effects. It is a legitimate political decision to trade off a somewhat costlier product for slightly cleaner air or safer working conditions.

Has the productivity of the American economy as a whole been adversely affected by government regulation? Has regulation eroded the international competitiveness of American industry? To the extent that it has, how much of the damage is attributable to avoidable inefficiencies in the regulatory process? The Commission's sectoral studies revealed specific cases in which regulation had a serious impact on performance, but we did not detect a major effect across the board. Studies of overall productivity growth have reached a similar conclusion. Although much environmental, health, and safety regulation was put in place during the 1970s, most economists estimate that this regulation was responsible for no more than 10 to 15 percent of the productivity slowdown during those years.[2] During the 1980s regulation has not generally become more stringent, and the effect on productivity growth has consequently diminished.

There have been few international comparisons of the economic impact of environmental regulation. According to one report, prepared by the Congressional Budget Office, the overall effect of regulation has been slightly more negative in the U.S. economy than in Canada, West Germany, and Japan, but in no case has it been a major cause of inefficiency.[3] Another recent study found that American industries that spent more on abating pollution tended on the whole to do less well in international trade, which suggests that environmental regulation may have been a source of competitive disadvantage for the United States, but the results were not conclusive.[4]

Many of the complaints about regulation voiced by U.S. industry focus not on the direct costs of control and monitoring equipment and the like but rather on the less easily measured costs associated with what are perceived to be inefficient regulatory processes. A common complaint is that American firms are burdened by overlapping regulatory jurisdictions, complex and lengthy procedural requirements, and excessively detailed, prescriptive regulations promulgated by inflexible regulatory institutions. It is also asserted that uncertainty about the future course of regulation has inhibited technological innovation and investment in research and development. It is difficult to estimate such indirect costs, and so far there have been few comparisons with experience in other countries. Some U.S. firms and industries have been seriously affected, but it seems clear they are a minority. In a recent survey of senior research and development officers of technology-intensive companies conducted by the Conference Board, less than a fourth responded that government regulation had been strategically important to their own firms. A somewhat larger number felt that the impact on the economy as a whole had been more important, but the problem was not regarded as an insurmountable barrier to U.S. competitiveness.[5] What seems generally true, however, is that relations between American industry and its regulators are significantly more adversarial than in other leading industrial countries.

More generally, our industry studies provide further support for the view that the American economy exhibits a lower level of cooperation among business, government, and labor than any of its major competitors. And however qualified our conclusions about the role of industrial policy in the successes of those competitors, what we do find significant is that closer cooperation has established a favorable climate for strategic and organizational change. Such cooperation may be stimulated by government and may even look like industrial policy, but we believe it is different.

Traditionally, U.S. industrial policy has involved the government in the design of national or sectoral policies, and industry and labor are brought into the process only to obtain information or to facilitate implementation of the government's grand design. In contrast, the cooperative arrangements we found to have been significant are characterized by power sharing, negotiation, and collaboration at all stages of the process. Equally important, the cooperative patterns differ from industrial policy with respect to what government provides. In the cooperative case, government facilitates the cooperation of many potentially divergent interests in projects from which all parties can benefit. In the case of traditional industrial policy, government action characteristically selects one firm or a few firms to receive subsidies and protection.

In many of the cases of failure that the Commission's industry studies examined, we found elements of weakness that few firms could remedy individually, even with infusions of public support. For example, in education and training only very large firms have the resources to make a significant impact by acting on their own. In general, the low level of educational achievement in the American work force, the inadequacy of postsecondary training, and the disastrous record of retraining programs are problems that will require cooperation among business, government, and labor to produce general improvement.

The Technological Infrastructure

Technology policy is another area of public-policy weakness that has contributed to the nation's productive-performance problems. The Commission believes that the nation needs to rebuild its technological infrastructure—broadly defined to include public laboratories and facilities, communication links, intellectual-property laws, technical standards, and other aspects of the environment within which the private sector moves to commercialize new technology. This infrastructure has grown haphazardly, without adequate regard for its strategic implications. It does not facilitate the rapid development and use of new technologies, and it creates serious competitive problems for some American firms.

Largely exempt from this criticism is the nation's basic-research system, which remains unexcelled. Federal support for basic research in the years since World War II has been crucial to the nation's current scientific and technological preeminence, and the importance of continuing this strong commitment to basic science cannot be overstated. The basic-research system is not without problems, such as aging university research facilities, a shortage of engineering faculty, and a risk that new big-science ventures like the space station and the superconducting supercollider will crowd out smaller but equally deserving research projects. But in our view the most serious problems in the nation's technological infrastructure lie elsewhere.

First, until recently the impact of technology on the economy was not seen as a legitimate focus of public policy. The federal government has invested heavily in technology development over the years, but primarily for specific public missions, such as national security, space exploration, and health. As we pointed out in chapter 5, the commercial implications of the technology have been considered only secondarily, if at all.

Second, the government is poorly organized to deal with questions of commercial technology policy. Responsibility for technology is dispersed widely throughout the executive branch and also in Congress.[6] No fewer than 12 federal agencies have responsibility for research and development. The White House Office of Science and Technology Policy could in principle provide a strategic focus and coordinate these agencies, but in recent years it has not done so. In Congress responsibility for the federal science budget is shared among 9 of the 13 appropriations subcommittees. Regulatory governance of commercial technology is dispersed still more widely. With such a decentralized organizational structure it is difficult to set priorities, pursue steady, coherent policies, and coordinate actions and policies of the federal government, the states, and the private sector.

One consequence of disorder in the technological infrastructure has been underexploitation of the federal laboratory system. This complex of more than 700 laboratories accounts for a sixth of the nation's total R&D spending. It could contribute more to meeting the technology needs of industry in such diverse areas as energy, materials, and information processing.

In the area of intellectual property, start-up companies often cannot get timely patent or copyright protection; thereafter, they cannot afford to contest infringements. International patent and copyright agreements to which the United States is a signatory do not prevent foreign firms from reverse-engineering American designs and then selling the resulting products in the United States or abroad, nor do they protect American firms from foreign businesses that copy manufacturing-process technology and sell the resulting output in the United States.

In recent years the federal government has taken several important steps to upgrade the nation's technological infrastructure, including measures to strengthen the intellectual-property regime, remove the main antitrust obstacles to joint research and development, increase the transfer of technology from the federal laboratories to private firms, and promote research linkages between universities and industry under the auspices of the National Science Foundation's engineering research centers. But many of the key underlying problems remain. As the Council on Competitiveness concluded in a recent report, these new policies have all too often been "piecemeal, *ad hoc,* and inconsistent. Throughout the government there is far too little coordination within the federal bureaucracy and among the federal agencies, the states, and the private sector."[7]

National Defense

The United States devotes a higher proportion of its national product to defense than most of its leading international competitors (6.6 percent of the GNP in 1985, in comparison with 5.3 percent in the United Kingdom, 4.1 percent in France, 3.2 percent in West Germany, and 1.0 percent in Japan).[8] Defense spending has a particularly important influence on research and development. About 46 percent of all U.S. research and development is sponsored by the federal government, and almost two-thirds of federal R&D expenditures go to defense.[9] The defense sector has both direct and indirect impacts on U.S. economic performance.

The direct costs of national security to the economy are measured by the sums paid for facilities, equipment, products, and services, and for the scientists, the engineers, and the many other people needed for such a large effort. The Commission did not address the question of whether our level of defense expenditure is appropriate. This is a political and military question that goes well beyond our scope. We concur, however, with several other studies (for example, that of the Packard Commission) that there is substantial opportunity to improve the efficiency with which goods and services are procured by the Department of Defense.[10] Desired levels of national security could be obtained at less cost, which would free resources for the domestic economy.

Beyond the direct costs of national defense, there are several indirect costs and benefits. They are significant to the domestic economy in terms of their absolute effects and also their recent trends. On the positive side, the Department of Defense has helped to create and has nurtured the growth of new activities that have had substantial commercial spillovers. A good example is the evolution of computer science and technology, a field that grew from nothing to nearly 10 percent of the gross national product in the past three decades.[11] The Department of Defense played a central role in the growth of this field through its Defense Advanced Research Projects Agency (DARPA), and it has funded what in retrospect can be regarded as more than half of the field's key innovations. These include time-sharing computers, artificial intelligence and expert systems, and computer networks.[12]

It may be that the great success of defense funding in fostering the growth of computer science and in generating so many spinoff ideas and commercial enterprises is due to the inherent versatility of computers. A time-sharing computer, an expert system, or multiprocessor computer system may be as useful to a business as it is to a military installation.

Some of MIT's own research programs provide further illustrations of the diffusion of military-funded technology into the civilian sector. At MIT's Lincoln Laboratory, Defense-sponsored developments in integrated circuits, laser technology, high-bandwidth communications, optical communications, and digital signal processing either have already found commercial application or have considerable potential to do so.

Another positive contribution of the Department of Defense has been the indirect effect of subsidizing and protecting defense markets. For example, in the commercial aircraft industry in the 1950s and 1960s, economies of scale, particularly for jet aircraft, were made possible by military procurement. (The situation was reversed in the 1980s, when the Air Force was able to buy a tanker version of the DC-10 airliner at a good price near the end of the DC-10 production run.)

Unfortunately, there are also serious indirect costs of defense spending. These costs arise from the inappropriate transfer of defense R&D or procurement practices to civilian industry, such as applying stringent military specifications and production standards to civilian processes and products that do not require military performance levels. Further, R&D sponsored by the Department of Defense (and to a lesser extent by other government agencies) may divert resources into technologies that have no conceivable civilian application and may foster an R&D environment that is not responsive to the needs of the civilian market.

The indirect benefits and costs of the military presence in the U.S. economy are complex and intangible. We have found it difficult to quantify them, but we have nonetheless observed a trend toward decreased indirect benefits, brought on by three factors. First, owing to a series of changes in the commercial U.S. economy and particularly in the electronics industry, the United States no longer has the manufacturing presence to take full advantage of military spillovers. Second, in an attempt to be fair to all potential contractors, large and small alike, the Department of Defense has increased its bureaucratic procedures for R&D procurement, thereby introducing greater delays in the R&D cycle. Third, there has been a consistent tendency toward short-term, mission-oriented contracts, which tend to reduce risks but also reduce the likelihood of big future commercial payoffs.

In conclusion, the inefficiency associated with direct Department of Defense costs and the trend toward fewer indirect benefits are causes for concern about the future impact of defense spending on the U.S. economy. The Commission believes that the nation can address some of these problems in a positive way, as we discuss in chapter 11.

Emerging Patterns of Best Industrial Practice

In the preceding chapters we identified several weaknesses that have prevented many American firms from effectively adapting to their changing economic environment. But the Commission's research on specific industries also identified firms that are responding successfully to the opportunities and constraints of the new environment. Each of our eight industry teams observed strong U.S. firms that, at least for now, are capable of holding their own in international markets. Two illustrative cases are Ford and Xerox. Both developed serious competitive weaknesses during the 1960s and 1970s and experienced major economic difficulties in the late 1970s and early 1980s, but both have made striking improvements in performance in the past several years. Ford rebounded from a loss of nearly $1.5 billion in 1980 to a profit of $4.6 billion in 1987, which makes it the most profitable auto company in the United States and one of the most profitable automakers in the world. Xerox cut its manufacturing costs by half, improved quality dramatically, and reversed the decline in its share of the copier market. Each company made radical reductions in its work force: Ford's labor force declined by over 40 percent from its peak strength in the 1970s, and Xerox cut its manufacturing work force by half. In neither case, however, would the employment cutbacks have been sufficient on their own to ensure recovery. Many other U.S. manufacturing companies made comparable layoffs, but to less avail. What distinguishes these companies is their commitment to making far-reaching changes in their production systems.

The specific practices adopted by these and other successful firms vary considerably. The solutions are tailored to each firm's markets and technologies and to the capabilities of its work force. The differences are important both for the firms themselves and for public policies designed to promote the spread of these best practices. But we have also found broad patterns of change that are common to many of the success stories. In contrasting industrial situations—old industrial-heartland firms and new high-tech manufacturers, large corporations and small niche producers, union and nonunion firms—certain characteristics recur, all the more remarkable in their similarity for the great diversity out of which they emerge.

We call attention here to six key similarities among the best-practice firms: (1) a focus on simultaneous improvement in cost, quality, and delivery; (2) closer links to customers; (3) closer relationships with suppliers; (4) the effective use of technology for strategic advantage; (5) less hierarchical and less compartmentalized organizations for greater flexibility; and (6) human-resource policies that promote continuous learning, teamwork, participation, and flexibility. The six responses are mutually reinforcing. Indeed, they form a single, integrated strategy. The specific changes in business aims and methods, internal organization, and supplier relations that characterize best industrial practice cannot be treated as individual items on a list from which firms can pick and choose at will.

Simultaneous Improvement in Quality, Cost, and Delivery

High quality, low unit cost, speed in moving new products from the design stage to market, speedy and reliable delivery of products and services—these are fundamental virtues in any business organization, and it is no surprise that they contribute to success. What we have found, however, is that our best-practice firms put particular emphasis on *simultaneous* improvements in quality, cost, and speed. Other firms have made partial improvements by trading off one dimension of performance against another; only the best companies have made significant improvements in all three.

Of course, the relative emphasis that firms give to each of these objectives depends on the particular characteristics of their markets. Chaparral Steel, in a commodity business, sets as its goal to be the lowest-cost producer in the world, and acknowledges that in such a business "you have to be more creative about *how* you make things than *what* you make." Niche manufacturers focus on carving out specialized markets for products that are distinguished by highly valued design or performance. Customers in such markets are commonly prepared to pay a price premium for quality or functionality.

Whatever the market, the successful companies are those that strive to be "best in their class" in all the main performance categories. The best of the niche producers set objectives for quality and product differentiation, but they also mount an intensive effort to reduce costs and establish competitive prices. Successful mass producers recognize that price competitiveness must be matched by attention to quality and service, and indeed, they stress quality of design and production engineering as a means of reducing manufacturing costs.

A characteristic of all the best-practice American firms we observed, large or small, is an emphasis on competitive benchmarking: comparing the performance of their products and work processes with those of the world leaders in order to achieve improvement and to measure progress. One of the keys to the turnaround at Xerox was a new focus on detailed comparison tests between Xerox copiers and competing models. When this practice was started in 1979, the tests revealed that Japanese producers could make copiers at half the production cost, with a development schedule that was half as long and involved only half as many people on the development team. The quality of the Japanese machines was also far superior; when measured by the number of defective parts on the assembly line, Japanese quality was from 10 to 30 times better than Xerox's performance in the United States. These dramatic findings provided both the motivation for Xerox's effort to overhaul its products and production processes and the target to be attained in that overhaul. At Ford the product-development team for the company's highly successful Taurus model was charged with surveying the practices of other firms worldwide in order to meet or better the highest existing specifications on more than 400 components.

Staying Close to the Customer

All of the successful firms that we observed are making a concerted effort to develop closer ties to their customers. These ties enable companies to pick up more differentiated signals from the market and thus to respond to different segments of demand. They also increase the likelihood of rapid response to shifts in the market.

Successful niche manufacturers know that finding a market niche and concentrating the firm's resources on producing for it are no guarantee of future competitive success. The best of these firms identify shifts in demand by staying in close and continuous contact with customers, then they rapidly redeploy their productive resources to new uses. Similarly, the most successful high-volume manufacturers combine a continuing emphasis on economies of scale with a new flexibility, reflected in shorter production runs, faster product introductions, and a greater sensitivity to the diverse needs of their customers. Today, when Du Pont thinks about its future products in composite materials, it thinks about formulating different products for different end users, in contrast to the way it developed such large-volume products as nylon in the past. Other leading firms in the U.S. chemical industry have divested or reduced the scale of their commodity chemical businesses and diversified into more profitable (or potentially profitable) downstream businesses like specialty chemicals, pharmaceuticals, biotechnology, and advanced materials; some of them have even gone into electronics or similar high-technology areas. Much of this change was achieved by acquiring small firms already present in these specialized niches along with divestment of other lines of business. As a result of the transformation, commodity chemicals represent a much smaller share of total sales in major U.S. companies. At Dow Chemical, for example, the share has fallen from 63 percent to 35 percent in five years, and at Monsanto it is down from 61 percent to 35 percent in four years.

Closer Relations with Suppliers

The closer and more tightly coordinated relationships with suppliers that we have discussed extensively in this book appear in all of the best-practice firms we have observed. In some cases, better coordination with suppliers has been achieved through the coercive power of market domination; in others, by new forms of cooperation and negotiation. No matter how it comes about, coordination with external firms is crucial in cutting inventories (and thereby costs), in speeding up the flow of products, and in reducing defects.

Greenwood Mills—a textile company with a commodity product, greige goods (undyed fabric), and a specialization in denim that accounts for 15 percent of the U.S. market—brought down inventory radically over two years, even as sales were doubled. To achieve this, the company tightened up its own operations and at the same time negotiated new arrangements with suppliers, who now deliver on a just-in-time basis. In exchange, Greenwood halved the number of its suppliers, forgoing the assurance of low prices that competition among suppliers had once produced in order to gain the advantages of closer collaboration. Ford and Xerox also greatly reduced their supplier base (in the case of Xerox from 3,000 companies to fewer than 400) and asked their remaining suppliers to participate earlier and play a larger role in the product-design process.

Using Technology for Strategic Advantage

Our industry studies revealed a trait common to the firms that are most successful in transferring scientific discoveries and new technologies into production and the marketplace: they have integrated technology choices into the rest of their business planning, including strategies for manufacturing, marketing, and human resources.

From a leading aerospace company the Commission learned that new technologies and systems will no longer be automatically incorporated into the designs of new aircraft. Instead, new technology must now, in the company's words, "buy its way onto the plane." Even in this engineering-driven company, the key test of a technology is, Is it the simplest and most efficient way to meet the *customer's* needs?

In the textile and apparel industry the creative use of information technology is now becoming an integral part of the marketing and purchasing strategies of leading firms. In the generally depressed domestic apparel industry, firms such as Model Garment and Levi Strauss are succeeding by investing heavily in new technologies that allow them to fill orders very rapidly and reduce inventory levels. Model Garment, for example, can ship out standard women's slacks three days after the fabric arrives at the plant. Computer hookups to their major fabric supplier, Milliken, and their major retail customers allow them to fill and refill orders far more quickly than an offshore manufacturer could. In a world of short product life cycles and rapidly changing consumer tastes, this "quick response system" is allowing these firms to overcome the labor-cost advantages of overseas competitors.

The U.S. automobile industry learned a hard lesson about the need to coordinate technology strategies with manufacturing and human-resource policies. The disappointing experience of General Motors with its highest-technology plants demonstrated that simply investing large amounts of money in new hardware is not the answer. Technology strategies that are tightly integrated with the manufacturing work force, the organizational design, and human-resource practices work far better. This lesson has had a powerful impact on the thinking of auto-industry executives and union leaders. General Motors, Ford, and Chrysler are all pursuing a strategy of linking investments in new plant and equipment to organizational changes that allow for teamwork, continuous learning, and the opportunity for employees to "give wisdom to the new machines."

IBM's decision to establish an R&D operation in Japan presents a different example of how firms seek to gain strategic advantage through technology. An important motivation for the decision was to learn firsthand how technology development and transfer work in Japan.

The Commission learned of other American companies that are trying hard to rid themselves of parochialism and now routinely scan the globe for new technology; frequently they experiment with new ways of transferring learning across national borders. Chaparral Steel's practice of sending its people all over the world to find the best new technology, along with its willingness to provide industrial sabbaticals and travel funds for that purpose, stands out in this respect. From Chaparral we also learned of the importance of links to universities for smaller firms seeking to exploit state-of-the-art technology. Chaparral uses its university linkages as a window on world-class technologies and scientific discoveries and seeks to be the best in its industry in *applying* the breakthroughs of others.

Flatter and Less Compartmentalized Organizations

Organizational structure—the horizontal division into departments and the vertical division into layers of management hierarchy—varies considerably from industry to industry and from small firms to big ones. In virtually all successful firms, however, the trend is toward greater functional integration and fewer layers of hierarchy, both of which promote greater speed in product development and greater responsiveness to changing markets.

Ford was the first American automobile company to experiment with the use of cross-functional teams to speed the development and introduction of a new model. The product-development team for the Taurus included representatives from planning, design, engineering, manufacturing, and marketing. The specialists worked simultaneously rather than serially, and the success of the Team Taurus project convinced Ford of the problem-solving potential of this approach.

Other American firms have also begun to implement the concept of simultaneous engineering. In most cases what this means is that the design of the product and of the manufacturing process overlap in time but are still handled by separate groups. A few companies, including Ford, have taken the idea further by completely integrating the two activities. A single multifunctional team is charged with developing both the product and the production process. At Boeing, "design/build teams" are now part of the lexicon. At Xerox, process and product design have been combined in the development organization, and the chief engineer on a project is also responsible for pilot production. Only after initial problems with both the product and process have been solved is the project turned over to the manager of production operations. This approach has helped Xerox to reduce its development time for copiers by almost 50 percent.

The benefits of simultaneous engineering are now acquiring the status of accepted wisdom in American industry. But setting up the right organizational structure is only half the battle. IBM, Hewlett-Packard, Ford, and other firms that have pioneered in these approaches stressed in discussions with the Commission that it is also essential to have a strong project manager who is capable of unifying the functions of the various team members. And it is important to ensure that the group has skills in problem solving, teamwork, and negotiation. Recent research by MIT faculty members on organizations in Europe, Asia, and North America provides further support for this last observation.[1]

The task of flattening deep organizational hierarchies goes hand in hand with the effort to dismantle functional barriers. A flatter hierarchy generally enhances organizational flexibility. It also promotes closer relationships with customers, for now the customer with a problem can often speak directly with the production group that has responsibility for the product, instead of going through a sales department.

In flatter, leaner organizations the number of job categories at each level is reduced, and the responsibilities associated with particular jobs are broadened. The net effect is often to decentralize decision making. For example, when production workers are given responsibility for quality checks, they must also be given the authority to stop the production line in order to stop the flow of defective parts. At Chaparral Steel, with almost 1,000 workers, there are only four job levels. Production workers are responsible for identifying new technologies, meeting with customers, maintaining their equipment, and training. Foremen and crews install new equipment. Security guards are trained as emergency medical technicians, and they input data while on their shift. At much larger companies like Xerox, Ford, and General Motors, experiments are underway to give production workers more information about, and greater control over, scheduling, quality control, and other management functions traditionally performed by supervisors, middle managers, or staff specialists.

Many companies have stated their intention to reduce the number of layers in their organizational hierarchy and achieve greater cross-functional integration but have had difficulty putting these ideas into practice. Successful implementation typically requires a change in company culture that encourages and supports participation, teamwork, and decision making at lower levels of the organization.

Innovative Human-Resource Policies

All of the changes in strategy and organization that we have described require departures from conventional job classifications, labor-management relations, career-progression ladders, and policies on employment security, training, and compensation. Best-practice firms have recognized that improvements in quality and flexibility require levels of commitment, responsibility, and knowledge on the part of the work force that cannot be obtained by compulsion or cosmetic improvements in human-resource policies. Quality circles do not work unless workers understand the overall production process and unless their wages, job security, or profit-sharing arrangements give them a sense that they have a stake in the firm's future. The most successful firms recognize that quality is the output of an entire production system, and not the result of an organizational gimmick.

Firms in industries as different as computers and office equipment, automobiles, steel, and aerospace have introduced innovative human-resource policies that promote participation, teamwork, trust, flexibility, employment security, and a sharing of economic risk. The companies adopting the new policies include some where labor unions have an important voice. A key element of Ford's successful turnaround was its decision to involve employees more in the affairs of the company and share more information with workers and union leaders. In parallel, the company negotiated new labor agreements with the United Auto Workers that introduced profit-sharing and employment-security provisions protecting the jobs and incomes of senior workers affected by technological change, plant closings, decisions to have work performed elsewhere, and other corporate restructuring actions. A Human Resources Center jointly administered by the UAW and Ford was established to offer training and retraining programs for current employees. In 1987 the company and the union at Ford (and also at General Motors) established plant-level committees on operating effectiveness and employment security. The committees share information on competitive conditions and costs and plan strategies for improving plant performance.

Big companies like Ford and IBM have the resources to train their own workers in special skills. They also have more incentive to invest in training, because they are more likely to capture the benefits of their investment. (Large companies have lower turnover, and so they are more confident of keeping the workers in whose education they have invested.)

Smaller companies draw more heavily on outside institutions for training, but even here there is often a major internal component as well. The Kingsbury Machine Tool Company once built dedicated equipment for high-volume production of power-train components for vehicles; it has successfully converted to building flexible machines and transfer lines controlled by software. Under the old regime the primary demand on the work force was for mechanical skills, but the new product line requires workers with knowledge of computers. To retrain the work force, the company provided everyone, from janitors to vice presidents, with computers to use at work or at home and offered classes to employees and their families. This approach to training produced general familiarity with computer technology rather than just narrow skills, and it smoothed the company's transition.

Sustaining a commitment to innovative human-resource policies is not easy when management is under pressure to reduce costs
quickly or when differences in compensation between top executives, workers, and middle managers are growing. The innovations
are likely to last only when they are reinforced by the business,
technology, and organizational strategies that make up the other
components of best industrial practice. Conversely, without changes
in human-resource practices, the benefits of the other restructuring efforts will remain elusive.

Obstacles to the Diffusion of Best Practices

What distinguishes the best-practice firms we observed from others
in their industries is that they see the various innovations we have
discussed not as independent solutions but rather as a coherent
package of changes. Competitive benchmarking, team-based
approaches to product and process development, closer relations
with suppliers and customers, increased emphasis on customer
satisfaction, flatter organizations, increased sharing of information, employee involvement in decision making, profit sharing,
increased job security, a commitment to training, and continuous
improvement—each of these features reinforces the others, and
the entire organization is affected by them.

Implementing such far-reaching innovations involves wrench-
ing changes at all levels of the organization and requires an
extraordinary commitment by corporate leaders. For every best-
practice firm there are many more companies that remain committed to outmoded principles and practices. Indeed, even within the
best-practice firms, acceptance of some parts of the package is far
from universal. Executives sometimes become complacent. They
see the benefits of innovation in one unit, but then they assume the
innovations will diffuse across the organization without further
intervention. Instead, innovations often become islands, isolated
from the rest of organizational practice and dismissed as special
cases by those not directly involved in the initial experiment.
Sometimes too the lessons drawn from the experiment are super-
ficial and the underlying message is not learned.

Thus, the best of the good news in the United States still leaves
much to be done. Our research also showed that a supportive
public-policy environment is in some cases a prerequisite for the
diffusion of best practices from firm to firm. For example, even the

very best of the small manufacturers must depend on external sources for new technology and new skills. The skilled work force of a small, specialized niche producer may achieve remarkable results in adapting machines and processes to the new needs of customers. In the best cases, a high level of continuous innovation in product and process may be achieved. But even the highly skilled workers of the best niche manufacturers are unlikely to achieve technological breakthroughs. It is rare to find such firms devoting substantial resources to research and development.

Similarly, the best of the small manufacturers are able to maintain and enhance the skills of their workers by assigning them broad responsibilities for whole operations and not simply narrow tasks. But unlike the best large manufacturers, whose extensive in-plant training programs provide both special skills and also a more basic education, formal training programs and the development of new skills require resources too great for most small firms. They have to draw on outside educational institutions, cooperative arrangements with other firms and local and state governments, or external labor markets to obtain many of the human resources they need.

The fact that there are different kinds of successful firms is important for the design of public policies intended to encourage the spread of best industrial practices. Government must recognize that no single set of policies will work across the board. For example, any system of tax credits that encourages in-plant training schemes might well elicit a bigger effort from large firms, but it is unlikely that it could stimulate the creation of such training programs in small niche manufacturers where they do not already exist. Rather, to improve the quality of skills in these companies, public resources have to be directed to programs that are in tune with the structures of these firms, for example, to programs designed to improve and multiply companies' relations with various colleges and universities. The diversity of firm types suggests that effective public policy ought to support different patterns of training by expanding in-plant training capabilities in some cases and encouraging better use of external educational programs in others.

Furthermore, what constitutes global best practice is itself a moving target, and even the leading American firms will have to continue to improve their performance in the areas of quality, cost, and product development. For today's best-practice companies, further significant reductions in production cost will require the adoption of a continuous-flow, waste-free production system—the just-in-time system. There are still only a few plants in the United States where the JIT system has been successfully implemented.

The key to major additional reductions in product-development time will be to make further progress in what manufacturing specialists term "design for quality" techniques. The challenge here is for product-development teams to arrive at a product design that has been systematically optimized to meet customers' needs as early as possible in the development project. The design must be robust enough to ensure that the product will provide customer satisfaction even when subject to the real conditions of the factory and customer use. The more problems prevented early on through careful design, the fewer problems that have to be corrected later through a time-consuming and often confusing process of proto-type iterations.

Design for quality and JIT production are each a key stage in the drive toward increased flexibility, which is emerging as a major new arena of manufacturing competition. As we discuss in the next chapter, in the longer run the goal of "total flexibility" may be within reach in some industries, though neither in Japan nor in the United States nor anywhere else is it close to being realized yet. Even so, it is already clear that adopting today's best practices will not be enough; American firms, working with government and educational institutions, will have to develop new approaches and practices that will enable them to achieve still higher levels of productive performance.

Imperatives for a More Productive America

The best-practice firms discussed in the last chapter demonstrate clearly that some American companies still have what it takes to be the best in the world. But many more still do not seem to have recognized that to achieve this status they will have to make far-reaching changes in the way they do business. They will have to adopt new ways of thinking about human resources, new ways of organizing their systems of production, and new approaches to the management of technology. And as we have seen, for these innovations to spread quickly through the large and diverse American economy, coordinated efforts will be needed by government and academia to supplement the actions of individual firms.

Because of the magnitude of the task, it is tempting to focus exclusively on the present predicament of American industry and on remedies that might be applied immediately. But the nature of industrial competition is changing rapidly, and new challenges are arising. Hence, we must look ahead before formulating recommendations. The Commission did not attempt to make detailed forecasts of technological and institutional changes in the business environment. Such forecasts are vulnerable to large error. (Who would have predicted two decades ago that the main commercial applications of the laser would be in compact-disc players and at supermarket checkout counters?) Yet even without a detailed vision of the future, the Commission did identify three major and pervasive long-term trends with broad implications for the productive performance of tomorrow's firms.

Long-Term Trends

First, it seems overwhelmingly likely that economic activity will continue to become more international. The ownership, location, work force, purchases, and sales of firms will all spread out beyond the boundaries of the nation in which the company originated. Only a major episode of protectionism could reverse this trend, and the main threat of such an episode appears to have passed, at least for the time being.

The further internationalization of business will almost certainly intensify competitive pressures. More and more countries will acquire the capacity to produce and to export sophisticated goods and services. Whenever the Latin American economy improves, Brazil and Mexico and perhaps other countries in the region are likely to emerge as players in world markets. The number of newly industrializing countries will surely increase, and some less developed countries will also participate. In the longer term there is the prospect that China will emerge as a potent force in international commerce. Many of these emerging economies will offer labor costs even lower than those of Taiwan and Korea, and far lower than those of the United States, Japan, and Europe. The obvious implication of this trend is that American firms will not be able to compete on the basis of cost alone. The future of American industry will of necessity lie in specialized, high-quality products; elementary commodities will be made in the United States only if their production is extraordinarily capital-intensive and technologically advanced. At the same time, competition among U.S., Japanese, and European firms in markets for high-value-added products will become increasingly fierce.

Second, partly because of internationalization and partly because of rising incomes around the world, markets for consumer goods and intermediate goods are becoming more sophisticated. In many countries, consumers and commercial buyers are becoming more knowledgeable and quality-conscious. Markets are also becoming more segmented and specialized; not everyone is prepared to accept the same designs and specifications. As this process continues, consumers will expect products progressively more customized to individual tastes.

Third, we expect the rapid pace of technological change to continue. Particularly rapid progress seems likely in three areas: information technology, new materials, and biotechnology. Information technology in particular has already permeated nearly every facet of the production of goods and the delivery of services, and we expect it to affect the business environment in a number of ways in the future. Markets will become more integrated. The matching of buyers and sellers will be less affected by geographical differences as computer networking expands. Manufacturing will be able to respond more quickly to market shifts, which in turn will spread more rapidly. Computer and communications technology will allow products to be tailored more closely to the needs and tastes of individual consumers.

Already the use of versatile workstations, rather than fixed, single-purpose machinery, enables short production runs of specialized products, with rapid switching between product types. In the limiting case of fully computer-integrated factories, a continuous stream of different products may be not much more expensive to produce on the factory floor tomorrow than a stream of identical products is today. (Some industries may combine decentralized computer-aided design with centralized foundrylike production, thus exploiting whatever economies of scale remain.)

In the longer run, the convergence of market forces, consumer preferences, and technological opportunities suggests the possibility of "totally flexible" production systems, in which the craft-era tradition of custom-tailoring of products to the needs and tastes of individual customers will be combined with the power, precision, and economy of modern production technology. In such a world the strategic objective will be to deliver high-quality products tailored to each customer at mass-production prices. Information networks and computer simulation techniques will expedite communications between customer and producer. Both purchasing and market research will be facilitated. Simulations will also reduce the need for creating prototypes and will greatly speed the product-development process. In some industries this trend may lead to a continuous flow of product improvements into the market, replacing the present bundling of many improvements into a discrete new product. To achieve this goal, manufacturers will have to move well beyond today's advanced flexible production systems to flexible but fully integrated product development, manufacturing, and marketing systems.

Five Imperatives

In a market economy it is individual firms that have the primary responsibility for correcting past deficiencies and for finding ways to compete successfully in the future. But for these efforts to bear full fruit and for the United States to succeed in building and sustaining an economy with high productivity growth, all sectors—

business, government, labor, and educational institutions—will have to work cooperatively toward this goal.

In the remainder of this chapter we set forth our vision of a more productive America in terms of five imperatives, each of which must be adopted by industry, labor, government, and the educational community. They are not detailed prescriptions but general goals; the next two chapters present our recommendations for how the goals might be achieved. The imperatives are these:

- Focus on the new fundamentals of manufacturing.
- Cultivate a new economic citizenship in the work force.
- Blend cooperation and individualism.
- Learn to live in the world economy.
- Provide for the future.

These goals are interwoven: each one reinforces the others, and all must be pursued together if they are to be effective. Achieving them will not be easy. In many cases, basic changes in attitude will be necessary. Indeed, accepting that there is a need for a sense of common purpose, of shared national goals, may require the biggest attitudinal change of all.

Focusing on the New Fundamentals of Manufacturing

Manufacturing, as we use the term here, encompasses a great deal more than what happens on a production line. It includes designing and developing products as well as planning, marketing, selling, and servicing them. The technologies and processes used in these functions are also part of manufacturing, and so are the ways in which technology and people come together. The United States needs to make a major new commitment to technical and organizational excellence in manufacturing after years of relative inattention. The focus on fundamentals in manufacturing has several subgoals, to which we now turn.

Put products and manufacturing processes ahead of finance. In the postwar years American managers took the production process largely for granted and ranked it below finance and planning in the hierarchy of managerial concerns. The management profession must now reassess its priorities. Managers can no longer afford to be detached from the details of production; otherwise, they will lose the competitive battle to managers who know their business intimately. Business schools must support this change by putting new curricular emphasis on the management of technology and of production processes.

Establish new measures of productive performance. Corporate management and the financial community must work together to develop indicators that better reflect how well companies are actually doing in developing, producing, and marketing their products. Currently, we believe, too much attention is being paid to indicators of short-term financial performance, such as quarterly earnings. At best, these are imperfect measures of longer-term prospects, and at worst, they preoccupy managers and discourage them from focusing on the basics of manufacturing. New measures might include indicators of quality, productivity, product-development time, and time to market.

Focus on the effective use of technology in manufacturing. Manufacturability, reliability, and low cost should be built into products at the earliest possible stages of design. Practices that can help in achieving these aims include extensive analysis of designs, computer simulation, and teamwork among product-planning and production people. Most important, new technologies should be integrated with, rather than thrown at, the work force that will use them. And technology should be integrated with business strategy, sometimes as servant and sometimes as master.

Embrace product customization and production flexibility. Increasingly sophisticated consumers throughout the world are no longer content with identical, mass-produced goods; they are seeking ever more sophisticated products tailored to individual needs. Both manufacturing and service firms will be forced by competition to learn to satisfy such demands. Developments in computer, communications, and manufacturing technology are pushing in the same direction.

In the longer run, as we have already suggested, the goal of "total flexibility"—high-quality, custom-tailored products at mass-production prices—may eventually come within reach. Such a world is still a long way off. But it is already clear that customizing products and being flexible enough to shift production smoothly and efficiently among a broad range of products are emerging as two of the main competitive arenas of the future for manufacturing firms.

Innovate in production processes. The notion that the United States should be content to dominate the inventive front end of the product life cycle is outdated and must change. Although the U.S. economy is still unmatched in its ability to open up new areas of science and technology for commercial exploitation, new products are more likely to originate overseas than they once were. More important, dominating only the front end of the product cycle is not enough to ensure high growth in productivity. The United States, with a fourth of worldwide production and consumption, cannot live off its research alone, just as most companies can get no more than a few percent of their revenue from research. Individual entrepreneurs may profit handsomely from being the first to bring a new product to market, but the biggest economic returns are generally realized later in the product cycle by firms whose strength is in designing better products, delivering them to the marketplace quicker, maintaining higher quality, and continuously improving both products and processes. Innovation must be applied to the processes of production as enthusiastically as it is now applied to products.

The primary responsibility for this must rest with private firms. But there is also an important role for government. Federal policy for science and technology has traditionally put more emphasis on basic research than on technology transfer and the commercialization of new technologies. That has begun to change lately, but there continues to be relatively little support for the development of advanced manufacturing process technologies and for strengthening downstream technical performance. More could be done through tax policy, procurement strategy, and a variety of other measures, as well as through policies for research and development.

Cultivating a New Economic Citizenship in the Work Force

Education for technological competence is crucial for raising the productivity of American firms. But improving productive performance is not the Commission's only objective. We see an unprecedented opportunity in the new technologies for enabling workers at all levels of the firm to master their own work environment. This marks a major change from even the recent past. The technologies for mass-producing standard goods consigned workers to tasks that made few demands on their mental capacities or skills or on their ability to work with others in planning and executing jobs. In a world of assembly-line workers, coordination and responsibility are located at the top of a steep hierarchical structure. In such a system the intrinsic satisfactions of work are few and material compensation is for many people the only motivator.

Today and in the future, effective use of new technology will require people to develop their capabilities for planning, judgment, collaboration, and the analysis of complex systems. In exercising these skills, workers will come to have a larger responsibility for organizing the production process. If American industry can seize this opportunity, individuals may experience a new measure of mastery and independence on the job that could go well beyond maximizing productivity and extend to personal and professional satisfaction and well-being.

Under the new economic citizenship that we envision, workers, managers, and engineers will be continually and broadly trained, masters of their technology, in control of their work environment, and involved in shaping their firms' objectives. No longer will an employee be treated like a cog in a big and impersonal machine. From the company's point of view, the work force will be transformed from a cost factor to be minimized into a precious asset to be conserved and cultivated.

The new economic citizenship will entail new relationships among companies, employees and technology. Learning, especially on the job, will acquire new importance. Greater employee breadth and responsibility are needed to facilitate the absorption of new and rapidly changing manufacturing technologies that span different processes. On the employer's side, greater caring for employees is essential, since under the rules of their new citizenship, employees will be expected to give so much more of themselves to their work.

Once again primary responsibility for achieving this goal rests with individual firms, but government, labor representatives, and educational institutions all have key roles to play as well.

We proceed to a discussion of three principal subgoals that, in our view, will lead to this new kind of economic citizenship.

Learn for work and at work. No matter how much a company invests in capital equipment, automation cannot replace human mastery of the production process, from conception to market. We have learned from foreign examples and from U.S. firms incorporating best practices that successful adaptation to the new economic environment involves workers, technicians, and managers using technology in ways that require good preparation and continuous learning on the job. Chaparral Steel in Texas, like Kyocera Ceramics in Japan and many other firms we visited, operate on the same two principles: technical knowledge must be broadly spread through the production work force to derive maximum advantage from new technologies, and the enterprise must organize its job rotations, career ladders, and training programs to promote learning.

Beyond the need for good basic schooling, which we discuss at the end of this chapter, education and training for work need major overhauling. The expansion of community colleges and other postsecondary educational institutions is a positive development that offsets the sad state of vocational training; it should be encouraged both by connections with the private sector and by public support. University education in the United States in general compares favorably with education in other countries, although there are opportunities for improvement here too, as we discuss in chapter 12. But if postsecondary education is relatively strong in the United States, on-the-job education is seriously underdeveloped. The Commission's research on America's most powerful foreign competitors shows the strengths of a system that offers large-scale training in the workplace, including training through experience in a range of different work responsibilities and frequent job rotations. As we have seen, the Japanese and the West Germans have demonstrated that in-plant training helps to develop a set of firm-specific skills in the context in which they will be employed, to inculcate in all members of the work force an understanding of the whole operation, and finally, by making learning a regular part of the job, to make retraining a normal part of work life. These assets are crucial to success in mastering the new manufacturing technologies. They are also assets that cannot be developed by schools alone, no matter how good the schools may be.

To improve education both in postsecondary institutions and in companies, a variety of contributions from both the private sector and the public sector will be required. Perhaps the most difficult challenge will be to find ways of encouraging more in-plant training and, in particular, training of the broad, general type that is needed over the course of an employee's entire working life.

The German and Japanese employers whom we interviewed feel they have a stake in maintaining a large national reservoir of highly trained workers. It is unlikely that American employers can individually reach this sense of collective responsibility for training workers. But it should be possible to devise incentives that would treat investment in human resources in ways similar to investment in plant and equipment. An equally important goal is to spread the kinds of partnerships among unions, employers, and state and local governments that, in some parts of this country, have begun to make real progress on providing training for the new technologies.

Increase employee breadth, responsibility, and involvement. The possibilities of flexibility, diversity, quality, and reliability offered by flexible computer-aided manufacturing systems can only be realized when the process of production is understood and controlled at all levels of the work force. Unless the jobs of production workers are broadened in ways that require them to understand and control a larger part of the whole process, the full advantages of this new technology cannot be exploited.

In the most successful firms today the role of production workers is shifting from one of passive performance of narrow, repetitive tasks to one of active collaboration in the organization and fine-tuning of production. Skill and flexibility are the result of work experiences in a variety of assignments, and not only or even primarily of courses taken in school or in the plant. Restructuring job categories, flattening hierarchies, broadening responsibilities, and taking on new tasks in regular job rotations—all of these produce a work force capable of responding rapidly and creatively to new problems. The objective should be continuous learning on the job, so that retraining is a normal part of work life.

Provide greater employment stability and new rewards. If people are asked to give maximum effort and to accept uncertainty and rapid change, they must be full participants in the enterprise. They deserve assurance that their striving to increase the productivity of the firm will not simply result in their becoming unnecessary and expendable commodities. The not-very-successful attempt to introduce the NUMMI pattern without NUMMI job security at the General Motors plant in Van Nuys, California, suggests how important this issue is.

Just as important as job security is a measure of participation in the company. In the best-practice firms we visited, participation took various forms, from profit sharing and bonuses based on overall firm performance to ownership of the firm's stock. Such rewards are important, for they focus employee attention on longer-term objectives.

In the longer term, the trends toward shorter production runs, shorter product cycles, a greater variety of products, and a shorter time to market for new products seem likely to result in profit instability, brought about by shifting demand and shifting productive advantage. A business environment of this kind may favor large, diversified firms. Alternatively, firms may become more viable if the risks of business are shared with workers (and suppliers too). In that case, however, workers and suppliers will insist on, and will be entitled to, compensation for their willingness to absorb some of the risks that used to be borne by the entrepreneurial firm. For suppliers, the adjustment might take the form of flexible pricing practices; workers might accept more of their compensation in the form of profit sharing or bonuses. Both developments will probably lead to some sharing of control as well as risk.

Blending Cooperation and Individualism

The challenge ahead is not to suppress individualism in favor of increased cooperation, but rather to combine these two attitudes into a unique mixture that is economically stronger than either extreme. Is this possible, and if so, how?

Americans have traditionally emphasized individualism, often at the expense of cooperation. The nation tends to see the economy as made up of individual persons competing for recognition within their company and of individual companies competing in the marketplace. This view is linked to deeply held national values of individualism and is reflected in the strength of American antitrust legislation and in a widespread suspicion of government intervention. Yet in the best American companies, as in other societies, values of group solidarity, community, and interdependence have led to important economic advantages. For example, they promote better relations with suppliers and customers, they facilitate agreement on common standards, and within a firm they can increase the quality and speed of production.

The presence of a strong tradition of individualism in the United States does not preclude cooperation. Consider the role of land-grant colleges and the extension services in American agriculture, the importance of support by the Defense Advanced Research Projects Agency in the development of the computer field, or the (TC)^2 project (Textile/Clothing Technology Corporation), which was funded by government, textile companies, apparel companies, and labor unions to sponsor research on automating sewing. There are also many examples of cooperation between state governments and local industry, and they seem to be growing in number. Within firms, we can point to examples, such as IBM's Proprinter project, where cooperation among scientists, technologists, and production people yielded tangible increases in productive performance. Thus, in our view there is nothing fundamental in American culture that is inimical to the blend of cooperation and individualism that we envision. We next discuss four ways for achieving this.

Organize for both cooperation and individualism. Deep organizational hierarchies, with their rigidity and compartmentalization, are an obstacle to cooperation. They should be replaced with substantially flatter organizational structures that invite communication and cooperation among different corporate departments. The related organizational change of reducing the number of job categories also promotes cooperation, since broadly skilled workers will generally overlap and share knowledge of manufacturing functions. The nation's best-practice firms are distinguished by such flat structures, which demonstrates their feasibility in the American workplace.

Another tangible step is to reward both cooperation and individualism in school. This could be done with team projects, which might receive two grades: one common to all team members that would measure the success of the overall project and another that would measure and reward individual performance. Companies could take exactly the same approach, using individual *and* team bonuses. This has already been tried by some best-practice companies with good results.

Promote better intra- and interfirm relations. We have already extensively discussed the paramount significance of strong and durable relations with suppliers and customers. Toward that end, companies should put less emphasis on legalistic and often adversarial contractual agreements, and promote business relationships based on mutual trust and the prospects of continued business transactions over the long term. Such a shift would not only enhance productive performance but would also help reduce costs.

U.S. firms must also develop cooperative relationships with their domestic competitors to evolve common standards. The lesson of the fragmented U.S. machine-tool industry and the standards-conscious Japanese has apparently not been fully understood.

Expand partnerships. Despite the many positive examples of partnerships here and abroad, Americans continue to regard cooperation among firms and other private and public agencies with suspicion. The nation is paying heavily for this unwillingness to recognize the potential importance of collaboration among the federal government, business, labor, universities, states, and localities in creating the conditions required for economic growth. Americans need to learn to think of cooperation among economic actors as a way of overcoming the defects of the market, which undersupplies certain collective factors that are essential to economic success.

Partnerships can take the form of research consortia or joint business ventures. They can and should also include collaborative efforts with government to promote the development of technologies for productive performance, much as earlier partnerships with the Department of Defense have stimulated new technologies for military purposes. Finally, partnerships should include consortia— especially among small companies and local governments—devoted to training and educating the work force at all levels.

Strengthen cooperation between labor and management. Innovative and cooperative labor-management relationships have emerged within many union and nonunion firms, but they remain fragile and are still at risk of being aborted by the broader adversarial model that continues to dominate labor relations in America. The prevalence of this adversarial model increases the political risks for union leaders who advocate cooperation, raises doubts among managers about the durability of cooperation, and slows the pace of further innovation.

American management, labor, and government therefore face a crucial strategic choice. Clinging to traditional values will mean an escalation of conflict and a diversion of resources away from productive uses. Endorsement of the new patterns of cooperation would create a climate in which further experimentation and innovation would flourish and expand across the economy. Management must accept workers and their representatives as legitimate partners in the innovation process. Labor leaders must become visible champions of the innovative model. And government must become an active party to the process by amending current laws that limit the scope and variety of employee participation and representation.

Learning to Live in the World Economy

Focusing on the technology of manufacturing, cultivating human resources, and encouraging cooperation are the indispensable first steps that Americans must take at home if the United States is to regain the productive edge. But they are not sufficient. To compete successfully in a world that is becoming more international and more competitive, Americans must also expand their outlook beyond their own boundaries. We list four subgoals that in our view will help foster America's international orientation.

Understand foreign languages, cultures, and practices. The ability to export successfully will call for a range of skills that American firms have not needed in the past (or have not perceived that they needed). Companies will have to cultivate knowledge of other languages, market customs, tastes, legal systems, and regulations: they will need to develop a new set of international sensitivities. The key fact here is that competition strengthens the hand of the customer, whose celebrated voice often speaks in languages other than English.

Much can be done toward the learning of foreign languages, customs, and business practices during primary, secondary, and postsecondary education. But schools are not going to embark unilaterally on such a foreign orientation without a strong signal that it is truly useful and in demand. Toward that end, colleges and industry could help directly by requiring a foreign language of those seeking admission or employment.

Shop internationally. American business and American workers must realize that cost considerations will increasingly dictate whether materials and components are best procured at home or abroad. It follows that not only marketing divisions will have to be knowledge-able about conditions abroad; purchasing agents and production managers will have to as well.

Many commentators, ourselves included, have noticed the damage done to American business by the "not invented here" attitude. Increasingly, things invented "there" will have been invented abroad. Thus, the technological net must be cast worldwide. Americans must learn to look for and shop for the best technologies wherever they happen to be.

Shopping internationally should go beyond materials and turn-key technologies to best practices and, particularly, best production benchmarks. Learning and imitating such practices and meeting or exceeding best standards will ensure the continued health of American productive performance within the world economy.

Enhance distribution and service. The history of foreign penetration of American markets suggests that efficient distribution networks and service facilities can be just as important as price and quality of product in getting customers and holding them. It is perhaps best to think of this as part of the general orientation to quality required by sophisticated consumers with money to spend.

Develop internationally conscious policies. All the evidence tells us that a country the size of the United States cannot help itself in the long run by widespread protectionism. Retaliation by others will only set off struggles between different interests at home. But the United States should also actively insist on open trade practices by others in Europe and Asia. It has been relatively ineffective at that so far, partly because of inexperience and ignorance both inside and outside of government.

We have neither the ability nor the wish to provide a manual for the export-competitive firm; we seek only to sketch the outlines of changes in orientation that seem to be required. Perhaps as important as any specific characteristic is America's general attitude about the surrounding world. Smaller countries have long known that the capacity to export at a profit is necessary for domestic success. With internal markets too small to allow full scope for economies of scale, and with resource bases so narrow that many goods and services can only be supplied by imports, which in turn have to be paid for, the smaller countries of Europe have always treated foreign trade as part of life. Japan, lacking domestic oil, minerals, and other resources, has rapidly acquired the same habit. The United States has never before felt that pinch. When the West German economy was being reconstructed after the war, a common slogan was "Exportieren oder sterben!" (Export or die!). The U.S. economy, because of its large scale and natural diversity, is not in quite the same fix. "Export or see your relative standard of living diminish" is not a slogan to set anyone's heart on fire, but it expresses the truth.

Providing for the Future

Many of the actions recommended in this book will bear fruit only in the future, perhaps the distant future. Changes in the organization of production and in the attitudes of producers will not happen overnight; if and when they do happen, the consequences will show themselves only with a further lag. We are talking, then, about investments. And while every one of the five imperatives presented in this chapter may be viewed as an investment, we focus here on providing for the future through a more conventional yet broad use of the term.

We consider in particular four major kinds of investment we believe are necessary to achieve a higher level of productive performance.

Invest in basic education and technical literacy. Americans must be provided with a fundamentally different education from what they receive today. Basic schooling from kindergarten through high school is seriously deficient to the extent that it leaves large numbers of its graduates without basic skills in reading, writing, and mathematics. Only a tiny fraction of young Americans are technologically literate and have some knowledge of foreign societies. Unless the nation begins to remedy these inadequacies, it can make no real progress on all the rest.

At the moment, responsibility for primary and secondary education falls chiefly on local and state governments. We believe, however, that if Americans are to achieve the breadth and depth of changes in education that they need, the federal government will have to provide leadership and incentives. If not, a few cities and states may move ahead, while many others remain at their current unsatisfactory status quo. The large majority of new entrants into the work force in the coming decades will be women, blacks, and Hispanics—groups with major educational and economic handicaps. This makes it all the more important to diffuse educational improvements widely throughout the country.

The Commission has no single, magical solution to America's educational plight. Numerous studies have analyzed the problem and have made their recommendations. In our view, several actions need to converge on this pressing and crucial national problem. The adoption of more rigorous educational standards; a greater focus on science, technology, and foreign languages; perhaps a longer school year; and greater incentives for teachers are some of the ways to begin work on this complex problem. In the next chapter we discuss some of these possibilities at the K–12 and postsecondary levels, where federal and state governments have a role to play, together with private interests.

Develop long-term business strategies. In chapter 4 we came to the conclusion that the shortsightedness of American business strategy goes beyond what can be explained by inappropriately high interest rates. Our case studies suggest that the internal reward systems in American industry are biased in favor of the quick payoff and against the patient exploitation of long-term investments, even when the latter are intrinsically more profitable. If this were a cultural trait, national economic policy might be helpless. However, we find irresistible the inference that the wave of hostile takeovers and leveraged buyouts encourages or enforces an excessive and dangerous overvaluation of short-term profitability. Limiting takeover activity would have efficiency costs as well as the benefits to which we are attracted. It seems clear from the evidence, however, that takeover activity is not entirely driven by efficiency. We believe that the national interest would be served by tax and credit legislation making it harder and more expensive to raise large sums of money for takeovers and buyouts. Among the more important benefits would be the redirection of entrepreneurial talent toward more productive activities.

The high expertise of certain companies in their own business has always been and will undoubtedly continue to be a source of strong competitive advantage. The acquisition, retention, and enhancement of specific expertise in U.S. companies is becoming even more important now that international competitors exhibit ever greater patience in investing for the long term. Thus, shutting down certain business activities and moving into fresh ones that appear to be more profitable may not be effective over the long run.

Another important way in which American businesses can provide for the long term is through investment in research and development. This type of investment may have the longest and least certain payoff period of all, yet it has been successfully pursued in the past, and it continues to be an important and large component of America's best-practice firms. Government, industry, and academic institutions must ensure not only that R&D investment continues strongly in basic research but also that it expands in the direction of productive manufacturing technologies and that it avoids becoming risk-averse.

Establish policies that stimulate productive investment. Reluctance to invest is one important aspect of the general short-windedness that we have identified as a common failing in American industry. An important goal of American economic policy should be to stimulate productive investment. This can be done in several ways. Investment is favored over consumption by a policy mix that combines a more expansionary monetary policy with "tighter" fiscal policy, rather than the reverse; by a fiscal policy that, other things being equal, taxes consumption more heavily than saving or investment when there is a choice; and by tax and other policies that encourage private and public saving, and thus increase the supply of capital to business. In all three of these directions U.S. policy has been perverse and is getting more so. The task of bringing the federal budget closer into balance should receive the highest priority in economic policy making.

Invest in infrastructure for productive performance. The transportation networks of highways, seaways, and airways and the worldwide telephone system are examples of infrastructures that have served their users well. In addition to preserving existing infrastructures, Americans should also consider investing in new infrastructures for tomorrow's changing businesses. One way of doing this is through partnerships among industry, universities, and government that pool their collective strengths but preserve their individual needs. Regional centers set up by state governments and industry would allow small companies to pool their resources for training and other needs that they cannot handle alone. Another possibility is a network of productive-performance centers that would give advice on best available technologies and foreign needs, supplies, and practices. We further believe that the time is right for American business and government to begin developing a national information infrastructure, which would eventually become a network of communication highways as important for tomorrow's business as the current highway network is for today's flow of goods—a prospect that we discuss in more detail in the following chapter.

To summarize, providing for the future is a matter of investing, in the broadest sense of the term. If Americans want the assets thus created to be owned at home, higher investment has to be accompanied by higher savings. It is (almost) as simple as that.

11

Strategies for Industry, Labor, and Government

The earlier chapters of this book have doubtless conveyed the general nature of the Commission's conclusions. In this chapter we state those conclusions in the form of recommendations addressed to industry and government. The next chapter presents our thoughts on what ought to be done by the nation's research universities, with a particular focus on MIT.

In speaking to "industry" we have in mind both workers and managers, and we address some additional remarks to the leaders of organized labor. Most of the recommendations to government will require the resources and the central authority of the federal government, but there are also a few areas where state and local governments can take part. Almost everything said in this chapter appears elsewhere in the book as well; we have, therefore, repeated certain material in telegraphic form in order to bring together in one place a concise account of the actions we believe are needed. The purpose of each recommendation is to suggest broad directions for action rather than to prescribe specific policy initiatives. The latter are left to those with greater involvement, experience, and qualifications in policy design.

We are mindful that it is often more difficult to implement worthy recommendations than it is to formulate them. The changes we propose are major ones, and putting them into effect will require the greatest management skill, particularly since there will be losers as well as winners in the process. We have no universal solution to the implementation problem, although we suspect that what will work best is a combination of methods, including both top-down and bottom-up approaches. We believe that concerted action on all of the recommended strategies will be more effective than a selective implementation of a subset. In our view, that is the key to improving the nation's productive performance.

Strategies for Industry

In the U.S. economy the principal responsibility for improving industrial productivity lies with the private sector, and most particularly with the individual firms whose economic survival is at stake. Our recommendations to industry are as follows.

• *Focus on the production process, with the objective of improving long-term productive performance.*

The management of industrial firms must recognize that improving productive performance is of overriding importance to the success of their firms. The chief executive officer must display leadership in setting high goals that meet the best standards of production worldwide. Management should adopt a long-range perspective but with the short-term flexibility needed to minimize the time to change. This means that firms must configure their production processes to allow flexible and rapid adaptation to changing market and production conditions.

• *Adopt as an explicit objective of the production process the delivery of high-quality products to market in a timely fashion at competitive prices.*

The modern market is diverse, competitive, rapidly changing, and international. In this environment, flexibility, speed, and design for quality become essential. The practical tests of business decisions are market relevance and customer satisfaction.

• *Develop techniques to measure and improve the efficiency and quality of the production process, and identify opportunities for progressive improvement in its performance.*

Current measurement methods reflect an older concept of productivity. Newer techniques must encourage engineers to design for manufacturing and to build quality in at the design stage. A dedication to continuous improvement both in the development of prototypes and in production can contribute to the speed-to-market objective by minimizing redesign and debugging delays. The most critical element is the ability to predict early in the product-development cycle that a new product will yield superior customer satisfaction in the actual marketplace.

- *Emphasize product variety and manufacturing flexibility in the development of production systems.*

The convergence of market forces, consumer preferences, and technological opportunities in flexible manufacturing suggest that future production systems should provide a wider range of products in a shorter time to satisfy a diversity of rapidly changing consumer needs. The earlier emphasis on minimizing cost and the more recent emphasis on improving quality should eventually result in closer parity with international competitors. Flexibility and variety to provide maximum customer satisfaction appear to be emerging as the primary areas of competition. This trend presents great challenges to product development, the factory floor, and marketing.

The above changes in production practices will require a much stronger spirit of cooperation within the firm. The managers and technical staff will need to work more closely and cooperatively with the work force. Closer relations will also be required with customers and suppliers.

- *Cultivate a more involved, less specialized, continuously learning work force.*

In the new systems of production, a worker's ability to contribute requires a knowledge that embraces much more than what is needed to perform a narrow set of tasks. All the other changes in the production system will depend ultimately on the ability and commitment of individual employees.

- *Flatten organizational hierarchies to give employees greater responsibility and broader experience.*

This step is both a part of the process of creating a more capable work force and a means of fully exploiting workers' talents.

- *Integrate and (where feasible) perform concurrently the functions of research and development, product design, and process design to achieve greater efficiency and a shorter time to market.*

This change requires the formation of product teams with strong leaders to carry products from the development stage through the production process. It presupposes that earlier recommendations have been carried out.

• *Cooperate with suppliers rather than treating them as adversaries.*

To achieve this end, firms must establish long-term relationships, be willing to take part in joint research, design, and development activities, and set standards both for the company and for the industry so that the benefits of improved performance will spread.

Beyond these changes firms should take explicit steps to adopt international strategies.

• *Insist that key employees have an adequate understanding of foreign cultures.*

Here a major share of the responsibility falls on educational institutions, but firms too have a part to play by providing incentives and demonstrating that they value international experience and knowledge of foreign languages and cultures.

• *Adopt the best practices of world industry to improve productivity and quality in the manufacturing process.*

American firms must be willing to learn from the best performers in their industry, whether those best performers be domestic or foreign. Industry associations should encourage wide understanding and rapid diffusion of concepts that have been demonstrated to work.

• *In the area of labor-management relations, support diffusion of cooperative industrial relations by accepting labor representatives as legitimate and valued partners in the innovation process.*

American managers must recognize that unions are a valued institution in any democratic society. Resources traditionally devoted to avoiding unionization need to be reallocated toward promoting and sustaining union-management cooperation. Yet management cannot be expected to adopt this approach unless union leaders demonstrate an equally strong commitment to a system of cooperative industrial relations, a point to which we now turn.

Strategies for Labor

• *Labor union leaders must become champions of cooperative and innovative industrial-relations practices and develop a new generation of leaders skilled in using these new practices to promote the long-run interests of their members and the firms that employ them.*

The entire inquiry of the MIT Commission has been dominated by the compelling importance of human-resource issues. Several of our recommendations require industry to reconsider deep-rooted values and traditions and take bold steps to elevate human-resource issues to a higher priority in organizational decision making. But labor leadership bears an equal responsibility. Innovative practices and a cooperative spirit will not diffuse widely unless they are supported and championed by labor leaders on the shop floor, at the level of the national union, and at the very top levels of the American labor movement. Involving workers in problem solving and in efforts at continuous improvement, encouraging investment in human resources and in lifelong learning by employees, and working cooperatively with managers in the design and implementation of long-term strategies for business and technology must become standard items on the negotiating agendas of labor.

We acknowledge that labor faces great challenges and will have to make difficult adjustments. But traditional principles governing work rules, job security, and compensation that may have worked well in the past now need to be revised to fit a world of changing technologies, international competition, and a more educated work force. The commitment of American management and labor to this new model must be matched by a corresponding commitment of government, a point we take up in the next section.

Strategies for Government

In this section we offer a number of suggestions directed to government. We stress again that the principal responsibility for improving industrial performance rests with the private sector. Too much direct governmental involvement in the process, at least in the American economy and society, could be counterproductive. Yet the government does have an important role in three broad areas: macroeconomic policy, education, and technology policy. Our recommended strategies deal with each of these areas in turn.

- *The federal government should pursue macroeconomic policies that reduce the cost of capital for private investment. This will require measures to increase private savings and reduce the federal budget deficit.*

The most important task for the federal government is to ensure that capital is available to American firms at a reasonable cost, comparable to that borne by the nation's major trading competitors. While the cost of capital is not the only determinant of growth in productivity, it is an important factor.

- *The federal government should continue to press for removal of trade restrictions and for equal access for U.S. firms and products to foreign markets.*

Equal access does not mean a perfect balance of trade with every country in each industrial sector. It does mean that consumers can purchase, and suppliers can offer, products in overseas as well as domestic markets, unencumbered by barriers that prevent customer satisfaction at least cost.

- *The federal government should adopt programs for K–12 education that will lead to greater technological literacy. This will enable a larger fraction of citizens to participate in and benefit from more productive working careers.*

The task of upgrading the primary and secondary schools is probably the single most important challenge facing the country. We join with others in calling for federal support of local programs that are intended to strengthen primary and secondary education. Commission members are acutely aware that the problems of public education in this country go well beyond the classroom to basic social and economic conditions. We believe several measures merit serious consideration: adopting more rigorous educational standards, establishing national examinations (which many other countries have), increasing the focus on science and mathematics in early grades, and lengthening the school year. Merely increasing standards or the time in school will not suffice, however; ways must also be found to better motivate students who do not currently see a good reason for staying in school.

- *The government should encourage continuous education and training for the U.S. work force, with special attention to the increased participation of women, blacks, and Spanish-speaking Americans.*

The federal role in adult education could include encouraging public-private partnerships for job training, working to retrain the unemployed, and perhaps giving corporations tax benefits for investments in education and training. We stress that the federal effort in this area must extend beyond policies that benefit workers in large corporations to include small and medium-size firms. The greater participation of women, blacks, and Spanish-speaking Americans in the work force should be recognized as an opportunity to benefit from the contributions of several disadvantaged groups. The federal government must consider these important participants in the work force in designing educational and training programs.

- *The federal government should endorse and seek to diffuse labor-management cooperation and worker participation in both union and nonunion settings. This will require enforcing current labor laws and modifying them to allow for more varied and flexible forms of participation and representation than were envisioned when the current law was initially adopted in 1935.*

National policy makers set the climate for labor-management relations. Leading companies and unions have demonstrated the feasibility of a new system of relationships. Government must now do its part to diffuse this new model by overcoming the adversarial climate and adopting a national labor policy that encourages continuous innovation and strengthens cooperation in labor-management relations.

- *The federal government should continue investing in basic research and should provide adequate support for operations, equipment, and modern facilities.*

Our first recommendation in the area of science and technology is motivated by the importance of preserving a healthy basic-research establishment. We share the widespread view that present U.S. difficulties in productive performance are due not to a loss of the ability to generate new ideas or technology but rather to difficulties in bringing these ideas to the marketplace and in exploiting technology effectively in the production of goods and services. But in the long run, a strong basic-research establishment is also vital to the competitiveness of the U.S. economy. Basic research conducted at American universities also provides the means for educating many of the leaders of tomorrow's scientific and technological enterprises. The government should therefore sustain its support for basic research. The nation's basic-research activities should be broadly conceived and should include social science, as well as science and engineering.

• *The federal government's support of research and development should be extended to include a greater emphasis on policies to encourage the downstream phases of product and process engineering and to clear any current obstacles to innovation.*

The federal government should launch new R&D programs directed toward improving manufacturing, product development, and process engineering. These programs ought to be undertaken by several agencies, including the National Science Foundation, the Department of Defense, and the Department of Energy. The federal government should also encourage innovation by increasing the speed of granting (or denying) patent applications and deciding patent-infringement cases; supporting intellectual-property rights, including rights relating to software, through international agreements; and encouraging collaborative relationships among universities, industry, and national laboratories that will lead to faster commercialization of new technology.

• *The government should encourage the establishment of a national information infrastructure.*

Such an infrastructure would connect a large number of personal, business, and government computers to a large number of information-based services. We believe that the creation of a national information infrastructure would allow business transactions to be carried out at greater speed and with greater knowledge than elsewhere and would thus establish an important competitive advantage for the United States. Just as the interstate highway system provided the means to move people and goods, an information infrastructure would facilitate the efficient flow of information.

- *The federal government should heed the many voices calling for greater efficiency in military research and development and military procurement to minimize the financial and human resources required to meet national-security needs.*

We believe serious attention must also be given to carrying out military research and development so as to encourage external benefits and minimize negative impacts. In particular, the Department of Defense should employ commercially available technology whenever practical (both for cost savings and to stimulate U.S. industry with economies of scale), and it should undertake R&D programs (such as manufacturing-technology programs) that can be anticipated to have benefits both for the military and the commercial sector. We encourage the department to expand the scope of its manufacturing-technology programs beyond hardware to include operational aspects that will improve quality and minimize production time.

This discussion of the federal government's role illustrates once again how science and technology considerations have become pervasive in government decision making. Of utmost importance, we believe, is that all federal agencies have people on their staffs with enough technical knowledge to properly inform decision makers and also to inform the public about the technical consequences of national policy.

Finally, we recognize that government policies change over time to reflect the will of the people and their elected leaders. This is necessary and appropriate in democracy. Yet just as industry must take a long-term perspective, so too should government. Abrupt changes in policy and regulatory action make long-term planning for corporate investment difficult. For the same reason, regulations arising from different agencies should be consistent and reinforcing rather than fragmented and conflicting.

12

How Universities Should Change

The winds of change that are sweeping through industry and the economy will not spare institutions of higher learning. In particular, the education of engineers and managers must be transformed. In this chapter we suggest ways in which educational institutions might respond to these new challenges. We focus on MIT because we were charged to do so and because we know it well, but we believe that much of what we have to say is also applicable to other universities if they choose to adapt our vision to their strengths.

Until recently we at MIT have shared a perception with older universities organized on the classical model, while taking a different path. The perception, Matthew Arnold's, is that coal, iron, and railroads have nothing to do with sweetness and light. The older universities have concentrated on the body of knowledge that represents "the best that has been thought and said in the world" and how it can be enlarged. For us, the concentration has been on the "hardware" of science and technology, sprinkled with our own brand of sweetness and light.

Today the older universities are struggling to fit the new science and technology into the body of their old learning, while MIT is struggling to determine what its students need to know in fields other than science and engineering. Both types of universities are trying to prepare their intellectual offspring for a world that is becoming more complex, a world whose doors can no longer be unlocked with the old-fashioned keys labeled "technologist" or "humanist."

But we want to do more than build a bridge between the two cultures. We also want to help our students discover a proper balance between individualism and cooperation, and to instill in them a richer understanding of the world that surrounds them—

attributes we believe they will need in order to cope with the challenges lying ahead. And as we made clear in sketching our vision of a more productive America, we would like to see our students derive more inspiration from, and delve more deeply into, real-world problems as they pursue their studies of design, production, management, and organization.

Many of the people in industry and government who have been making the decisions or following the practices we so sternly criticize are graduates of our own or sister institutions. We and our peer universities must share the responsibility for having influenced these alumni on how to do research, how to design and build products, how to manage, how to sell, and how to form strategies. By changing the way we educate these leaders of tomorrow's productive enterprises, we aspire to contribute our share to the solution of the national productivity problem. We begin with our principal recommendation for MIT.

• *MIT should broaden its educational approach in the sciences, in technology, and in the humanities and should educate students to be more sensitive to productivity, to practical problems, to teamwork, and to the cultures, institutions, and business practices of other countries.*

In projecting the effects of our recommendations on the future composition of the MIT faculty and student population, two contradictory objectives drive us. We want to broaden the community in accordance with the vision we have outlined, yet in doing so, we do not want to endanger or damage the Institute's strengths in the pursuit of scientific discovery and analysis or its expertise in particular technological specialties. Accordingly, we recommend developing a new cadre of students and faculty, rather than trying to induce wholesale changes in the existing population (which in any event would be difficult to do). More specifically, we recommend the following.

• *Create a new cadre of students and faculty characterized by (1) interest in, and knowledge of, real problems and their societal, economic, and political context; (2) an ability to function effectively as members of a team creating new products, processes, and systems; (3) an ability to operate effectively beyond the confines of a single discipline; and (4) an integration of a deep understanding of science and technology with practical knowledge, a hands-on orientation, and experimental skills and insight.*

We envision that this new cadre would gradually evolve as a result of changes in instruction and research. We would like to see a greater emphasis on real-world, hands-on experience, and we would also inject an international context into courses where it makes sense to do so. We think students in the engineering school should be exposed to real problems that go beyond the idealized abstractions that have dominated texts and homework since the 1950s. In calling for this change, we do not wish to return to the past educational focus on "handbook" engineering at the expense of fundamentals. Instead, we see a great challenge in advancing and using engineering science to tackle pressing, real problems. In addition, we would like to see students become more internationally aware through knowledge of an appropriate foreign language and become more oriented toward teaching as a management practice. Toward these ends our recommendation is as follows.

• *Where possible, revise subjects to include team projects, practical problems, and exposure to international cultures. Encourage student teaching to instill a stronger appreciation of lifelong learning and the teaching of others. Reinstitute a foreign-language requirement in the undergraduate admissions process.*

A good example along these lines is the proposal, currently under discussion within the engineering school, to institute a one-year practical team project that could substitute for the undergraduate thesis. Every undergraduate would choose one project, and every faculty member in the school would supervise a project team perhaps once every four years. The projects would explore subjects of immediate interest to the professors in a real-world context. Typical examples would be drawn from broad themes that would continue over several years, like the design of a computer system for a nursing home, robots for cleaning Boston harbor, a solar home, or a manager's workstation for a manufacturing plant.

Such projects would bring students and faculty closer together, give the participants an opportunity to apply abstractions to practical problems, stimulate them with real needs, and promote teamwork. The importance of teamwork could be emphasized by giving each student two grades: one for individual contributions and the other for the effectiveness and success of the overall project. All of these are essential ingredients in our recipe for increasing industrial productivity.

Changes in the Engineering Curriculum

Over the last several years, undergraduate education in engineering at MIT has been redefined to reflect a broader agenda.[1] As now envisaged, the basic purpose of the four-year educational process is to prepare its graduates for leadership in technology, for professional excellence, and for rich lives of learning and reflection. This is to be achieved through education in science and engineering with an emphasis on the fundamentals, in essential partnership with the social sciences and the humanities.

Future baccalaureate graduates of MIT's School of Engineering should (1) have obtained a firm foundation in the sciences basic to their technical field; (2) have begun to acquire a working knowledge of current technology in their area of interest; (3) have begun to understand the diverse nature and history of human societies, as well as their literary, philosophical, and artistic traditions; (4) have acquired the skills and motivation for continued self-education; (5) have had an opportunity to exercise ingenuity and inventiveness on a research project; (6) have had an opportunity to perform an engineering synthesis in a design project; (7) have developed oral and written communications skills; and (8) have begun to understand and respect the economic, political, social, and environmental issues surrounding technical developments.

The biggest danger associated with broadening MIT's educational programs lies in the potential dilettantism of students who may end up being lightly exposed to diverse courses of instruction. We know from our experience as educators that reducing the depth of knowledge leads to professional weakness and should be avoided. We are thus led to the conclusion that if we are to preserve depth and expand breadth, we have no alternative but to increase the number of years for a basic engineering education.

• *The MIT School of Engineering should offer as an alternative path to the existing four-year curriculum a broader undergraduate program of instruction, followed by a professional degree program.*

The preprofessional undergraduate program would be discipline-based, but it would be broader than current undergraduate engineering programs. Additional instruction would be offered in allied technologies, science, economics, history, and management. The program might well attract nonengineering students. For those aspiring to become professionals in law, medicine, management, and other nontechnical disciplines, it would offer a technology-based alternative to today's liberal-arts-based preprofessional education. For tomorrow's technologist, this major change in basic engineering education would transform the stereotype of a specialist who cares only about a narrow technical field into an engineering professional with the same technological depth in one engineering discipline as before but with a broader educational background.

Attorneys and physicians understood the need for a longer professional education many years ago. By analogy, the Commission envisions similar breadth, strength, and leadership prospects for engineering students, but based on an education that is rooted in technology.

In calling for this change, we want to ensure that the traditional route for obtaining masters' and doctoral degrees is preserved. The proven successes in research, higher education, and professional work deriving from this existing educational template must not be sacrificed. In time and if the new model proves successful, it will gradually and naturally seek its proper balance, perhaps even becoming someday the dominant curriculum for all of MIT.

Finally, we want to ensure that the experience and wisdom of the MIT faculty will be used to carefully lay out both strategic and more detailed plans for these programs. Our broad vision leaves a great deal unspecified and many questions unanswered. It may be, for example, that five, six, or seven years is the preferred duration of the extended professional engineering program and that the mix of disciplinary and general subjects is different from that envisioned by the Commission today.

Changes in the Management Curriculum

Historically, business schools, including the Sloan School of Management at MIT, have not taught that technology or human resources are as important or central to the task of managing as finance, marketing, or other traditional disciplines of management. Moreover, the predominant values, theories, models, and case studies presented to students were derived from American sources. Comparisons with practices from other countries were given scant attention. These views must change if managers are to be prepared to work in, and help create, the types of organizations and institutions that we envision as crucial in the future.

The Sloan School faculty recently examined many of these issues as part of a broad review and reappraisal of its mission. We draw heavily on the vision and programs that have been generated by that process.

Managing internationally. Because of the increased dispersion of technological and managerial innovation among countries and the need for firms to match *global* best practice, management training must embody deeper exposure to international issues. We believe that future managers must be skilled in all of the following: (1) operating in an international economic, political, legal, social, and information era; (2) operating in a number of national environments and social structures; (3) managing international flows of goods, people, technology, information, and financial resources and the institutions that facilitate or regulate these flows; and (4) learning across borders, by which we mean identifying, analyzing, and adapting the world's best management practices wherever they happen to be found.

To develop these skills in students, three changes are needed in educational programs. First, the international content must be deepened in the required core courses taken by all management students. Second, linkages with regional-study programs and with universities in other countries should be strengthened to foster broader exchanges of ideas, knowledge, students, and faculty. Third, students need deep exposure and direct interaction with the people and cultures of other countries. Summer, semester, or year-long internships abroad could be provided.

To provide this deeper international exposure and skill to students, more management faculty members will need to be directly exposed to, and expert in, international developments, practices, and theories in their specific discipline or specialty. Faculty exchanges with universities abroad, faculty leaves to do research and to teach in other countries, and multinational research teams will need to be encouraged. For this to happen, the reward criteria used to evaluate faculty for promotion and tenure will need to be revised to reflect the longer lead times required to do high-quality scholarly work of this kind.

Managing technology. For too long business schools have taken the position that a good manager could manage anything, regardless of its technological base. If technological judgments were necessary, experts could be consulted, but it was not essential for top executives to understand the technologies they were investing in or managing. Among the consequences was that courses on production or operations management became less and less central to business-school curricula. It is now clear that this view is wrong. While it is not necessary for every manager to have a science or engineering degree, every manager does need to understand how technology relates to the strategic positioning of the firm, how to evaluate alternative technologies and investment choices, and how to shepherd scientific and technical concepts through the innovation and production processes to the marketplace. For more and more firms, effective performance in developing, adopting, and using technological innovations is becoming vital to success in the marketplace. A solid understanding of how to combine the technical, organizational, and human dimensions of the innovation process is at the heart of effective technology management.

MIT is currently attempting to give business students a firmer foundation in technology through a number of new initiatives. One of the most important of these is the Leaders for Manufacturing Program, involving the Schools of Engineering and Management in partnership with industry sponsors. This two-year master's program is designed to create a new intellectual paradigm for the study and practice of manufacturing and to train a new generation of managers skilled in applying state-of-the-art managerial and engineering knowledge to manufacturing operations.

Managing human resources. In many business schools, courses in organizational behavior and human-resource management are viewed as the "soft" side of the curriculum. Because human-resource management was not on the fast track to the top of organizations, courses in these areas were downplayed by both students and business-school faculty. As the labor movement declined and government regulation of the workplace receded from the forefront of public debate, the prominence of courses in industrial relations and human-resource management receded even further.

Partly in response to the vocal criticism of the business community itself, nearly all business schools now recognize the shortsightedness of this attitude. But incorporating deeper understanding of, and skill in, the management of human resources and organizational change into an already crowded curriculum is no easy task. As with the issues of technology and internationalization, the best way to educate managers in these concepts and skills is to integrate them into the core curriculum. Students should gain insight into such matters as the principles of effective teamwork and labor-management cooperation, alternative models of worker participation and representation, problems of human-resource management, and solutions associated with organizational change and differences in race, gender, education, and cultural background. If teamwork is to be encouraged in the organizations of the future, teamwork skills and experience need to be part of our educational programs in both management and engineering.

In recent years a number of business schools, including the Sloan School, have brought leaders from labor and management to campus for extended formal and informal dialogues with faculty and students. Invariably, these experienced leaders stress the importance of human and organizational dimensions to the management challenge. Much more of this needs to be done; getting closer to the customer is good advice for educational programs as well as for businesses!

Research

At MIT, education has always consisted of a rich mixture of instruction and research. We believe that this important pattern must continue and should be enhanced. Moreover, we would like to encourage research in the area of productivity, including not only the productivity of factories and service operations but also productivity in the office, where more than half of the 120 million employed Americans carry out their work. To that end we make the following recommendation.

• *Establish a major interdepartmental research center on industrial productivity, possibly to include existing efforts, with a broad research program spanning from office productivity to factory-floor productivity.*

We recommend establishing this major interdepartmental research center to focus and coordinate ongoing research in industrial productivity in the broadest sense and to coordinate and encourage interdisciplinary courses and educational programs relating to industrial productivity and its applications. The research of the center would not only span blue-collar, white-collar, and service-worker productivity but would also involve interdisciplinary studies of organization, technology, and culture, as well as more specialized engineering and management programs.

Existing MIT centers, such as the Leaders for Manufacturing Program and the MIT Laboratory for Manufacturing Productivity, are already beginning to carry out several of the tasks that we consider important. We believe that there are additional and major opportunities for productivity research beyond these activities. For example, the use of computers to enhance human productivity is a topic that research has barely begun to tackle. In the dawn of the industrial era a great deal of effort was expended to develop and apply productivity measures to the use of machines that replaced or augmented human muscle power. Today the augmenting machines are computers, but it is proving more difficult to measure their effects, partly because the value of information is harder to quantify and partly because the field is young and still growing. Yet the opportunities are there for addressing the productivity leverage of this important tool, in which America still retains world leadership, and we believe that they can be properly addressed by this center.

Beyond these challenges in the new area of computer productivity, we believe that there are intellectual challenges and opportunities in the analysis and design of manufacturing processes, in the study of organizational practices and management procedures and in changing those practices and procedures to increase productivity, in the technologies of manufacturing, in labor-management relations, and generally in the multitude of factors that affect industrial productivity.

We think that MIT is the right place for launching this new kind of enterprise because of its preoccupation and involvement with such technologies as computers and advanced materials that will figure dominantly in tomorrow's productive enterprises, and because of the Institute's past experiences in putting together interdisciplinary laboratories for new enterprises such as computer science. A final reason for establishing the center at MIT is the combination of strength and willingness to change found in the schools of engineering and management, where our principal recommendations are directed.

As in the case of our recommended curriculum changes, we do not want to overspecify the structure and functions of the productivity research center; we prefer to leave this task to the faculty members and researchers who will make it happen. It is conceivable, for example, that the center would be tightly linked to, or indeed consist of, other centers now at MIT. Alternatively, it could be an entirely new entity, which might eventually become for the civilian industrial needs of the nation what the Lincoln Laboratory is to the defense sector.

Awareness

In closing, we make a final recommendation based on our personal experience as members of the MIT Commission on Industrial Productivity.

• *Increase the MIT community's awareness of the critical problems surrounding national productivity and university education.*

In our everyday work lives at MIT we would not have learned what the concentrated activities of the Commission have taught us during the past two years. We feel that the changes we have undergone in our own thinking through our participation in this Commission have been profound, and we would like to impart a sense of our new experiences to our colleagues.

Finally, going beyond the question of how universities can contribute to the goal of strengthening industrial productivity, we believe that our own productivity as an educational institution is hampered by many of the weaknesses that we have discovered in American industry. For example, we are subject to short-term pressures in setting goals and in measuring the success of students, faculty members, and programs; we do not use as much creative energy as we might in measuring the quality of our product (students); we do not have adequate resources and mechanisms in place to manage educational change effectively; and we could do more to cultivate closer relationships with our "clients," who hire our students, and our "suppliers," the secondary schools that provide them. In short, we call on the MIT community to reflect on what this book says about industrial productivity in the context of our own educational and research enterprise.

13

Conclusion

When our Commission began its investigation of American industrial performance, we set out to understand a topic that from the perspective of our individual specialties seemed complex, vague, and full of unanswerable questions. Now, with our two-year study behind us, we feel able to draw four major conclusions.

First, relative to other nations and relative to its own history, America does indeed have a serious productivity problem. This problem in productive performance, as we call it, is the result of major changes within and outside the United States in the past four decades. It is manifested by sluggish productivity growth and by shortcomings in the quality and innovativeness of the nation's products. Left unattended, the problem will impoverish America relative to other nations that have adapted more quickly and effectively to pervasive changes in technology and markets.

Second, the causes of this problem go well beyond macroeconomic explanations of high capital costs and inadequate savings to the attitudinal and organizational weaknesses that pervade America's production system. These weaknesses are deeply rooted. They affect the way people and organizations interact with one another and with new technology; they affect the way businesses deal with long-term technological and market risks; and they affect the way business, government, and educational institutions go about the task of developing the nation's most precious asset, its human resources. They introduce rigidities into the nation's production system at a time of extraordinarily rapid change in the international economic environment.

Third, some American firms have adapted well to the new environment and are capable of holding their own in highly competitive international markets. But there is little cause for complacency. This is so because the diffusion of what we have identified as best industrial practices from the most successful U.S. firms to others is being inhibited by ingrained beliefs, attitudes, and practices; because a more rapid diffusion of best practices will require changes in the policies and practices of governmental and educational institutions, as well as the actions of individual firms; and because the world is not standing still—addressing yesterday's weaknesses offers no immunity from problems caused by tomorrow's changes.

Fourth, just as there is no reason for premature celebration, so there is no cause for despair. The American production system is enormously resilient and has many great strengths, the most important of which are the creativity, entrepreneurship, and energy of individual Americans. Our Commission believes that if industry, government, and the educational system can build on these strengths and unite in steady pursuit of a few basic, interrelated, and, in our view, feasible goals—goals that we have called imperatives for a more productive America—this nation has every chance of entering the twenty-first century displaying the same dynamism and leadership that characterized its industrial performance throughout much of the present century.

Toward that end, we close with a suggestion inspired by our own experience in carrying out the work of the MIT Commission: We call on interested groups throughout industry, government, and the educational system to ask themselves, as we did, what have been the recurring weaknesses and strengths of current industrial practice in the domains most familiar to them and to ask what they in turn might do to help improve the nation's productive performance. We hope that this book will serve as a guide for such efforts and that those who embark on such a course find the process as enriching and rewarding as it has been for us.

INDUSTRY STUDIES

A

The Automobile Industry

For several decades a foreign-made automobile was a rare sight on American roadways. The Detroit carmakers totally dominated the domestic market, and up until the 1950s they led the world in auto exports. Even in the late 1960s the United States maintained a slight export surplus in international automobile trade. The situation since then has changed dramatically. In 1987 more than 30 percent of the automobiles sold in the United States were made overseas, and the trade deficit in motor vehicles reached almost $60 billion, a third of the total U.S. deficit for merchandise transactions (see figures A.1 and A.2). How did the auto industry, a bulwark of the American economy, lose its strong competitive position? What are the prospects for a recovery?

In retrospect, it appears a crucial event was Detroit's decision to concentrate on the "family-size" car, which allowed overseas competitors to capture other market segments. The most important other segment was that of compact cars, imports of which grew rapidly after the oil crisis in the early 1970s. First the Europeans and then the Japanese offered compacts in the United States, while American carmakers stuck to more profitable midsize and large luxury models. During the 1970s the Japanese took over the compact market, while the Europeans shifted to luxury vehicles smaller than those being made in Detroit. In 1987 European manufacturers built about a sixth of the autos imported into the United States, but because most of these cars were expensive models, the European share of the import market was roughly a third in terms of dollar value.

A summary report of the Commission's Motor Vehicle Industry Working Group. A longer working paper by James P. Womack, "The U.S. Automobile Industry in an Era of International Competition: Performance and Prospects," appears in *The Working Papers of the MIT Commission on Industrial Productivity*, 2 vols. (Cambridge: MIT Press, 1989).

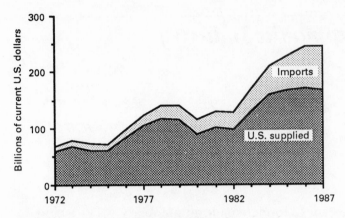

Figure A.1   Total U.S. automobile sales
Industry defined by Standard Industrial Classification (SIC) 371.

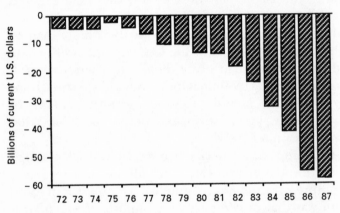

Figure A.2   Trade balances in the U.S. automobile industry
Industry defined by Standard Industrial Classification (SIC) 371.

Japan now builds about two-thirds of the imported vehicles. From a strong base in smaller cars and compact pickup trucks, the Japanese producers are now expanding their product offerings to cover all of the American market. They have been building plants in the United States, and they are rapidly repositioning their products into the higher-price segments of the market. Higher profit margins for luxury cars can help the Japanese make up for lesser returns on compacts, where prices have been squeezed by the stronger yen. Honda's success with a line of luxury cars sold under the "Acura" model name has encouraged Nissan and Toyota to follow, and Mazda and Mitsubishi are adding larger cars to their lines. These luxury entries might succeed at the expense of European vendors, but many industry observers think they will also take market share away from U.S. luxury models. Since these models are currently a key to Detroit's profitability, there may be another crisis in store for the U.S. firms.

Meanwhile, inexpensive cars from several newly industrializing countries (Korea, Brazil, Mexico, and Yugoslavia) are pouring into the United States, capturing 5.3 percent of the market in 1987, up from zero three years earlier. Since the Detroit manufacturers make few small cars, this new presence in the market is a threat mainly to the Japanese and to the "transplants," factories set up in the United States by Japanese companies. In fact, many of the new entries are being orchestrated by U.S. carmakers filling in the low ends of their lines.

All is not bleak for the U.S. auto companies. Productivity and quality, which have been strong factors in the success of imports, particularly those from Japan, have begun to rise significantly in the United States. The improvements were achieved first in American factories run by Japanese companies, but more recently some American-owned plants have improved dramatically as well. There are also signs of an effort to improve relationships in the industry that have traditionally been weak, such as those between assembler and suppliers, unions and management, and technical specialists and general management. For example, recent agreements between American firms and the United Auto Workers give the companies greater flexibility, while assuring the workers greater job security. American manufacturers are also beginning to export to Europe and other parts of the world in significant volume for the first time in decades.

At the same time Japanese assembly plants in the United States are rapidly increasing the fraction of their components obtained from American factories. Honda has announced plans for what it terms a "self-reliant" manufacturing system in North America by the mid-1990s. According to this plan, final assembly will be done here, components will have a very high level of local content, and the company will establish a full R&D organization to design new products. Nissan and Toyota appear to have the same intention. As a result, a larger fraction of the value of these companies' "American-made" products will be added in the United States.

In the next few years a strong recovery for auto manufacturing in the United States seems likely; what is not certain is whether the recovery will benefit the American carmakers or the Japanese companies producing cars and trucks in North America. Trends in currency exchange rates favor factories in the United States, but so far these trends appear to have had little impact on the trade balance in automobiles, as figure A.2 shows. (Their major effect may have been to hasten the Japanese movement to set up facilities in the United States.) In any case, it will take more than a cheap dollar to restore the Detroit manufacturers to global competitiveness. The entire system for designing and building motor vehicles must be overhauled; piecemeal reforms of the kinds attempted so far will not do.

The Structure of the Auto Industry

An automobile is, of course, a complex product; there are typically 15,000 parts per vehicle. Manufacturing automobiles in volume requires a wide range of skills, organizations, and technologies. Even the smallest of the world's mass producers (Jaguar, Porsche, and Saab) employ about 40,000 people in final assembly plants and in the components-supply chain. General Motors employs about 1 million workers worldwide in the largest of the production systems. (There are 700,000 on the General Motors payroll and another 300,000 in supplier companies.)

The motor-vehicle industry is one of the largest manufacturing activities in the United States, employing 1.04 million workers in 1986 in the design, fabrication, and assembly of cars, trucks, buses, and replacement parts. The United States is also the world's largest market for motor vehicles (16.3 million units out of a worldwide total of 45.3 million in 1986). Consumers spent $243 billion on vehicles and parts in that year, 8.7 percent of all U.S. consumer spending.

The three major U.S. carmakers, the Big Three, are General Motors, Ford, and Chrysler. These companies were formed by the consolidation of many smaller firms in the early days of the industry, a process that is still going on: Chrysler acquired American Motors in 1986. In recent years, alliances with foreign manufacturers have increased. Some of the alliances take the form of partial ownership (Ford has a stake in Mazda, Chrysler in Mitsubishi, and General Motors in Isuzu and Suzuki); other arrangements call for joint-manufacturing facilities (General Motors and Toyota set up a plant in California); and still others involve subcontracting overseas for the manufacture of vehicles to be marketed through the U.S. dealer network.

The Japanese program of building manufacturing facilities in North America continues at a rapid pace. By 1991 transplants in the United States and Canada will account for roughly a fourth of North American production.

An Obsolete Production System

The decline of such a major and highly visible industry as motor vehicles inevitably draws forth a variety of diagnoses. Most analyses point to one of three factors: unimaginative management with a short-term view, myopic unions demanding more than the industry could afford, or an unsupportive, perhaps even hostile, government. Some analysts blame all three.

There is truth in each of these perspectives. The U.S. auto companies have at times been dominated by "bean counters," who looked inward to the U.S. heartland rather than out to global markets and who favored short-term returns over long-term investments. Unions did demand wage increases that could not be sustained as growth in productivity slowed. Government policy was inconsistent and sometimes harmful. But there appears to be an underlying cause of stagnant productivity and declining market share that goes much deeper and will be more difficult to cure. Specifically, the system of production organization and the accompanying market strategy that was developed by the industry in the 1920s and perfected with brilliant success over the next 40 years finally became obsolete and was overwhelmed by foreign competition.

The American system of car building arose in the 1920s when Alfred Sloan of General Motors transformed an approach that had been developed earlier by Henry Ford. Ford had found great success by developing an assembly-line method of manufacturing low-cost automobiles for a mass market. To maximize economies of scale, Ford concentrated production on a single design. At General Motors, Sloan countered this approach with a decentralized corporate organization and a broad product range (for "every purse and purpose"). By the late 1940s, the U.S. auto industry had adopted the structure and strategy it would pursue for nearly 40 years. Here's how the system worked.

Market concept. Detroit assumed that consumers liked variety as long as it didn't cost too much. Large-scale production was the route to keeping costs down, and cosmetic changes could offer variety in appearance while concealing the use of the same major parts, such as engines and transmissions, in many models. The industry converged on "standard-size" cars and trucks and turned to dedicated automation to produce them.

Human resources. In the early days of the industry, skilled laborers were in short supply and their wages were high; management therefore simplified jobs so that cars could be assembled by a relatively unskilled work force. On the basis of methods of time-and-motion study developed by Frederick Taylor, jobs were precisely defined and delineated. The emphasis on narrow subdivision of work went beyond the factory floor into engineering, management, and administrative functions as well. Consequently, even professionals in the industry developed deep but very narrow skills. Such very narrowly defined job content became so instilled in the industry that eventually it was even built into union contracts.

Being highly cyclical, the industry also faced the problem of massive cutbacks in every business downturn. The United Auto Workers turned to an elaborate seniority system to protect middle-aged members, who might be harder hit by layoffs than younger workers. More-senior workers also had the option of accepting or rejecting assignments, so that even small cutbacks might lead to a large number of changes as older workers took the jobs they wanted and bumped younger ones.

Production machinery. Well-defined tasks eased the burden of automating, since a dedicated machine could be assigned to each specific task. This policy led to inflexible automation, so that by the

1960s even a small change in the dimensions of an engine would require millions of dollars for new tooling. Until the mid-1960s this "hard" automation steadily boosted productivity by 5 percent per year, about double the increase for the rest of manufacturing. Once most of the defined tasks had been automated, however, productivity growth dropped back to the rather low average of 2.5 percent per year found in other U.S. manufacturing sectors. Wages, meanwhile, continued to rise at a 5 percent annual rate. The high cost of design changes also led to reluctance to diversify product offerings when European automakers introduced compacts in the late 1950s.

Production coordination. Orchestrating the activities of tens of thousands of workers and many plants is a formidable organizational problem. Each of the American manufacturers found its own solution, but they all shared the practice of putting heavy pressure on their component suppliers. General Motors had central management to coordinate the final assembly of automobiles, while the decentralized component groups were supposedly kept efficient through the pressures of competing in the marketplace. Chrysler, too small to integrate vertically, bargained hard with fiercely competing independent suppliers working on short-term contracts. Ford initially went the furthest in vertical integration, even making its own steel, glass, and rubber. But management difficulties eventually led to a mix of decentralized divisions and short-term contracts with independent suppliers. Over the course of business cycles, suppliers were treated much as production workers were: as marginal assets to be utilized at times of peak demand but jettisoned during troughs. These arrangements could not foster loyalty and trust. Assemblers feared that their suppliers might shift to competitors, revealing inside information like plans for future models. Hence, the assemblers kept their plans secret and did little to advance the skills of suppliers.

The management of production. A set of widely shared beliefs about the "best way" to produce cars and trucks evolved among suppliers, union leaders, and the management of the assembly companies. Each worker or supplier was expected to do an assigned job, but no one expected them to make any effort to improve the way their job was done. Instead, the task of monitoring and improving performance became yet another narrow specialty assigned to a professional group of industrial engineers, planners, and data gatherers.

The production system had to be "robust," so that breakdowns would not stop an assembly line. To avoid stoppages, the builders kept buffer stocks at each step of production and developed alternative sources of supply. They also overbuilt plants in case future changes were needed, and they retained pools of reserve workers to fill in for absentees so that production volume could be maintained. The level of quality was thought to depend on the amount of checking and reworking devoted to the product, and of course luxury models got more of it than economy cars. It was assumed that workers would not share knowledge about defects as they occurred and that in any event it was better to fix the problem later rather than to stop the assembly line.

Product development. Under the American system of production, a new model proceeded sequentially through a set of steps, each with its own set of experts, from market assessment through final assembly. The design cycle took five years or more, a length of time that encouraged the companies to keep basic designs in production as long as possible with occasional cosmetic "face lifts." Financial experts at corporate headquarters, often with little knowledge of the marketplace or the factory floor, drove the industry toward standard, long-run products to minimize capital costs and maximize short-term profits.

In retrospect, the American system might seem cumbersome, but it worked splendidly for decades. In fact, it worked so well that Europe and Japan tried hard to copy it. Because of major differences in their markets, however, they were forced to make changes. That wasn't easy, because changing only parts of such a carefully wrought system is disruptive, as American carmakers are now discovering. The Europeans stressed product diversity and advanced technology in their designs, whereas the Japanese devised a new manufacturing and marketing system that could deliver diverse, high-quality products at low cost.

Automaking in Europe

In the 1920s European industrialists visiting American assembly plants expressed concern that their craftsmen would not agree to assembly-line working conditions, but they proceeded to imitate Ford's production system anyway. American marketing methods and product strategy could not be copied, however, because of the differing demands of the various countries in Europe. At the extremes, Sweden was largely rural and had low gasoline taxes and severe winters, whereas Italy had crowded cities, high gasoline taxes and registration fees based on engine size, and a mild climate. When trade barriers suddenly fell in the 1950s and 1960s, the European industry found itself with a very wide range of products to sell in European and world markets.

In the United States, by contrast, a large and unified domestic market, long distances, and low gasoline prices encouraged the Big Three from an early date to concentrate their efforts on a large, standard-size car. This gave the Europeans an opportunity to capture an unserved sector of the American market with cars such as the Volkswagen Beetle.

European preeminence in compact cars started to erode in the mid-1960s, when cheaper Japanese small cars began to catch on with American consumers. Using a production system similar to that of the U.S. carmakers, the Europeans tried unsuccessfully to compete against a highly efficient new manufacturing approach developed in Japan. Finally, to sidestep direct competition, several European vendors shifted to luxury cars, exporting a new class of smaller, sportier models than the American companies offered. European assemblers were greatly aided by a small group of technologically advanced components suppliers, led by Robert Bosch in Germany. Developments such as electronic fuel injection and antiskid brakes gave European products a high-tech image unmatched by American cars.

Automaking in Japan

During Japan's postwar reconstruction, Japanese automakers also tried to copy the Ford-Sloan system. With a small and fragmented domestic market served by many manufacturers, however, high-volume production and vertical integration were not feasible. Neither was the American practice of laying off and rehiring workers at the convenience of management. To ward off a Marxist union movement, Japan's automakers offered lifetime employment to workers in company unions.

Over the next two decades, through sometimes chaotic experimentation rather than any grand plan, the Japanese forged a new production and marketing system that turned these seeming weaknesses into strengths. The government tried to push the

industry toward a system more like Detroit's, but the conglomerates taking shape in Japan saw the opportunities in the market, and
each followed its own course rather than acquiesce to the urgings
of the Ministry of International Trade and Industry (MITI). The
Japanese system differs considerably from the American one. Here
are its main elements.

Market conception. Japanese executives doubted that the high-
volume manufacturing of the big American carmakers was feasible
in Japan. Demand was fragmented: different trucks were needed by
farmers and by industry, small cars were appropriate to crowded
cities, but officials and industrialists wanted larger models. Furthermore, there were many competitors backed by strong conglomerates so that no one company could count on capturing a majority
share of the market. Of necessity the firms looked for cost-effective
ways to produce in low volume. To be competitive, they decided
that factors such as quality and close attention to consumer needs
would be important.

Production machinery. Instead of dedicated automation, the Japanese carmakers developed flexible machinery that could be switched
quickly from one product to another. Metal stamping is a prime
example. In Detroit, stamping is centralized in gigantic facilities,
and an entire press line might be dedicated to a single part, such
as a right-front fender for a standard Chevrolet. The line is kept
running as steadily as possible, and its output is shipped by rail to
many assembly plants around the country. Dies might be changed
only a few times a year. The Japanese, building more models in
lower volume, realized that they would have to produce a variety of
parts on each stamping line. Since they might have to change dies
several times during a shift, they developed machines that allowed
fast changeovers. By the 1970s they could change dies in five
minutes, compared with eight to 24 hours for American stamping
presses.

Making small batches with frequent die changes turned out to
reduce defects and improve productivity. The reason, paradoxi-
cally, was that a production system with no inventories could not
tolerate bad parts. Stamping shops were located close to body-
welding areas, rather than hundreds of miles away, and there might
be only two or three hours of inventory in any given part. The
absence of buffer stocks made it essential to avoid bad parts or

unexpected breakdowns. Simple inspection mechanisms built into machinery allowed defective parts to be spotted immediately. In the U.S. there were occasionally long runs of bad parts; the Japanese system made this less likely to occur, because it could not tolerate such waste.

Human resources. An offer of lifetime employment turns labor into a fixed cost, but it also encourages investment in the work force. Japanese management emphasized training to upgrade skills as workers gained seniority. Steep rises in wages compensated the workers for their increasing value to the organization and helped to build loyalty.

Organization of the production chain. American plants are organized around individual workers and their tasks, but the Japanese discovered that it is more effective to organize in groups operating as teams. They extended this concept beyond factory workers to product-development teams, component-supply groups, and even the conglomerate group. In the factory, instead of assigning specific tasks to individuals, a set of tasks is assigned to a team. The team divides up the work, which is clearly defined and standardized as in American plants, but everyone is expected to be able to do any job. This versatility allows for quick changes in product mix and work flow. There are still quality-control specialists and industrial engineers, but they serve as consultants to the teams.

Product-development teams are much broader than they are in the United States; they include product planners, product and process engineers (from suppliers as well as from the assembly plant), and manufacturing specialists. Each such team, typically under a strong leader, stays together from the conception of the product well into manufacturing, a period of perhaps four years. Including suppliers in product development is much easier because of the concept of component groups linked to the assembly company. The largest of these is the Toyota group, which includes about 225 first-tier suppliers linked to the auto company. The companies in each group develop a sense of shared destiny as a result of holdings of one another's stocks, loans of machinery and personnel, and collaborative design exercises.

The auto companies have other ties through the conglomerate group (*keiretsu*), which may consist of the auto assembler, a bank, a trading company, an insurance company, materials processors, and a host of manufacturing enterprises in other sectors of the economy, all linked through equity holdings. This structure adds strength to firms in a cyclical industry like automobiles. For example, Mazda went into a tailspin when it chose a fuel-hungry rotary engine just before the oil shortage of 1974. The Sumitomo Group stepped in, replaced Mazda's management with executives from elsewhere in the group, and provided sufficient financing to develop a new model range and a new family of engines in short order. Mazda emerged stronger and larger than ever. In the United States, by contrast, Chrysler's bankers and creditors took no action until the firm was almost bankrupt, and then, even with government help, the company only developed one new model (the K car), which is still carrying it in the marketplace.

Like the American approach to production and marketing, the Japanese approach constitutes a total system, with each part reinforcing the others. In contrast to the U.S. approach, however, the Japanese system allows manufacturers to produce a variety of models with minimal downtime and low inventory requirements, and it permits fast, flexible responses to market changes.

The Three Production Systems Compared

The American automotive market has shown a persistent trend toward more distinct products and fewer average sales per product. The number of American models has risen only slightly since 1973, and Europe's total entries have also remained fairly steady (with a shift toward the luxury end). But the number of Japanese offerings has raced past the Europeans' and caught up with the Americans'. Between 1973 and 1986 the Japanese accounted for almost all the net increase in platforms (groups of cars with the same wheelbase) in the U.S. market. At the moment, as American producers are consolidating their entries in the high-volume segments to gain economies of scale in production, the Japanese are pushing to expand their lines, and they have the flexible manufacturing systems needed to achieve greater product differentiation efficiently.

Although the U.S. auto companies have now invested in automated machinery that has the potential to be highly flexible, they have tended to use it in the same dedicated manner as their older, "hard" automation. Management has tended to view flexibility as a means of reducing downtime (since there are alternative paths through the factory if a workstation develops a problem). Thus, automation has become another buffer against a dreaded work stoppage rather than a means to greater variety in the marketplace.

Even highly automated General Motors plants in Delaware and New Jersey (where robots were installed at a cost of about $350 million per plant) achieve only average productivity, and although the automation is flexible, they produce only two body styles of one product. European factories also rely largely on dedicated automation. The Japanese automakers made less use of automation in creating their first flexible systems. Now they are pursuing interesting experiments in more advanced automation. Honda, for example, recently announced plans to triple its manufacturing productivity in the next few years.

The American producers, on the average, have kept slightly ahead of the Japanese and the Europeans in R&D spending per vehicle. But the results of that spending are a different story. Japan's share of U.S. automotive patents has been rising steadily, and by 1985 the total for Honda, Toyota, and Nissan exceeded that for General Motors, Ford, and Chrysler, even though the Japanese were spending much less on research. A broad range of product innovations are following, with four-wheel steering and multivalve engines being some of the more recent advances entering the marketplace. Not all of the innovations are of Japanese origin; in fact, the Japanese are frequently first to commercialize developments from elsewhere. Japan appears to be taking over the technology lead in the industry, and technology is particularly important at the higher end of the market, where U.S. production is now concentrated.

Japanese achievements in the product-development cycle are even more notable. A study of cars introduced over the past five years showed that the Japanese took an average of 43 months to go from initial conception to the consumer, whereas the American and European companies took 62 months. That puts the Japanese manufacturer about a year and a half closer to the consumer. Data from recent studies suggest that with the same manpower the Japanese can develop twice as many models in about two-thirds as much time as it would take either American or European product-development groups.

Three major factors were identified by Kim Clark and his associates at the Harvard Business School to explain this dramatic difference. First, Japanese product-development teams include a "heavyweight" project manager to champion the product. Second, potential conflicts over objectives and roles are resolved at the outset of product development. Third, some development activities are carried out simultaneously.

American carmakers have followed a complicated product-development process in which one group of experts determines the design and general specifications of the vehicle, another group of experts does the actual product engineering, and a third group determines how the car will be manufactured. As each group finishes its work, the project is turned over to the next group in a process frequently described as "throwing it over the wall." Project managers are assigned to coordinate the project at each stage, but they have little authority over the various functional departments involved in getting the job done: engine, transmission, chassis, body, production tooling, and assembly. Furthermore, a new model is typically assigned a series of project managers during its development.

The Japanese drastically revamped this system, designating a program manager with great authority to coordinate the functional departments. This manager (the *shusha*) assembles a core development team that remains with the project throughout the development cycle and for some time into production. A key task of the program manager is to uncover disagreements about how to proceed before the actual development work begins. This gradual approach to consensus may make it appear to an outsider that a great deal of time is spent at the outset of a program with little progress. But the approach helps avoid problems such as the one General Motors recently faced when it canceled the GM-80 program in midstream after several hundred million dollars had already been spent. The Big Three have had a number of such aborted programs.

To speed the development cycle, the Japanese work simultaneously rather than serially on various design tasks, with extensive communication between functional groups. Die makers start work on approximate dies, for example, while keeping informed of changes that might require variations in their designs. The American system, by contrast, not only works serially but also erects barriers to communication as a result of adversarial relationships between assemblers and their vast arrays of component suppliers. Design is concentrated in the central offices of the assembler, and drawings and specifications are sent to in-company divisions and independent component firms a year or so before assembly is to begin. Short-term bids are sought, and the carmakers may shift orders to cheaper suppliers on short notice. The automakers keep their plans secret, and the vendors in turn typically have a "my plant is my business" philosophy. Defect levels are set for components, and suppliers are expected to meet them. Bad parts are simply thrown away.

The Japanese companies also insist on strict conformance to parts specifications, but in contrast to the American assemblers, they bring their first-tier suppliers into the design process and even help them retool their factories. When bad parts are received, instead of merely rejecting them, reasons for defects are carefully sought out so that the process can be corrected. General Motors needs 6,000 buyers to deal with its network of outside suppliers, whereas Toyota has only 337. An average General Motors plant deals with 1,500 vendors, in comparison with only 177 first-tier suppliers for the average Toyota plant.

These structural differences in the way the motor-vehicle industry operates in Europe, Japan, and the United States have resulted in widely different performance ratings, as recently measured in a worldwide survey of automobile assembly plants done by MIT's International Motor Vehicle Program (see figures A.3 and A.4).

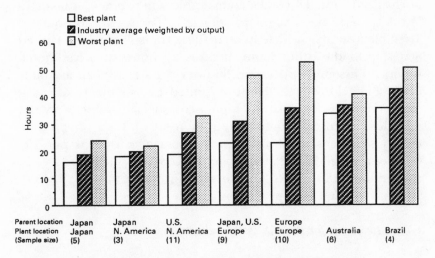

Figure A.3   Production effort in automobile assembly plants
Production effort is the total number of hours for both management and hourly workers, direct and indirect, needed to accomplish standard manufacturing activities on a standard vehicle in assembly plants running at full output. The data were obtained from a survey conducted during 1986 and 1987. Source: The MIT International Motor Vehicle Program.

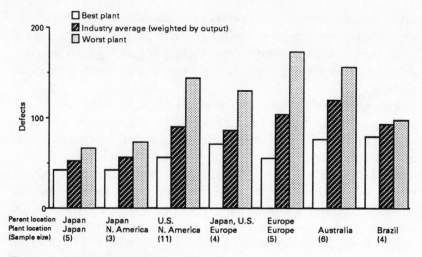

Figure A.4 Automobile defects
Defects are the number of owner-reported defects per vehicle in the first three months of use, per 100 vehicles. The data were obtained from a survey conducted during 1986 and 1987. Source: The MIT International Motor Vehicle Program.

Manufacturing steps and the complexity of the vehicles were normalized to make results comparable. On average, it takes 19 hours to assemble a standard vehicle in Japan and 20 hours to assemble a similar vehicle in a Japanese transplant in the United States. On the other hand, it takes 27 hours at a traditional American assembly plant and 36 hours in a European assembly plant. (The European data are limited to assemblers of mass-market vehicles. Producers of higher-cost specialty vehicles are not included to ensure compatibility of results.) Data on product quality show a similar range of performance. Defects per 100 vehicles average 52 in Japan, 56 in the U.S. transplants, and 90 in conventional U.S. plants. The worst performance was a high of 173 in a mass-market European plant.

Future Prospects for the U.S. Auto Industry

American auto companies, while taking the first steps toward a more competitive manufacturing system, realize that they have far to go. Progress is most evident at the plant level, where some American-owned assembly plants are now slightly *more* productive in their use of labor than the average Japanese plant, as shown in Figure A.3. This is an extraordinary achievement for old plants with an existing work force, and we believe that improvements in the performance of most American-owned assembly plants will now proceed at a rapid pace.

In the area of supplier systems the evidence is more difficult to quantify. It appears that the arrival of the Japanese transplants is having a dramatic effect on American suppliers at the same time as the Big Three are rethinking their supplier systems. Many suppliers are developing more productive relationships with assemblers and are moving toward a more "Japanese" approach to components supply, with earlier supplier involvement in the design process and contracts awarded to one or two suppliers for the production life of the product.

In the areas of product development and research and development, the American companies have become aware of the productivity and development-time gap only within the past two years. Every company is now making efforts to streamline its development system and to revitalize its approach to new-product technology.

On the basis of recent experience with the transplant assembly plants, it appears that American firms learn fastest not through reading books or gathering intelligence overseas but by being directly confronted with a competitor performing at a much higher level using American employees in America. Thus, dramatic improvements in Big Three performance in research and development are likely when Japanese firms set up R&D facilities "right across the road," but that may not happen until well into the 1990s.

In summary, the American-owned *firms* are now heading in the right direction, and American-based *industry* (including the Japanese-owned firms operating in the United States) is improving its international competitive position very rapidly. The trade deficit may remain at the current level for the next few years as the transplant assembly plants come on stream and before North American sources for components are developed. In the early 1990s, however, it is likely that the U.S. trade balance will begin to improve substantially and that "Made in America" will again be a respected phrase in motor-vehicle export markets.

A number of challenges lie ahead, particularly for the weaker American firms. Can their new and more cooperative labor-management relations survive a deep recession? Can American-owned supplier firms learn quickly how to supply the Japanese assemblers? And can American-owned firms, both suppliers and assemblers, move fast enough in improving their total manufacturing system to avoid being overtaken by the Japanese firms in their own country?

B

The Chemical Industry

After a long period of spectacular growth fueled by a steady stream of technological advances, the U.S. chemical industry began to slow down in the 1970s, and it went into a serious decline about a decade ago. In the past few years, however, the industry has begun to make a strong comeback after an extensive restructuring of major American chemical firms.

The slowdown began as the long tradition of rapid advances began to fade. Both innovation and growth in productivity began to decline, along with financial performance. Recognizing that momentous changes were reshaping the business, executives of leading American companies reduced the scope of their commodity chemical operations while diversifying into specialty chemicals and into such emerging areas as biotechnology, pharmaceuticals, and advanced materials. They transformed what had become largely a commodity industry into a more research-intensive, market-driven industry with an emphasis on product innovation. As a result, prospects are bright for the U.S. chemical industry in spite of intense global competition.

This turnaround was accomplished while the industry had to deal with problems similar to those facing other sectors of the U.S. economy. For example, there were pressures from financial markets for short-term returns on investment. Management also had to cope with an array of government regulatory policies, steeply rising costs of production, and a squeeze on profits.

What were the fundamental causes of the slowdown, and what were the critical factors that led to a relatively quick turnaround? What lessons could other American industries learn from the initial

A summary report of the Commission's Chemical Industry Working Group. A longer working paper by Kirkor Bozdogan, "The Transformation of the U.S. Chemicals Industry," appears in *The Working Papers of the MIT Commission on Industrial Productivity*, 2 vols. (Cambridge: MIT Press, 1989).

decline and the subsequent recovery? A brief review of the industry's structure and history will be helpful in finding answers.

Structure of the Chemical Industry

The production of chemicals and allied products is the largest of the industries studied by the Commission. In 1987 it had sales of $210 billion, compared with $126.5 billion for automobiles. Employment in chemicals, 805,000 in 1987, was exceeded only by employment in textiles and apparel (1.73 million) and in automobiles (1.04 million). The industry's output encompasses many thousands of products, most of them industrial intermediates that are further processed before becoming familiar industrial and consumer products. More than a fourth of the output is consumed within the industry itself; roughly half goes to other industries, and the remaining fourth is sold for final consumption by households.

The chemical industry is very capital-intensive ($92,300 per worker, compared with $42,900 for all of manufacturing in 1985) and research-intensive (4.7 percent of net sales versus 2.8 percent for manufacturing as a whole in 1985; the pharmaceutical segment of the chemical industry invested 8.4 percent of revenue in research and development). As a rule, raw materials are not converted directly into finished products but instead go through a sequence of operations. Feedstocks (such as crude oil and natural gas in the petrochemical business) are converted into building-block chemicals (such as ammonia or benzene or ethylene), which in turn are used to make a wide variety of final products (such as solvents, pesticides, plastics, and adhesives). Often one raw feedstock or intermediate can substitute for another, which intensifies competition. Different raw materials (such as benzene or naphtha) might be used to make the same product, which gives processors considerable flexibility and puts pressure on prices. Different finished products can also compete for the same end-use applications, which enables vendors to compete through product differentiation.

There are many large, highly diversified, and vertically integrated chemical companies (Du Pont, Dow Chemical, Union Carbide, and Monsanto are among the largest), but there are also a large number of smaller, specialized firms. Some market segments are highly concentrated. The eight biggest companies, for example, account for more than 50 percent of production in 14 of

28 major market segments. But even in the broad market segments where concentration is high, competition is intense. In the plastics industry there is tough competition in products and processes not only among producers of the same material but also among makers of different plastics that contend for the same applications. In pharmaceuticals, a field where Congress once investigated possible abuses of monopoly power, there is increasing competition between patented and generic drugs as well as between American manufacturers and many foreign firms marketing drugs in the United States.

A recent development is the rapid expansion of overseas companies, particularly large European chemical companies, in the American market. About a fourth of the U.S. chemical industry is owned by foreign companies. The European firms have acquired American companies (particularly in specialty chemicals), expanded existing operations, set up joint ventures, and stepped up R&D activities, sometimes through links with universities. Japanese companies have begun to make similar moves. About a dozen European companies now have annual sales of more than $1 billion in the United States, and six of them now rank among the top 20 U.S. chemical companies: Britain's Imperial Chemical Industries (ICI), Royal Dutch/Shell of the Netherlands, Switzerland's Ciba-Geigy, and West Germany's three giants: Hoechst, Bayer, and BASF. (The three German firms and ICI are the largest chemical companies in the world. They are each from 30 to 50 percent larger than Du Pont, the largest U.S. company.) Investments in the United States became more attractive as the value of the dollar declined after 1985, and they were also encouraged by the lower cost of capital outside the United States. They give the foreign firms a strong strategic presence in the American market, which is stable and much larger than their own domestic markets. The investments also provide opportunities to acquire new technology.

Recent Performance Trends

During most of the period since World War II the U.S. chemical industry has been a world leader, with firms expanding rapidly to serve growing markets and at the same time achieving impressive gains in profitability. Much of this extraordinary growth came from the substitution of chemical products, particularly polymers, for natural materials. Polymeric synthetic rubbers, coatings, adhesives, fibers, and a wide range of plastic products supplanted traditional materials such as wool and cotton, natural rubber, animal and vegetable glues, paper packaging and fabricated wood, and metal parts. The American firms built many new plants all over the world to serve these burgeoning markets both at home and abroad.

Over the past decade or two almost all segments of the industry have slowed down, and the output of some segments has been steadily declining since 1978. Among these troubled areas are such key sectors as inorganic chemicals, plastics, and industrial organic chemicals. The only significant exception has been the drug segment. Employment too has dropped sharply, particularly in plastics and organic chemicals.

Exports have also sagged in the 1980s. Throughout the 1970s there was a dramatic rise in chemical exports, but the 1980 trade surplus of $14.6 billion turned out to be the peak (see figure B.1). Imports, which had always been a small portion of American chemical consumption in the past, have progressively increased since about 1972, especially in agricultural and organic chemicals. As a result of these trends, the U.S. trade surplus in chemicals fell to a low of $8.3 billion in 1985.

Productivity in the industry rose steadily until the mid-1970s. The rate of growth was 3.4 percent per year from 1960 to 1967, then it accelerated to 4.4 percent until 1973. In the interval from 1973 to 1979, however, productivity not only stopped improving but actually declined at a rate of 2.4 percent per year. It continued to decline at a rate of about 0.5 percent per year through the early

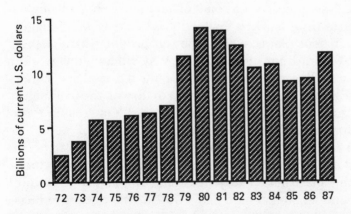

Figure B.1   Trade balances in the U.S. chemicals industry
Industry defined by Standard Industrial Classification (SIC) 28.

1980s. All of these figures are based on the broader multifactor measure of productivity (i.e., with respect to both capital and labor), rather than simply on output per labor hour. Lagging productivity in the industry was a global phenomenon, but the decline was especially pronounced in the United States.

Accompanying the nosedive in productivity was a slowdown in innovation: there were fewer advances in products, process equipment, and instruments. Spending on research and development as a percentage of sales was also lower, although this has begun to turn around recently. According to one study, there were 63 major advances in the chemical industry between 1930 and the early 1980s, including major plastics and fibers and such products as fiberglass, herbicides, flame retardants, epoxy adhesives, high-nitrogen fertilizers, and catalytic converters for automobiles. Of the 63 advances, 40 came in the 1930s and 1940s, 20 emerged in the 1950s and 1960s, and only 3 in the 1970s and early 1980s. A similar slowdown has been reported in the rate of improvement in processes for making chemical products.

The financial performance of U.S. chemical firms also deteriorated steadily over the years since 1973, but it has begun to recover in the past few years.

What Caused the Decline?

For more than a century the chemical industry was driven by technological innovation, both in products and in processes. The great chemical companies of Europe, such as Bayer, BASF, and Hoechst, were all founded as a result of laboratory breakthroughs. The rapid growth of markets enabled producers to build bigger and more efficient plants, which boosted productivity and provided the R&D funds for new advances. Why did an industry with such a strong tradition of innovation slide into a period of decline?

The causes were both external (having to do with the market for chemicals) and internal (affecting production). One reason for a slowdown in demand was the gradual saturation of potential substitution possibilities for plastics, polymers, and similar products in end-use markets. There were also important structural changes taking place in such major customer industries as automobiles, steel, and apparel. These heavy users of chemical products were already facing fast-rising import competition when they were hit hard by the energy crises of the 1970s. Sharp jumps in costs for both process energy and feedstocks caused chemical prices to rise in real terms for the first time in decades. In response, demand began to fall, which was something new to the industry. Finally, the recession of the early 1980s, the worst in 50 years, dealt another heavy blow.

On the supply side, the decline in innovation and productivity can be attributed to three major causes: the industry's growing technological maturity, the upheaval stemming from the energy crises of the 1970s, and overcapacity (which was exacerbated by the energy crises). In the 1970s and the early 1980s all three of these factors contributed to a worldwide decline. In the United States there may have been a fourth factor (although the evidence is less conclusive): the adverse effects of government regulation. The four possible causes are discussed in turn.

Technological maturity. By the 1970s the chemical industry had matured technologically and had become largely a commodity business. Process technology was roughly comparable worldwide. New entrants into the market, particularly the large oil companies, led to sharpened competition and lower profit margins. This discouraged large R&D expenditures with distant and uncertain payoffs. Feedstocks were cheap (until the 1973 oil shortage), and there were large, complex plants in place to process them. These factors also shifted incentives away from significant new R&D efforts toward maximizing current production and return on existing investment. Some companies also diversified outside the chemical business. All of these moves reduced innovation in the industry.

Another factor leading to reduced innovation was increasing reliance on engineering contracting firms for plant construction. These giant contractors became the leaders in diffusing process technology around the globe, especially in newly industrialized countries, during the 1950s and 1960s. For the most part these firms did little research and development themselves and relied instead on licensing technologies from leading oil and chemical companies. The worldwide diffusion of technical know-how may have reduced incentives to innovate among companies that had previously been able to appropriate more of the benefits of their R&D spending.

The energy crisis. The oil shortage of the 1970s hit the chemical companies with a double blow: prices rose both for major feedstocks and for the fuels used to process them. Unable to pass on the full cost of these increases to downstream users or consumers, the industry suffered a profit squeeze. Falling demand put still more pressure on chemical producers, who had to cover not only the steeply rising input costs but also the fixed costs of large plants. The firms therefore tried to maximize their use of existing capacity, creating surpluses that further intensified price competition. Meanwhile, fluctuations in foreign-exchange rates, which resulted in part from the global economic disequilibrium brought about by the energy crisis, created uncertainty for international pricing and investment decisions.

Overcapacity. Adding to the industry's difficulties was the emerging problem of global overcapacity, which stemmed from several causes. The great success of the chemical companies in the 1950s and 1960s prompted the major oil companies to integrate downstream, or in other words, to process their feedstocks into more-finished products. At the same time large chemical companies, aiming for more upstream integration, were moving into feedstocks. The big chemical firms also projected fast growth for bulk chemical sales into the 1970s, a serious miscalculation. As noted above, demand declined instead, for reasons rooted in the energy crisis. Still more capacity came from new petrochemical plants being built in such oil-rich areas as the Middle East, Indonesia, and Mexico. And yet another factor contributing to overcapacity was the continuing subsidizing of the European chemical industry in spite of growing losses. With government help, some European companies actually expanded capacity when demand was stagnant.

Government regulation. Increasing U.S. government regulation in the areas of toxic chemicals, pollution control, resource conservation, and worker health and safety may also have contributed to the decline. During the 1970s a growing array of government regulations increased the cost of developing new products and building new plants. At a time when profit margins were already narrow, scarce capital was diverted to meeting regulatory requirements, which thus reduced the amount available for productive investment.

The dramatic slowdown in innovation in drugs and agricultural chemicals has been attributed, at least in part, to the impact of 1962 amendments to the Food, Drug and Cosmetic Act and the more recent Federal Insecticide, Fungicide, and Rodenticide Act. These regulations increased the costs of developing new products and lengthened the time needed to bring them to market. The extended period required to get approvals and the consequent shortening of the patent-protected life of the products reduced the profit potential for research and development, which was already considered high-risk. Although regulation increased around the world, U.S. restrictions were considered more severe.

From a longer-term perspective, the huge success of the industry in the 1950s and 1960s probably sowed the seeds for overbuilding and other troubles later. Price cutting was common because of a steady stream of more efficient processes, and falling prices encouraged a growth rate much higher than the aggregate growth rate of the whole economy. The confidence engendered by this rapid and sustained buildup led management to expect the trend to continue, and so construction of large-scale plants went on even after the first oil crisis in 1973. Such large and complex plants made the supply structure rigid. When prices for chemical products jumped (in real terms) instead of continuing their steady decline, demand sagged. Under the impact of the deep global recession in the early 1980s, the industry went into its worst slump in 50 years.

Restructuring the U.S. Industry

Major American chemical companies appear to have responded to the worldwide upheaval as well as their counterparts in Europe and Japan, or perhaps even better. They sold or reduced the size of many parts of their businesses. At the same time, they diversified into more profitable (or potentially more profitable) downstream businesses, such as specialty chemicals, pharmaceuticals, biotechnology, and advanced materials, and even into electronics and similar high-technology areas, mostly through acquisitions. Dow Chemical, for example, sold more than $1.8 billion in assets, mostly in basic chemicals and plastics, pulled out of several joint ventures, wrote off most of its oil and gas business, and reduced its global work force by nearly 20 percent between 1981 and 1986.

This restructuring has consolidated the commodity chemical business in the United States and brought major changes in ownership patterns. Major oil companies, with a few exceptions, have expanded and strengthened their positions in commodity chemicals. Product lines have generally been narrowed to those where a particular chemical or oil firm is strongest, and other operations have been either sold off to competitors or, in the case of some marginal operations, shut down. In the 1970s, for example, Union Carbide strengthened its dominant market position in polyethylene and ethylene oxide through the development of the Unipol process for making linear low-density polyethylene; at the same time it withdrew from weaker positions in vinyl chloride, styrene, polystyrene, and all of its commodity-chemical operations in Europe (which were sold to European companies). In general, major U.S. oil and chemical firms have withdrawn from commodity-chemical production in Europe, which they had dominated in the 1950s and 1960s.

Some divestments took other forms. Key employees bought chemical operations from Georgia Pacific, Tenneco, and Conoco. European companies bought some American chemicals firms and sold them off piecemeal, as ICI did with Stauffer Chemical.

While operations in bulk chemicals were being reduced or consolidated, the chemical companies (and some of the big oil companies as well) diversified into higher-value-added downstream markets. Capital-intensive operations emphasizing process technology gave way to new emphases on science, research, product development, and meeting the needs of the market. The primary targets of the diversification included the following:

- Specialty chemicals, including gasoline additives, dyestuffs, catalysts, industrial coatings, diagnostic aids, enzymes, food additives, and many more
- Pharmaceuticals and biotechnology products, including not only drugs but also agricultural chemicals and new types of products based on advances in biotechnology
- Advanced materials, including fiber and metal-matrix composites, engineering plastics, ceramics, and materials for the electronics industry
- Medical instruments and other instruments, devices, and systems

The shift was not an easy one, because most of these areas were already dominated by specialized firms. Big drug companies were already established in pharmaceuticals; specialty chemicals had strong firms such as W. R. Grace, Rolm and Haas, and Lubrizol; advanced materials were the province of Corning Glass, 3M, and the major aircraft companies; there was a wide array of instrument, system, and device manufacturers. The major route to entry was through acquisition. In specialty chemicals, for instance, acquisitions rose from 35 in 1981 to 128 in 1986.

As a result of the transformation, commodity chemicals account for a much smaller share of total sales of major U.S. companies. At Dow Chemical the proportion dropped from 63 percent to 35 percent in five years; at Monsanto it went from 61 percent to 35 percent in four years. As capacity has shrunk and demand has started to pick up, prices and profits have begun to rise, aided significantly by the decline of oil prices since the early 1980s.

The Response Abroad

In most other countries government came to the rescue of distressed chemicals firms, but in many cases government intervention turned out to be an encumbrance rather than a help. It slowed down change at a time when quick and decisive action was required.

In France and Italy the adjustment process became highly politicized. Huge government subsidies or nationalization made size reduction and consolidation a protracted and painful process. In Britain a more imaginative approach involved capacity swaps, but it was not any quicker, because of regulatory policies. West Germany's industry managed to reduce its capacity in commodity chemicals relatively quickly without government assistance. Royal Dutch/Shell also showed agility in adjusting to changing market conditions, narrowing its chemical operations to those where it had the greatest strengths, and making the change without government help. It aimed to be the lowest-cost producer of ethylene after excess capacity had been trimmed from the market, and it emphasized building a competitive position in derivatives as part of its restructuring strategy.

Japan had overcapacity even greater than that in Europe. To scale back the industry a program of complex, carefully bargained swaps between major companies was initiated in 1983 under the direction of MITI. Unlike other Japanese industries, the chemical makers were not globally oriented. They had concentrated on serving local markets, which put them at a disadvantage in competition with major producers in the United States and Europe. The Japanese companies had deemphasized research and development, preferring instead to acquire technology from overseas (particularly the United States). This attitude has recently been changing, however. As Japanese companies concentrate on particular market segments, especially in biotechnology and pharmaceuticals, and increase their R&D efforts in those areas, they may become formidable competitors.

The American Strategy

Early indications are that the U.S. chemical industry has been relatively successful in adapting to the global upheaval of the past decade or two. Here are some major reasons for this success. The companies have developed a strategic corporate vision based on both their strengths and their weaknesses, as well as on competitive conditions and evolving market opportunities. They have renewed their emphasis on long-term R&D investments as part of a broader technology-management strategy; in some cases this strategy also includes collaborative research links with universities, joint ventures, acquisitions, or licensing agreements. The companies have become market-driven; products are developed to meet specific customer needs or preferences. They emphasize productivity, quality, and management of human resources, particularly in organizing the workplace for effective integration of technology and people. Finally, new organizational systems have evolved that allow quicker response to market changes and encourage technological innovation.

In the successful companies these were not isolated factors but were knitted together by an overall corporate strategy. Developing a corporate vision was not a simple, predictable process, since each company had its own strengths and weaknesses, each faced a different set of problems, and changes had to be made in a rapidly evolving environment. In some cases, major shifts in corporate culture and organizational structure were necessary. Strengthening the firms' ability to adapt was the market knowledge they gained in decades of global operations. Also, management was steeped in the century-old scientific and technological tradition of the industry. Chemical firms have typically been led by technologically experienced executives who have seen past innovations produce spectacular success. Such knowledgeable leaders may be better equipped to map out new directions than the managers of other industries, where top executives have little background in a company's technology or in the specifics of its business.

Most U.S. chemical firms have increased their R&D spending in recent years as a central feature of their strategic thrust. They have taken a long-term view and have shifted from an emphasis on process improvement to product development as they moved toward a more market-driven strategy. This new emphasis appears to be part of a pronounced shift in the U.S. chemical industry toward what might be called an American model of corporate research and development, typified in the past by Bell Laboratories and IBM. The central feature of this model is extensive research activity outside the firm's core business to spawn new basic technologies and products. Companies such as Du Pont, Monsanto, and to an increasing extent, Dow Chemical have stepped up their commitments to such an approach. Several have recently entered into major R&D joint ventures with universities.

The large European firms also invest heavily in research, but so far there have been few research relationships between the industry and universities comparable in scale to the largest American ones.

The Japanese chemical firms have traditionally given a back-seat role to corporate research, preferring to acquire, improve, and commercialize technology from abroad, particularly from the United States. Only recently have Japanese chemical firms become more research-oriented. Also, in recent years more foreign chemical companies have begun entering partnership arrangements with American universities and research institutions to explore emerging areas of science and technology.

The shift toward a market-driven mode of operation was aided by the major companies' transition from commodity products to specialty chemicals and other narrow-application products, which typically require close attention to customer needs. In some cases the importance of listening to the customer was learned by bitter experience. For example, General Electric's European Group worked to develop plastic automobile bumpers to open up a new market for its polycarbonate products; the company was able to shift to other plastics, however, when polycarbonate did not work well in tests for Ford's division in Cologne, West Germany. By contrast, Monsanto, though once a leader in providing plastics to the auto industry, continued to rely on its technological leadership (focusing particularly on ABS, or acrylonitrile-butadiene-styrene) while losing market share. General Electric's greater experience in responding to customer needs helped the company overtake

Monsanto in this market. Monsanto has since adopted a much stronger market focus, by opening its Automotive Plastics Marketing Group in Detroit in early 1986, for example.

Another factor helping management to carry out rapid, far-reaching changes was the hands-off attitude of the U.S. government, which, unlike many other governments, did not take part in the restructuring process. This allowed management greater flexibility in redeploying corporate resources.

The Outlook

The radical transformation of the chemical industry is continuing, and further changes can be expected over the next decade. Diversification will continue, and global technological alliances will take shape as major companies build strengths across international markets. The large-scale entry of European and Japanese companies into the American market is likely to continue. International competition is also likely to increase greatly in Europe, as American and Japanese firms stake out positions in the fully integrated Common Market that will be created when remaining trade barriers are removed in 1992. Competition will be particularly intense in such emerging areas as biotechnology, specialty chemicals, and pharmaceuticals because of the large number of new entrants. With access to advanced technology becoming crucial for international competitiveness, there is likely to be an expansion of large-scale cooperative R&D programs as well as further links between industry and universities. Collaborative research programs have already been established by Du Pont and Harvard University, by Monsanto and Washington University, and by Hoechst and Massachusetts General Hospital. Technological progress in such areas as advanced materials and instrumentation is also likely to lead the chemical companies toward even wider diversification into electronics, life sciences, and other allied industries.

C

The Commercial-Aircraft Industry

Among all the industries studied by the Commission, the commercial-aircraft industry is the strongest exporter and has the healthiest trade balance. Since World War II the manufacture of large commercial transport aircraft has been dominated by American companies.[1] Indeed, until the 1980s the U.S. airframe builders held a virtual monopoly, and they still command about three-fourths of the worldwide market. Continued American preeminence is now in doubt, however. Only two U.S. companies remain in the commercial-airframe business: the Boeing Commercial Aircraft Company and McDonnell Douglas Aircraft Company. They now face serious foreign competition in a business environment that has changed drastically.

For many years it was technological leadership that sold large commercial transports. Today, partly as a result of deregulation in the American airline industry, purchase decisions are based more on price and credit arrangements. Another fundamental change has turned the commercial-aircraft industry into a thoroughly international enterprise. Although the U.S. market is still the world's largest (with 40 percent of revenue passenger miles), foreign airlines are wielding more clout, and foreign governments are taking a more active role in aircraft-purchase negotiations. Not only the market has become international; so has the production system. All airframes and most engines are now developed and built by multinational consortia, both to share risks and to satisfy the demands of national governments.

A summary report of the Commission's Commercial-Aircraft Industry Working Group. A longer working paper by Artemis March, "The U.S. Commercial-Aircraft Industry and Its Foreign Competitors," appears in *The Working Papers of the MIT Commission on Industrial Productivity*, 2 vols. (Cambridge: MIT Press, 1989).

The most important change is the emergence of a foreign competitor: Airbus Industrie, a consortium formed by aerospace firms in four European countries. Airbus has overtaken McDonnell Douglas in new orders, and it has begun to challenge Boeing's 30-year hegemony in the world market.

Up to now the American builders have retained a lead in technology, but that too may be threatened in the long run. International partnerships inevitably tend to diffuse new technologies among the cooperating nations. Moreover, aviation research in the United States is not receiving the emphasis it once did. The space program has eaten away at NASA funds once devoted to aviation, while the divergence of military and commercial needs has reduced the value of military-technology development for commercial aviation. At the same time, other countries have greatly increased their aviation research, and according to a recent government report, "In a growing number of aviation-related areas, foreign technical capabilities are now comparable, if not superior, to those of the United States."[2] Though most of the major competition has been coming from Europe, the Japanese government has designated aerospace as one of three key technology areas for the twenty-first century, and Japan looms as a potential independent competitor.

The Structure of the Industry

The aircraft industry has the structure of a pyramid, with a few prime contractors (the airframe integrators) orchestrating the work of thousands of subcontractors, both domestic and foreign. The airframe manufacturers design the aircraft, integrate all its systems, manage the vast network of suppliers and subcontractors, complete the final assembly, market the airplane, and provide customer support for the 20 to 30 years of its life. Engine manufacturers design and build propulsion systems in close association with the airframe manufacturers and maintain their own marketing and customer-support networks. Risk-sharing subcontractors do detailed design and use their own tooling to assemble major subsections of new transports. Finally, layers of suppliers develop systems and equipment for aircraft, including cockpit displays, computers, hydraulics, seats, and galleys, and they rely in turn on a wide range of component manufacturers.

The number of large-transport integrators has been reduced to five: Boeing, McDonnell Douglas, and Airbus deliver more than 95 percent of the aircraft, while Fokker in West Germany and British Aerospace build smaller, short-range transports. Other early contenders (such as Martin, Convair, and Lockheed in the United States) have been winnowed out by the enormous financial risks that must be borne by integrators of jet transports. In the days of piston-engine transports, airlines would request bids for a few aircraft at a time, and multiple manufacturers would respond, often offering airplanes derived from military antecedents. Today it takes sales of 400 to 500 units and a minimum of 50 sales per year to break even on a completely new aircraft. Few companies can survive 5 or 6 years of negative cash flow, last 10 to 14 years until breakeven (if it ever occurs), and ride out the industry's extreme cycles in sales and employment. Because of the high breakeven hurdles for large jet transports, only two or three models can be supported in any one market segment, and an airframe manufacturer must have multiple models with overlapping product life cycles competing in different market segments. One group of industry analysts has concluded that "economic failure is the norm in the civil aircraft business" and has estimated that jet transports lost their manufacturers some $40 billion on revenues of $180 billion through 1984.[3] At that time, even Boeing had not quite broken even.

The risks and demands of the engine business are similar to those of the airframe business. The engine manufacturers—General Electric, Pratt & Whitney, and Rolls-Royce—work with the airframe manufacturers in specifying power-plant performance, and they market their products both to the airframe builders and the airlines. Most airframes are now offered with a choice of engines, thereby intensifying competition. Engine technology is extremely demanding, and in complex interaction with aerostructure and system developments it is the principal pacing technology for new-generation aircraft. It usually takes longer to develop and certify engines than new aircraft. The cost of developing a new jet engine is more than $1 billion, and some 2,000 sales over 10 years may be required to break even. Replacement engines and spare parts are an essential element of the business and its most profitable aspect; during the lifetime of an airplane, the cumulative cost of its engines and their replacement parts is equal to the purchase price of the airplane.

As with airframes, engine makers must have multiple overlapping product cycles and participate in multiple market segments.

Because no one firm can afford to participate in every segment on its own, the companies have formed international alliances to codevelop, manufacture, and market engines. For example, General Electric and its French partner, SNECMA, split the development and manufacturing of the CFM-56 series; Pratt & Whitney, Rolls-Royce, Fiat, MTU, and a Japanese consortium share development, manufacturing, and marketing for the V2500 engine.

While the airframe integrators and engine makers are the most visible component of the industry, thousands of subcontractors fabricate between 60 and 70 percent of the value of American airframes. (The proportion is less for engines; subcontractors also have a lesser, though still substantial, share of Airbus production.) Subcontracting now extends throughout the world, partly at the insistence of overseas customers or their governments. To sell airplanes in many countries, airframe manufacturers must accept offset agreements that give a share of production to firms in those countries. Offsets have reduced the business of some domestic suppliers and have also hastened technology transfer abroad.

Although subcontracting got a big boost during World War II, international revenue-sharing and risk-sharing partnerships are more recent. The partnerships reduce the manufacturers' risks because partners tap other sources for working capital, including foreign governments. The international arrangements also improve market access by raising the probability of sales to countries where part of the aircraft or engine was built. Finally, they facilitate the financing of export sales. Of course, the partnerships may also have detrimental effects, particularly by diffusing proprietary technologies. American partners try to structure these agreements so that they share interfaces rather than the internal details of their designs, and they try to stay ahead on yet newer technologies, but many observers believe these will turn out to be Faustian bargains in the long run.

Relationships with Customers

Commercial aviation has been marked by very strong working relationships between manufacturers and airlines, particularly those major carriers whose early orders allow the development of a new aircraft to be launched. Transports are sized and designed to meet the multiple and usually conflicting demands of these "launch customers." In return, the manufacturers used to receive launch payments that provided from 20 to 30 percent of their working capital.

Deregulation, Airbus competition, and the growing importance of foreign markets have made such payments the exception. Instead of providing capital, the airlines now look to the manufacturers to finance the sale, or they choose to lease aircraft. By 1986 one-third of the fleets of the major domestic airlines were leased, and fully half of the airplanes delivered between 1982 and 1984 were leased. Though the flexibility of leasing is attractive to the airlines, it passes risk back to the manufacturers and forces them to replace the working capital no longer provided by progress payments. Leasing separates the user from the buyer, and weakens traditionally close customer relationships.

At the heart of those relationships were large airline engineering staffs who worked closely with the manufacturers and played a lead role in making fleet-purchase decisions, establishing design geometries, and choosing airplane systems. Airline engineers spent thousands of hours evaluating designs from suppliers, suggesting alternatives of their own, and making strong arguments for the choices they felt best fit their own airline's needs. The power of the engineering departments, in conjunction with the regulated business environment, exerted strong customer pull for technology-based performance improvements in new airplanes and engines. During the past decade, however, many airlines, especially in the United States, have drastically reduced the size and role of their engineering staffs. Purchase decisions are increasingly made by marketing and financial staff. This trend is being accentuated by the rapid rise of leasing companies.

The ever growing importance of foreign sales also changes the nature of customer relationships. Most foreign carriers are owned or supported by their government, which is involved in approving purchases or in negotiating such conditions of purchase as offset and coproduction agreements. Export financing and financial concessions are important for international sales, and export credit agencies play a key role. Some of the policies and practices of the U.S. Export-Import Bank, compared with those of European export credit agencies, put American manufacturers at a disadvantage with respect to their foreign competitors.

Government Support

Because of the high risk and the enormous staying power required until the company breaks even, commercial-aircraft producers cannot survive without government backing. And governments have strong incentives to provide support: the industry is a user and driver of advanced product and process technologies; it is thought to enhance national prestige; and it has obvious importance in the event of war. Governments have therefore played a substantial and indeed essential role in both the development and marketing of commercial aircraft.

On the development side, in the United States NASA provides direct funding for technology development—but not for product development—in civil aviation, though the space program now claims 95 percent of its budget. The Department of Defense reimburses some industry research that has potential military payoff, but such research is less than 5 percent of Boeing's research and development. While military contracts were extremely important in the past, particularly for validating high-risk, expensive new technologies such as swept wings and turbojet propulsion, military and commercial needs have diverged since the mid-1960s, which reduces the commercial benefit of military work on airframes. As a result, airframe companies fund most of their commercial research and almost all development costs. For jet engines the gap between military and civilian technology is narrower, and so engine companies recover a larger share of their research and development from the Pentagon. It is important to note that all of the direct government support is for technology development, not product development, tooling, or production costs.

In contrast, the Japanese government funds half of both the development and the production costs of its aviation consortia in both airframes and engines as long as the companies are working as a consortium (and thus are obtaining technology). European governments provide most of the working capital for development and production of the Airbus programs in the form of low-cost loans whose repayment is contingent on a revenue stream. Thus, the tremendous risk and the cost of working capital are borne primarily by European governments rather than by private industry. Airbus is said to have received close to $10 billion in government aid for its first three models and another $4 billion to $5 billion for launching work on its new A330/340 program. American producers claim these subsidies are illegal violations of the General Agreement on Tariffs and Trade (GATT), because there is no expectation of repayment, which gives the Europeans an unfair pricing advantage and allows them to make outrageous financial deals. Airbus denies the charges, asserting that its objective is to achieve a 30 percent share of the global market by the mid-1990s to become self-sustaining.

On the market side, the U.S. government has taken an active interest in commercial aviation from the outset. Post Office regulation of airmail routes laid the foundation for passenger service and led to the emergence of a few strong carriers in the 1930s. From 1938 to 1978 the Civil Aeronautics Board created markets and stimulated airline demand for advanced technology by controlling entry, pricing, and route structure, thus preventing price competition and encouraging service-based competition. Each airline sought to get an edge in performance through rapid adoption of advanced-technology aircraft and engines. Manufacturers could pass on the costs of this technology to end customers via CAB-approved fare increases. Moreover, the slow increase in the initial cost of new aircraft was accompanied by an order-of-magnitude decline in operating costs and gains in performance.

With deregulation the role of the U.S. government has been confined largely to maintaining the infrastructure of civilian aviation (such as airports and the air-traffic-control system). Elsewhere in the world the airline business has traditionally been highly politicized; this situation is changing somewhat in European nations, where private firms are taking over management of national airlines.

Performance of the U.S. Industry

Large commercial aircraft remain the single largest net contributor to the U.S. balance of payments, providing between 4 and 7 percent of the nation's total exports (see figure C.1). In 1987 civil exports of aircraft, engines, and parts amounted to $16.2 billion, and the lion's share of this amount could be attributed to large transports, their engines, and parts. Trade flows in aircraft parts, engines, and engine parts are climbing rapidly as a result of the internationalization of production, the importance of spares and parts, and increasing Airbus penetration of the market. Exports still greatly exceed imports in all of these areas.

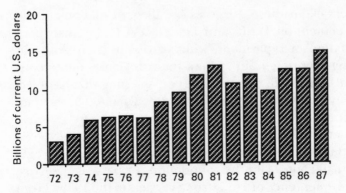

Figure C.1   Trade balances in the U.S. commercial-aircraft industry
Industry defined by Standard Industrial Classification (SIC) 372.

The U.S. share of the world transport market remains commanding, but the effects of Airbus competition are beginning to show up. Boeing's share of deliveries has hovered around 60 percent for two decades, but its share of recent orders has been slipping (see figure C.2). While Airbus production rates, and thus deliveries, have remained low, its orders, led by the new A320, have shot up, and a long-planned production increase is now under way. Airbus orders surpassed those of McDonnell Douglas in 1986, and Airbus accounted for 23 percent of new orders in 1987. Even apart from the capture of market share, the presence of Airbus has had a larger effect. It increases the bargaining power of airlines, cuts into Boeing's profit margin, and forces McDonnell Douglas to compete on price. The net effect is to reduce American capacity for funding new development.

Though the U.S. share of the world engine market also remains commanding, American manufacturers must rely increasingly on foreign partnerships to reduce risk and gain access to markets. As a result engine technologies diffuse more rapidly.

Company Performance

The Boeing Commercial Airplane Company established its hegemony by means of its technological leadership. It has maintained its position by having the right product ready for the market at the right time, by building a family of excellent airplanes that cover most payload and range segments of the market, by establishing an outstanding reputation for integrity and commitment to safety,

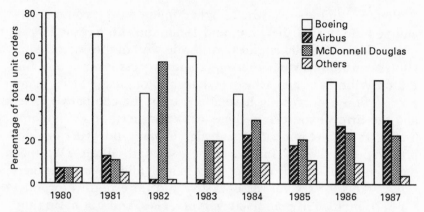

Figure C.2   Shares of the world commercial-aircraft market
Shares for 1987 are to July 31. Sources: The Boeing Company; *Wall Street Journal*, September 2, 1987.

and by offering unparalleled product support to its customers throughout the world. The company took a major leap in 1957 by introducing the 707, which became the first successful commercial jet, and it made another leap with the giant 747 in 1969. It hesitated a long time before introducing two new-generation airplanes, the 757 and 767 in 1982, and it appears to have indefinitely postponed its all-new 150-seat transport, the 7J7. The eventual success of the 727s, 737s, and late-model 747s have kept its business afloat through the deep valleys of the early 1970s and early 1980s. Only Boeing remains committed to being a full-line producer.

The Douglas Aircraft Company (the commercial side of McDonnell Douglas) has become a niche player that has made no commitment to a new-generation plane in more than 20 years; it competes on price and financing of its derivative planes. Although preeminent in the piston era with the DC-3 through DC-7 series, the first Douglas jet transport, the DC-8, lagged behind the 707 and was later withdrawn in favor of the larger DC-10. The latter split its market with Lockheed's L-1011, an epic struggle that eventually drove Lockheed from the commercial field, and (in combination with the DC-8 decisions) threatened to do the same to Douglas. Douglas managed a resurgence in the early 1980s through aggressive financing and leasing for its MD-80 series, a derivative of the small DC-9, which was itself stretched to create multiple models. Douglas's planned MD-11 will be an enlarged derivative of the DC-10, built on the same production line but with many advances in materials and systems.

Pratt & Whitney overwhelmingly dominated the commercial-engine field during the 1950s and 1960s and still has the largest installed base (18,000 engines worldwide). All of the engine companies continuously make product and process innovations, but Pratt & Whitney remains the overall technology leader. New materials and their processing have always been the company's forte, and the firm's expertise in these areas was given added impetus during the development of the high-bypass-ratio JT9D engine, built to power the 747. In spite of these strengths, Pratt & Whitney has been steadily losing market share in both military and commercial markets for several reasons: slow and unresponsive product support, inefficient manufacturing practices, and not having the right product at the right time. The beneficiary has been General Electric, which is now the market leader in commercial as well as military engines. Its market share has been pulled up of late by soaring orders for the 737-300 and the Airbus 320, both of which use the CFM-56.

General Electric has been a major force in military jet engines since World War II. It first achieved commercial success with its CF6 series (used on the DC-10 and later on the Airbus 300) and then with the small CFM series, produced with SNECMA. The cores of both engines are derivatives of military engines, a strategic choice that has helped General Electric to become the low-cost producer. Manufacturing efficiency has also been aided by the reorganization of its plant system in the 1980s, which focused each plant on particular processes. General Electric's forte has been mechanical design and blade cooling.

The Rise of Foreign Competition

American companies enjoyed a virtual monopoly in commercial aviation from the end of World War II into the 1980s. The enabling conditions for this situation were a combination of historical and political factors; those conditions were actively exploited by pilot-managers who loved flying. Military projects helped in many ways: by helping to fund and validate new high-risk technologies,[4] by underwriting development of the jet engine, and by providing orders for aircraft that could later be transformed into transports. The war created a legacy of production capacity, tooling, and skills in project management and engineering, and the aviation companies built on this advantage. The managers thought for the long term, and they repeatedly bet their companies in this "sporty game."[5] The 747 nearly bankrupted Boeing and Pratt & Whitney, for example, and General Electric and SNECMA each sunk a great deal of money into the CFM-56 before it showed signs of repaying the investment. Lockheed lost its bets on the turboprop Electra and the L-1011 and had to pull out of the commercial-aircraft business.

As pointed out above, the growth of the American aircraft industry was fostered by close relations between manufacturers and their customers and by CAB regulations that encouraged competition in service or performance rather than price. The U.S. companies also developed excellent global product support, which is critical in this business. Still more factors favoring the American industry were geography (widely scattered cities) and a postwar growth economy. The Europeans, in contrast, were short of capital, and their efforts were fragmented. They designed for their domestic market rather than for global markets, and they could not provide the required level of product support. The Germans and Japanese were prevented from rebuilding their aviation industries for many years. Nevertheless, the American monopoly is now gone forever.

It has taken the Europeans several decades to recover from the war, to rebuild their separate industries, and then to learn to cooperate effectively. The European aviation companies have invested substantially in research and development, first to catch up and later to develop expertise in particular areas. Small domestic markets often compelled the companies to specialize, which gave them particular competencies to bring to multinational consortia. British Aerospace, for example, is outstanding in wing design, while Messerschmitt-Bolkow-Blohm is developing expertise in the processing of composites and in flexible automation for the manufacture of body sections. In the past several years each of the major European companies has invested heavily in new flexibly automated equipment and computerized systems. These investments have boosted productivity and reduced delivery times and costs, which enabled the Europeans to bid successfully for major pieces of many programs, of which Airbus is but one. European nations are now seeking a bigger share of the world aerospace market, and specialized expertise is a cornerstone of each of their strategies. The Germans and the British have rationalized their industries considerably, but companies still remain small compared to American aerospace firms. The consolidated firms find it essential to participate in both military and commercial markets, in aviation, and in aerospace.

The French organizational mechanism used by Airbus Industrie has allowed the Europeans to pool their resources and create a decision-making structure that could bring them commercial success as well as technical achievement in large commercial transports.[6] The participating companies from France, West Germany, the United Kingdom, and Spain retain their independence and technical strengths but have the benefit of a single-point marketing and customer-support organization. The partners are free to pursue independent projects and other consortium projects. They are both shareholders of and subcontractors to the collective entity, Airbus Industrie. The partners are responsible for financing (with the help of their governments) and for conducting research, design, development, and manufacturing. Partners compete with one another during design and development for particular work, and thus different shares of work are subcontracted to the partners for each program.

Though government assistance has given Airbus the ante to enter and stay in this high-stakes game, it would not have succeeded without a good product and a good business strategy. Coming late to the game, Airbus felt it had to have something to offer in order for airlines to switch to a new supplier with no track record. Its strategy for overcoming the enormous entry barriers emphasizes aggressive use of advanced technology, particularly in materials applications, systems for flight control and safety, and aerodynamics (for example, it has developed wing designs that push out the point at which local airflow over the wing becomes supersonic). A second leg of the Airbus strategy is to develop a family of airplanes for markets not served by new aircraft or not served at all. Airbus took the initiative first in targeting two segments of the market with wide-body twin-engine aircraft, then in developing a new-generation airplane for the 150-seat market, and now in going after the market below the 747 for a long, thin airliner.

Airbus transports constitute a family not only in covering multiple payload and range segments but also in their very substantial design commonalities. This is not to say that Boeing and McDonnell Douglas do not employ commonality; Airbus, however, has made it a cornerstone of its approach to both design and marketing. Airbus is also very conscious of using new product technologies to stimulate thinking about how design and manufacturing are carried out. For example, when it decided to make a vertical fin from composite materials in order to reduce weight, it rethought the design and reduced the part count from 2,000 to 100, thereby reducing the overall cost of making the fin.

Airbus is replicating two elements of the old Boeing strategy: technology leadership and a family of airplanes. What it has not yet achieved are two other capabilities that have long made Boeing the envy of every competitor: outstanding product support and the ability to manage changes in production levels and high levels of output. Lagging product support has been Airbus's Achilles' heel, and it clearly hurt early Airbus sales. But support is now improving. Production at Airbus has been very slow: the consortium delivered only 32 airplanes in 1987, and its plans called for delivery of only 28 heavily backlogged A320s in 1988. (In contrast, Boeing has recently been planning to increase production of 737s from 14 to 17 per month.) Airbus's investments in flexible automation appear to be laying the groundwork for increased rates of production, but so far these have not been in evidence.

In addition to the Europeans, there is a wild card in the industry, the Japanese. Opinion is sharply divided over the potential of the Japanese to become an independent force in commercial aviation. Although their capabilities in both airframes and engines have grown enormously during the past two decades, they are far from having the requisite infrastructure. Furthermore, the aviation business differs structurally from the types of industries the Japanese have preferred to target. The Japanese domestic market is small, there is no potential for high volume, and production levels are highly variable. But it can also be argued that the particular nature of aerospace industries as a driver of new base technologies and a disseminator of advanced product technologies to other industries makes it precisely the right industry for the Japanese to target. And indeed, MITI designated aerospace in 1970 and again in 1980 as one of three key technologies for the twenty-first century. By the early 1980s government aid to jet engines almost equaled that given to computers and exceeded that for telecommunications, energy, and new base technologies. One pair of researchers believes that the Japanese are drawing from multiple base technologies in materials processing, electronics, and computers to develop their military aerospace industry and that these developments will be used to provide a foundation for commercial aviation and other commercial industries.[7] In this view, the fact that Japanese aerospace firms are small divisions of giant firms becomes an advantage, rather than, in the more popular view, a disadvantage.

Technological Leadership

The revival of the European aviation industry and the possible emergence of a Japanese industry are not in themselves cause for alarm. What is alarming is the appearance of weaknesses in the infrastructure of the American industry. The Aerospace Industries Association (AIA) is concerned about America's "eroding competitive and technological edge" because the United States has been exploiting its technology reserves without replenishing them. The products on which the current aerospace trade surplus is based draw on technologies developed from 10 to 25 years ago. The American government has since reduced its support of aeronautical research and development both as a percentage of GNP and as a percentage of the NASA budget. Technology validation, the longest and most expensive stage in new-technology development, has become the weakest link in the American R&D chain. With the military providing much less validation and NASA not filling the gap, commercial developers no longer have a solid foundation on which to apply new technologies, and there are fewer new technologies in the pipeline. The situation with regard to process technologies is even bleaker. Seed funding for programs aimed at validating risky new processes and transferring them to the shop floor has been sparse and is shrinking. No coherent policy at the Department of Defense has guided such programs, and DOD has too often supported narrow cost-reduction projects. The result, in the view of many, is a deteriorating industrial base.

The direction, coordination, and funding of product and process research and development is not the only issue. Deregulation has drastically altered the U.S. marketplace and is charting a path that the Europeans are taking as well. Deregulation has shifted the primary arena of competition for both airlines and manufacturers from performance to price. The effects are salutary insofar as manufacturers are being forced to rethink their design and development processes, to design for manufacturability, and to reorganize their operations more efficiently. But there are serious drawbacks as well. The demand pull for technology has diminished, airline engineering has declined, progress payments from launch customers have dried up, and close customer relationships have been weakened by leasing intermediaries. The long-run implications of declining technical sophistication among users and buyers has been demonstrated in other U.S. industries, such as machine tools. Competitiveness is not all that may be in jeopardy. There is also cause for concern about technologies that do not show a direct economic benefit, including safety-oriented technologies.

Competing in the New Environment

The American manufacturers find themselves in a very different world from the one in which they wholly dominated commercial aviation. The nature of the competition in large transports has been altered. Whereas success used to depend on such factors as technical performance and product support, now competition has expanded to include a variety of financial and political factors. Manufacturers are expected to offer creative financing, which may take the form of buybacks, offsets, leases, expanded warranties, insurance, training, or very low interest rates. Export financing policies and terms offered by export credit agencies are also an essential marketing tool. In some cases sales are coordinated with political deals, often involving senior government officials who can negotiate trade agreements and route awards, landing rights, or regional economic assistance.

To compete effectively today, the manufacturers must also take part in multinational development and production programs. Careful judgment is needed in choosing their partners and timing their participation. The programs serve to accelerate the international flow of technology and program-management skills, and they place a premium on leadership in critical technologies.

Under the changed economic conditions, applications of a new technology must demonstrate direct economic benefits. No matter how ingenious an idea is, if it does not lower total system cost, the airlines may continue to operate less efficient but highly depreciated or low-priced used airplanes, or they may buy less-advanced aircraft at lower prices.

A new imperative for manufacturers is cost-effective management of development and operations. By reducing their own needs for working capital, they will be able to negotiate from a strong cost position and to meet growing pressure from customers for lower first prices and for financing assistance. To help meet these challenges, the major U.S. aviation firms are all making significant changes in their operations. They are also putting pressure on their suppliers and subcontractors for higher quality without cost increases.

There still exist enormous opportunities for the development and exploitation of aeronautical technology, yet civil and military research have not been strategically directed or well coordinated. The AIA, however, has gone forward with its own effort. Its Technical Council (composed of members) has developed an industry consensus around eight key technologies for the 1990s, which is based on the highest potential payoff, leverage, and the broadest application. The council is now expanding that consensus through meetings with policymakers and university scientists in order to forge a cohesive, strategically targeted effort among industry, government, and academia. So far, however, there has not been an effort to increase funding levels.

D

The Consumer-Electronics Industry

Among the industries studied, consumer electronics provides the clearest illustration of an innovative, high-growth industry that has been virtually eliminated in the United States by overseas competition. The U.S. market has grown at a compound rate of 15.2 percent per year since 1976, reaching an estimated $30 billion in factory sales in 1986. Yet the share produced domestically by American-owned firms, which was close to 100 percent in the early 1950s, had shrunk to about 5 percent by the late 1980s. Consumer electronics contributed about $11 billion to the U.S. trade deficit in 1986 (see figure D.1), with imports from Japan responsible for 74 percent of the total.

The loss of the consumer-electronics industry was not due to a lack of inventiveness by American manufacturers. In fact, many of the foreign products that took over U.S. markets depended on technology licensed from American manufacturers. Most of the American-owned companies that left the market did so voluntarily. Executives in these firms were seeking to maximize return on investment for their corporations. As foreign competitors, particularly those from Japan, targeted the huge U.S. consumer electronics market, the managers recognized that their firms could earn higher returns in other businesses.

American firms dropped out of consumer electronics in stages, giving up functions and products one by one. The withdrawal by function started with manufacturing. Initially the American firms contracted with offshore producers for hand assembly of simple products, then for the manufacture of components, then for

A summary report of the Commission's Consumer Electronics Industry Working Group. A longer working paper by David H. Staelin et al., "The Decline of U.S. Consumer Electronics Manufacturing: History, Hypotheses, and Remedies," appears in *The Working Papers of the MIT Commission on Industrial Productivity*, 2 vols. (Cambridge: MIT Press, 1989).

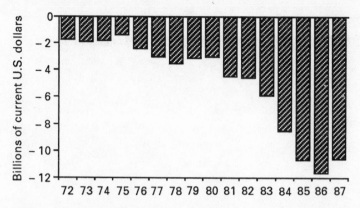

Figure D.1   Trade balances in the U.S. consumer-electronics industry
Industry defined by Standard Industrial Classification (SIC) 3651.

production of complete systems. After abandoning most manufacturing, the firms gave up research and development, then managerial control, and finally marketing. A few firms retained this last function and became marketing outlets for products designed and manufactured overseas. The abandonment of products followed a similar sequence: first portable radios, followed by passive components (such as resistors and capacitors), then audio and high-fidelity equipment, television sets, and finally video recorders and video cameras.

Along both dimensions of this retreat the sectors conceded by American firms required progressively greater technological capabilities and financial resources. The progression took place as the Japanese (and more recently others like the Taiwanese and the Koreans) steadily increased their own skills, technology, and financial strength. A number of factors contributed to this remarkable trans-Pacific migration of an entire industry:

- Lower labor costs in Asia provided an initial advantage. (The difference has been greatly reduced in recent years.) Not only were factory wages lower, but such professionals as engineers and managers also worked longer hours at lower salaries.

- Skills were initially higher in the United States, but capabilities in Japan and other Asian nations became progressively more sophisticated. Engineering levels are now about equal between the United States and Japan, but there are many times more consumer-electronics engineers there.

- Capital costs were higher in the United States, and the difference increased sharply over the period in which the industry was being abandoned (the prime interest rate in the United States passed 20 percent in the late 1970s). American companies mainly financed their operations internally, but as the big U.S. firms left the business, any new entries would have required higher-cost external financing and would have been competing against foreign firms with much lower capital costs.

- The Japanese emphasis on teamwork and quality gave them advantages over American firms. In the United States poorer teamwork between product-development and manufacturing activities often contributed to delays in bringing new products to market. Lags in U.S. automation and other factors also resulted in roughly one fault per television set in 1977; at the time the defect rate was worse in the United Kingdom but markedly better in Japan.

- American technology and patents were initially licensed by foreign competitors, but as U.S. firms cut back on research and development and as overseas companies increased theirs, the patent advantage turned heavily to the Japanese.

- Materials costs were about equal. The United States did have an advantage in wood, but that has almost disappeared from consumer products.

Trade policy has been strongly tilted against the United States. Protectionism overseas has recently diminished somewhat, but only after the U.S. industry was essentially eliminated. While Japan and Europe nurtured and protected their consumer-electronics industries, U.S. policies in many cases actually contributed to the American decline. Deliberate Japanese targeting of sectors of the industry, with prices set to drive out U.S. competition, was allowed to persist until virtually all U.S. manufacturers conceded, either leaving the market or selling out to foreign competitors.

The United States had protective mechanisms that might have helped to prevent the loss of such a major industry, but they did not work. Cases filed under antidumping laws were tied up in litigation for so long that even if adequate remedies had been awarded, they would have been too late. Tariffs of 15 percent on color-television picture tubes probably helped to preserve limited production of this product in the United States, but lower tariffs on other items were evidently insufficient. Antitrust regulations effectively prevented major American firms from joining forces (and perhaps from thereby preserving at least parts of the industry), but the laws failed to stop powerful foreign competitors with small market shares in the United States from buying up American consumer-electronics operations. Import limits worked out in Orderly Marketing Agreements proved ineffective, because foreign firms simply shifted assembly to other countries (including the United States). Consequently, this approach was abandoned in 1982.

Except for their unsuccessful attempt to obtain dumping relief, American firms were reluctant to admit publicly that their position in the industry was in serious jeopardy or to acknowledge their growing reliance on overseas manufacturing capabilities and technology. This reluctance presumably stemmed in part from fear of disapproval by customers, stockholders, and employees. The companies' silence, however, made remedial government action less probable, and none occurred.

The outlook for the consumer-electronics industry in the United States is dim. Unless vigorous action is taken to restore competitiveness, action that would require investments of at least hundreds of millions of dollars, even the minuscule share of manufacturing retained by American firms is likely to shrink further. As yet there is little sign of any strong government commitment to U.S. industry that could bring such a resurgence, even though the long-term economic benefits to the nation should be substantial.

Apart from the impact on employment in the United States, the destruction of such a large manufacturing industry has strategic consequences as well. Many of the components required for consumer products also have military uses in areas such as communications and radar. More than 90 percent of America's domestically owned and located consumer-electronics manufacturing capability was lost over the past few decades through economic attrition, a loss comparable to that experienced in wartime by direct combatants. This setback must be considered in evaluating U.S. economic sovereignty and national-defense readiness.

Even though consumer electronics accounts for about only 15 percent of the total electronics marketplace (computers, telecommunications, and industrial electronics are the dominant segments), it has special value because it emphasizes the mass production of sophisticated devices at low cost. The skills and equipment required to do this successfully can contribute to the efficiency of making other electronic products, from computers to military systems. Making components for the consumer market also helps to achieve economies of scale in the electronics business; for example, consumer products use roughly half the semiconductors produced in Japan.

An additional concern is the ability of foreign interests to influence decision making through ownership of U.S. firms. An example is the broadcast industry, which expects eventually to shift to high-definition video recordings. The U.S. Advanced Television Systems Committee voted by a narrow margin (a two-thirds majority was required) to accept a Japanese (NHK) production standard for the format of these recordings. Adoption of the proposed standard could lead American consumers and broadcasters to spend more than $100 billion on new equipment, most of which would probably be Japanese. Although most American broadcasters opposed the NHK standard, 15 percent of the votes in the committee were by Japanese firms operating in the United States, and another 18 percent of the votes were abstentions. According to observers of the industry, some abstainers had concerns about potential economic retaliation from foreign customers, suppliers, or partners.

The Structure of the Industry

Three major segments of the consumer-electronics industry each account for roughly a fourth of total sales: audio products, television sets, and video recording. The remaining fourth of the business ranges over an assortment of products, such as home computers and software, calculators, electronic watches, video games, satellite earth stations, telephones, and a few others. Total estimated U.S. factory sales in 1987 were $30 billion, with retail sales of roughly $40 billion.

Consumer electronics is a low-margin, mass-production industry. For most products it would cost more than the price of the final product just to buy all the components in small lots. Typically, assembly costs now amount to 10 percent or less of the value of radios or televisions.

Factories in the United States accounted for only 23 percent of U.S. consumer-electronics sales in 1985 (plus 2 percent in exports). Today the few American firms that remain in the business are primarily marketing outlets that either manufacture offshore or buy products from foreign producers and relabel them for sale here. Zenith is the only American manufacturer still producing television sets in the United States, and even it has recently come under pressure from investors to leave the market. A few companies, including Zenith, produce some home computers domestically, but they too are under intense competitive pressure.

Why the Domestic Industry Declined

U.S. leadership in consumer electronics was based on a sequence of technological developments that go back to Edison's invention of the phonograph in 1877. These inventions enabled American companies to develop innovative consumer products of increasing sophistication. But during the 1960s and 1970s, spending on research and development followed trends in market share. Other nations, particularly Japan, stepped up their investment in research and development as investment was being cut back by the declining number of U.S. manufacturers. By the early 1970s the Japanese consumer-electronics firms employed roughly twice the R&D manpower of their American competitors. As a result, Japanese and European companies have gradually taken over technological leadership, which, in turn, allows them to develop new generations of fast-growth products. Recent product introductions, mainly or exclusively from overseas sources, include pocket radios, pocket televisions, small portable videocassette and compact-disc players, and small television terminals for direct-broadcast satellites. Innovations by foreign producers also extend to low-cost manufacturing techniques and machinery. Introductions by U.S. firms of comparable new consumer products (other than computer products) are no longer expected unless government policies become much more supportive.

The recent failure to innovate is only one symptom of serious industry problems that began as early as the late 1940s. These problems stem from aggressive penetration of the U.S. consumer-electronics market by well-managed and well-financed foreign firms supported by their own governments' policies and economic postures. The history of these developments follows.

Radios and television sets. The postwar rise of the Japanese consumer electronic industry was achieved with a good deal of American help. In the late 1940s U.S. manufacturers sought to cut costs by assembling radios and other products in Japan and elsewhere.

Technology transfer steadily increased as the American firms, hoping to reduce their costs even further, encouraged Japanese and other manufacturers to develop capabilities to manufacture parts. The Japanese then began independently to develop and sell first parts and then complete receivers in the U.S. market. They started with transistor radios, which American producers were slow to pursue because they offered lower margins and entailed higher risks than vacuum-tube sets. This Japanese initiative opened a whole new market segment.

The takeover in television manufacturing followed a similar course. The Japanese took advantage of lower labor costs and their increasing capabilities in parts manufacturing and assembly operations to compete in the U.S. market even after American manufacturers developed alternative low-cost suppliers. Repeating the earlier Japanese initiative with transistor radios, Sony introduced a miniaturized television in 1960, taking a high risk with a low-margin product. Sony's success with this innovative eight-inch monochrome set established the microtelevision market segment and helped to build the company's reputation for high-quality products.

One important innovation in manufacturing techniques for consumer electronics has been the development of flexible and programmable equipment for automatically inserting components on circuit boards. Much of the early work on these machines was done by American firms. Nevertheless, aggressive design for manufacturing and early investments enabled the Japanese to fully exploit the machines several years earlier than most U.S. firms. Today Japan leads in innovation in this area.

The loss of domestic manufacturing by American industries such as consumer electronics is sometimes attributed primarily to higher wage rates in the United States. There is reason to doubt this explanation. In the late 1960s, when domestic television manufacturers were being underpriced in the marketplace by the Japanese, assembly labor was less than 15 percent of direct costs in the United States. During this period U.S. import duties were 8 percent, and the costs of transportation and insurance added about 10 percent more to imported goods, for a total cost differential of 18 percent. Thus, the lower prices could not be attributed solely to lower Japanese labor costs. Nonetheless, areas where labor costs less still remain attractive to the industry. The popularity of Mexico even for highly automated plants arises partly from the approximately

$15,000 in annual savings per employee in comparison with U.S. labor.

In the late 1960s Japanese television sets cost about twice as much in Japan as they did in the United States. High prices at home helped the Japanese manufacturers to generate the capital they needed to maintain a healthy growth rate in spite of the low prices they were charging to gain market share in the United States. At that time American television makers were prevented from selling their products in the protected Japanese market. It was suggested that American firms were not being deliberately excluded but rather that they "didn't know how to market in Japan." It is certainly true that the Japanese market, with its labyrinthine distribution system, was difficult to penetrate. But even Japanese companies manufacturing at lower costs in other countries did not export back to Japan at low prices. In 1962 Zenith tried to sell its television sets in Japan through C. Itoh, a Japanese trading company, but the Japanese Ministry of International Trade and Industry (MITI) refused to allow C. Itoh to export dollars to buy the Zenith products. Zenith also learned that leading Japanese department-store and appliance-store chains were pressured by MITI not to distribute Zenith products too aggressively. In 1973 Motorola tried to sell its Quasar color-television consoles in Japan through Aiwa, a Sony-controlled company, at prices about a third lower than Japanese sets. Matsushita bought out Motorola's television-manu-facturing operations for $100 million in 1974, eliminating this potential threat.

In court proceedings that stretched over many years, American vendors charged that in 1963 the leading Japanese television manufacturers set up a Television Export Council and a Television Export Examination Committee with the approval of MITI. These groups were alleged to have established a "check price," which they felt was the lowest price they could charge and still avoid antidump-ing fines. Then, even though the check price was typically so low that matching it would have made U.S. sets unprofitable, still lower prices were allegedly attained by awarding illegal rebates to U.S. retailers, including Sears. When Sears stopped buying from War-wick, which had been its U.S. supplier, the American company left the business and sold its assets to Sanyo at liquidation prices.

In Japan's home market the Japanese Federal Trade Commis-sion conducted a number of investigations. One of these looked into the activities of three secret consumer-electronics groups that each met monthly for many years. The groups included representatives from Matsushita (Panasonic), Hitachi, Mitsubishi, Sanyo, Sharp, and Toshiba—most of the major television manufacturers. (Sony remained more independent and did not participate.) This major Japanese price-fixing investigation ended in the 1970s, owing in part to "the passage of time," according to the Trade Commission. American firms alleged that the collusion had produced enormous profits that were used to subsidize dumping in the United States.

Even though American manufacturers began antitrust and antidumping litigation in the late 1960s, it was 1986 before the case was decided. The Supreme Court overturned a lower court's antitrust finding, which had favored the U.S. companies. The Supreme Court did leave open the antidumping aspect, but when Zenith tried to press this issue, the appeals court decided that antitrust and antidumping were intertwined, and the Supreme Court declined to rehear the case. The U.S. government joined with the Japanese government in opposing Zenith's reappeal.

Attorneys involved in this decades-long case speculated that both Democratic and Republican administrations concluded that it was better to settle trade disputes between governments rather than through litigation. In fact, an antidumping complaint was finally issued by the U.S. Customs Service, assessing duties of $800 million to cover all Japanese color television sets imported into the United States from 1964 to 1979. This assessment was based on the allegedly low check price in effect over the period. The annoyed Japanese then revealed a secret letter from the U.S. ambassador to Japan in which the Carter administration had promised to stop customs-fraud and dumping investigations in partial exchange for a Japanese agreement to limit imports into the United States under an Orderly Marketing Agreement. In 1980, near the end of the Carter administration, the Commerce Department took over the negotiations with the Japanese and eventually settled for payments of $67 million plus an $11 million fine.

By that time most American makers of televisions and parts had left the market. Emerson, Magnavox, and Quasar had ceased to be American brands by 1975, and Admiral was in severe decline. To U.S. management the consumer-electronics industry had taken on the appearance of a war zone, to be avoided if less risky investments could be made in areas such as industrial electronics, computers, or defense work.

Videocassette recorders. As both radio and television manufacturing were being abandoned by American companies, video recording was being developed by U.S.-based Ampex Corporation. First demonstrated in 1956, the technology enabled Ampex to become a leader in high-cost, high-performance video-recording systems for professional and industrial markets. There was wide speculation that if the cost could be reduced to a few hundred dollars for a simple, reliable video recorder, a huge consumer market would develop. Motivated by this promise, Ampex demonstrated a prototype of Instavision in 1970. Instavision was a cartridge-record-and-playback system that could record up to 60 minutes of color video. Ampex planned to price it at about $1,500 and a five-pound camera for an additional $500.

Two years later Ampex abandoned the project. The company's manufacturing operation in Japan, a joint venture with Toshiba, failed to transfer the design to mass production. The company suffered a $90 million loss, and management decided to focus its limited video resources on the lower-risk broadcast equipment market, where price was less important than quality. As is well known, the Japanese went on to perfect their own videocasette-recorder (VCR) technology, and they now totally dominate the consumer market for video recorders and cameras. No American firms participate. Moreover, the Japanese are now entering the market for professional and broadcast recorders, capitalizing on the profits, technology, and economies of scale they have built up in consumer video-recording operations. Ampex has recently been pushed toward smaller-niche video markets, such as special-effects generators.

An abortive attempt to pioneer the videocassette market was launched in the early 1970s by Cartridge Television, Inc. (CTI), a U.S. firm. With limited financial backing from Avco (the principal manufacturer) and a public stock offering, the firm tried to commercialize its product through large retailers, such as Montgomery Ward and Sears. CTI's video-recording-and-playback unit with a primitive cartridge was sold as a built-in feature of console television sets made by Warwick, Admiral, and Packard-Bell. The color console was offered by Sears in 1972 at $1,350, with an optional monochrome camera for $250. Some 200 films to be provided by Columbia, United Artists, Time-Life, and perhaps others were to be rented at $3 each. The plan was to offer stand-alone VCRs at $900 in 1973. But sales were hurt by frequent problems with the hardware and the tape cartridges as well as by a shortage of films, so that CTI finally had to declare bankruptcy. Avco's limited financial commitment may have led the company to a premature introduction in the hope that it could raise enough cash from sales to improve and promote its innovative product.

RCA, the biggest U.S. consumer-electronics company in the 1960s and 1970s, pursued an effort to develop a VCR up to the mid-1970s and built up a strong capability in the technology. The program foundered, however, when the recorder proved too difficult to manufacture. By then Sony was having success with its Betamax, and Philips was making progress in manufacturing a VCR product. So RCA canceled its own R&D project and in 1977 agreed to acquire outside technology. Rather than licensing Sony's Beta-max technology, which would have enabled it to make a quicker entry into the market, RCA chose to buy a VHS license from JVC and arranged to have its VCRs made in Japan to its own specifications. RCA's retention of its own design capability was unique; Zenith and General Electric, for example, chose to market VCRs of Japanese design.

Although RCA dropped its VCR development work, it continued a videodisc effort, expecting that the cost of making videodisc players would be half that for VCRs. RCA chose a capacitive stylus pick-up rather than the laser-disc technology pursued by the Japanese and the Europeans. The capacitive microgroove technology proved more sensitive than expected to environmental factors such as dust and oil, so that introduction was delayed. As in so many other cases, part of the problem was a weak coupling between product design and the manufacturing group. Meanwhile, VCR sales expanded, and prices dropped to levels that fatally undermined the videodisc market. RCA later wrote off perhaps half a billion dollars invested in its attempt to introduce a videodisc product and other efforts in video recording. In 1987 RCA (including NBC) was bought by General Electric for $6.4 billion, and the consumer electronics units were sold later that year to the French firm Thomson. The Princeton laboratories responsible for thousands of RCA's innovations in consumer-electronics technology were given to Stanford Research Institute, a contract research firm.

Even though it is clear that the competitive environment forced many American manufacturers to capitulate, there were also missed opportunities; in many cases U.S. firms initially had the technological lead, and they failed to exploit it. Perhaps management and investors with more vision and willingness to take risks could have achieved such great successes as RCA once had with monochrome and then color televisions, for example. In consumer electronics, attracting customers through innovative products is an alternative to competing strictly on price. Success in the industry depends on opening up new growth markets as older markets level off.

Winners and Losers

The American retreat from the consumer-electronics market should not be attributed to mere incompetence or to poor judgment. The managers of U.S. firms acted rationally, guarding the interests of their shareholders. And yet there were alternative strategies the American industry might have adopted. Obviously, the Japanese experience offers one model for emulation. The European response to events of recent years also bears examining.

Japan. In just four decades the Japanese consumer-electronics industry has progressed from making a few cheap, low-quality parts and radios to leading the world in market share and technology. Japan's ascendancy has come primarily at the expense of the U.S. industry. Although Japanese companies competed intensely with one another in the marketplace, their collaborative strategies and the help of their government were vital factors in their enormous success. With the help of low-cost loans, Japanese firms were willing to take huge risks on innovative products. Because Japan's resources were limited, they had to be carefully allocated to where they would be most effective in lifting the nation from the devastation of World War II.

In the late 1940s Japan took advantage of low-cost labor to assemble radios and manufacture such simple parts as resistors and capacitors in small factories. Then with the improved education of engineers in Japan and with the help of American firms seeking cost savings, Japanese capabilities improved rapidly. Manufacturers first concentrated their efforts on transistor radios and then took on greater and more economically significant technological challenges. By the 1960s Japanese firms had tackled and then dominated the manufacture of electron tubes and transistors, home and auto radios, high-fidelity equipment, and monochrome television sets. By the 1980s they had moved on to color television sets, integrated circuits, and video-recording technology.

With MITI often supporting and coordinating Japanese industrial efforts at critical junctures, in many cases the succession from entry to dominance of a market segment took no longer than a decade. At the same time American firms retreated in every area where the Japanese (or other competitors) chose to advance. A major reason was that the risks were higher and the potential profits were lower for U.S. manufacturers in these contested areas, and the marginal return on investment was greater elsewhere.

Talented managers at American companies exploited the freedom and fluidity of the American economy to orchestrate these retreats, shifting resources to gain higher returns on investments. (With the aggressive pricing strategies of the Japanese, even U.S. Treasury notes would have earned better returns than were available from many consumer-electronics product lines.) Denied patent monopolies and patent pools by laws and regulatory restrictions, firms such as RCA and AT&T marketed their technologies to offshore companies in exchange for royalties, lower costs for parts and subassemblies, joint-venture ownership, and other forms of compensation. As soon as any product or service became available at a lower price and at acceptable quality elsewhere in the world, American managers took advantage of the opportunity to improve return on investment, even though it generally meant exiting from that element of the business. Resources were often shifted to the service sector not because the companies had greater skills in those areas but because there was less competitive pressure, so that returns could be greater.

In recent times other Asian nations like Taiwan and South Korea, which were used by both the American and Japanese firms as sources of low-cost labor, have steadily moved up scale. They are now attempting to emulate the Japanese success in the U.S. market.

Europe. European nations employed a variety of mechanisms to protect their consumer-electronics markets, first from the United States and later from Japan. Three broadcast standards for black-and-white television, all different from the U.S. standard, were established for the United Kingdom, France, and the rest of Europe. Then in 1966 the SECAM color standard was chosen by France and a few others, including the U.S.S.R., and PAL was adopted by the rest of Europe. The Japanese first licensed PAL technology in 1970, but under restrictions that effectively limited production and required European sales to be under Japanese labels. This kept Japan's penetration of the television market low throughout Europe (14 percent in the United Kingdom and 8 percent or less in other European nations by 1977, although typically the percentages were higher for picture tubes). Meanwhile, European manufacturers consolidated, until by the late 1980s only Philips and Thomson remained dominant in the television business.

European governments have regularly supported commercial enterprises, including some in consumer electronics. The recently organized EUREKA program, for example, involves multinational R&D projects among members of the European Economic Community and other nations in Europe. One large project is devoted to high-definition television, and cooperative work in this area has resulted in recommended European standards. Yet even with all this government support, Europe has still seen a steady loss of market share to Japan and other Far East nations.

The Fate of the U.S. Industry

Without a subsidized and well-planned national effort, it appears that the consumer-electronics industry is doomed in the United States. But the costs in lost trade and manufacturing capabilities of not reestablishing the industry could be substantially greater. If such an effort were organized, targeting emerging areas of technology would appear to hold the greatest chance for success. There are a number of important developments taking shape in consumer electronics that could offer large market opportunities in the future. They include the following:

- Flat-plate displays that will allow substantial reductions in the size, weight, power requirements, and cost of television sets. Improved low-cost displays for high-definition television will also be important.

- Improved television recording and transmission formats and signal-processing methods for enhanced-definition and high-definition television.

- Increased use of digital circuitry for enhanced picture quality and controllability. High levels of integration will reduce the number of semiconductor chips needed. New types of memory devices are also being developed for this market.

- Linking computers and other media, including video, sound synthesis, and compact laser discs, to create new modes of interactive entertainment and education, such as going on simulated flights or exploring artificial environments.

At present many observers expect Japanese companies to lead the way in both the invention and the product-development phases for these technologies because of their much larger R&D programs. For the United States to pursue these prospective markets aggressively, joint-development programs involving a number of companies would probably be required. Since the remaining U.S. producers are few and weak, low-cost, long-term funds from federal or other sources seem essential to success. Consortia might be formed to carry through development to manufacturing, and antitrust barriers might be relaxed to allow collaborations or mergers that could reach the critical corporate size. Yet as recently as 1983 the Department of Justice advised the Center for Advanced Television Studies, a new U.S. television-industry consortium, that their university collaborators could perform long-range basic research, but they were specifically forbidden to develop any products.

If Philips is taken as a reasonable model of a viable world-class enterprise in this industry today, an annual R&D budget of perhaps $320 million would be required (about 4 percent of Philips's sales of $8 billion in consumer electronics). Use of world-class technical teams to leapfrog competitors in new areas could lower reentry costs substantially. The Japanese teams developing videocassette recorders were of this class and were relatively small. From 10 to 15 years could be required for such an enterprise to become self-sustaining with over $8 billion in annual sales. Even then, one such enterprise would account for only about a fourth of U.S. consumption. Additional investment would also be needed to build up the component-manufacturing and process sectors to sustain a revived consumer-electronics industry and to support other sectors.

The high cost of capital in the United States and the handicap of weak or even antagonistic government policies make private investment in consumer electronics highly unlikely. Therefore, unless significant policy changes are made in these areas, the outlook is grim for the survival of this dying industry, let alone its revival.

E

The Machine-Tool Industry

The American machine-tool industry collapsed in the early 1980s, when imports surged just as demand slumped. Orders dropped 60 percent between 1981 and 1983. Since then the market has been steadily recovering as American manufacturers resume capital spending. But the recovery has given American machine-tool builders little cause for celebration: industry has been buying only half of its new machine tools from domestic suppliers.

The machine-tool industry stands at the heart of the nation's manufacturing infrastructure, and it is far more important than its relatively small size might suggest. All industries depend on machine tools to cut and shape parts. The entire industrial economy suffers if a nation's machine tools are too slow, cannot hold tight tolerances, break down often, or cost too much. If American manufacturers must turn to foreign sources for machine tools (or for other basic processing systems, such as those for fabricating semiconductors or making steel), they can hardly hope to be leaders in their industries, because overseas competitors will often get the latest advances sooner.

Yet the trend toward overseas dependence is increasing. Of 100 new presses recently ordered by General Motors, 88 will come from West Germany and Japan because the foreign models offer greatly improved efficiency. (Die changes, for example, take five minutes rather than eight hours.) General Motors has also bought large computer numerically controlled (CNC) horizontal milling centers from Sharmann in West Germany because of their superior ability to hold tolerances over a wide range of part sizes. Pratt &

A summary report of the Commission's Machine Tools Industry Working Group. A longer working paper by Artemis March, "The U.S. Machine Tool Industry and Its Foreign Competitors," appears in *The Working Papers of the MIT Commission on Industrial Productivity*, 2 vols. (Cambridge: MIT Press, 1989).

Whitney increased its purchases of foreign machine tools from 10 percent to 25 percent during 1986. Creep-feed grinders were bought from West Germany because no U.S. supplier makes such machines, and five-axis milling machines were bought from Japan because of fast delivery.

Growing American dependence on foreign machine-tool vendors is already putting some U.S. manufacturers behind their foreign competitors. The director of a recent machine-tool study at General Motors observed, "If you buy the very best from Japan, it has already been in Toyota Motors for two years, and if you buy from West Germany, it has already been with BMW for a year and a half." Thus, if U.S. manufacturing industries want to lead rather than be perpetually trying to catch up, a strong American machine-tool industry will be essential.

Much of the American machine-tool industry has been in decline for a decade or two. The Commission found a pattern of interrelated causes for the decline, most of which are characteristic of the entire industrial economy. In other words, not just the builders of machine tools are responsible; the buyers and users are too. Briefly, the causes are these:

- A sharply declining interest in the manufacturing process as a strategic advantage within industry and as an intellectual keystone within universities
- Weak user demand for innovation and declining user sophistication in new process technologies and equipment
- Short-term investment strategies fostered by Wall Street
- The absence of commercially oriented government policies

Although a few American machine-tool makers remain leaders or contenders, broad leadership has been taken over by Japan and Europe; within the European community, West Germany is the leader. The West Germans and the Japanese have taken quite different approaches to advancing their machine-tool industries. German firms stress high precision and special capabilities, whereas the Japanese concentrate on offering fast delivery of reliable, standard machines at low prices. Contrasting the recent history of the industry in the United States with these more successful nations, however, reveals some common elements for success, including an export orientation, continuous innovation with rapid

adoption of advanced technology, mechanisms to propagate information across the industry, high levels of cooperation, and sophisticated user communities.

Structure of the U.S. Industry

The U.S. machine-tool industry has historically been fragmented,
with small firms, mostly family-owned, clustered in regions where
user industries are concentrated. Each firm tended to specialize in
a narrow product line for a particular market. Cross built transfer
lines and Gleason built gear-cutting machines for the automakers;
Bridgeport produced milling machines for tool rooms and machine shops; and Hardinge Brothers made lathes for super-preci-
sion work. Each firm built its reputation on certain models and
gained economies of scale by producing the same models for many
years. This habit of long production runs, together with the high
costs for a user to switch vendors, led to long life cycles for equipment and discouraged innovation.

Since the mid-1960s the industry has been consolidating as
smaller companies have been bought by larger firms, particularly
conglomerates. By 1982, 85 percent of machine-tool production
had become concentrated in just 12 firms, and the number of active
companies had shrunk steadily until only about 500 remained.
Even with the consolidation, however, nearly two-thirds of domestic machine-tool builders still have fewer than 20 employees. The
acquiring firms, for the most part, have continued to operate their
acquisitions as separate units rather than rationalizing product
lines, integrating manufacturing facilities, and combining marketing efforts.

Performance of the Industry

After a worldwide economic boom that crested between 1979 and
1981, orders and shipments for machine tools nose-dived. Orders
have been rising again since the mid-1980s, but the industry has
rebounded less strongly in the United States than in the other
major producing nations (see figure E.1). U.S. shipments peaked
at $5.1 billion in 1981, and after the slump of the early 1980s they
rose to only $2.8 billion in 1986. From being the world's largest
producer with over a fourth of world production in the 1960s, the
U.S. industry's share had shrunk to less than 10 percent by 1986.

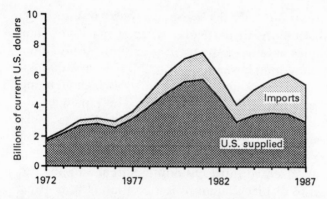

Figure E.1   Total U.S. machine-tool sales
Industry defined by Standard Industrial Classifications (SIC) 3541 and
3542.

Japan, meanwhile, with only 7.5 percent of world production in
1968, exceeded 24 percent in 1986.

A major problem facing American machine-tool builders is that
demand by U.S. manufacturers appears to have permanently
shrunk. Many metalworking companies in a broad range of industries have shut down domestic factories. Other materials, such as
plastics and fiber composites, are increasingly replacing metal.
Some process improvements (such as powder-metal near-net-shape
casting) have reduced the need for machining. (Some machine-
tool builders, such as Cincinnati Milacron, have become large
manufacturers of machines for working with plastics and other
alternative materials.)

At the same time the share of imported machine tools in the U.S.
market rose from 4 percent in the mid-1960s to nearly 50 percent
in 1986 (see figure E.1). Penetration has been greatest in metal-
cutting machines, which are about three-fourths of the market,
especially in CNC lathes and machining centers in the low- and
mid-price ranges. That was the first sector of the American market
targeted by the Japanese. In contrast, for grinding and polishing
machines, imports are strongest at the high-price end of the
market, because the U.S. depends on precision equipment from
Europe in this category.

Globalization of the business has also worked against the American industry, which has not been export-oriented. During the past
two decades the share of worldwide machine-tool production that
is exported rose from less than 30 percent to almost half. All

European countries trade extensively, especially with one another, based on special strengths in particular types of machines. The European companies have been strong in precision, custom-engineered machines that often have unique capabilities. Japan, which is now the world's largest producer of machine tools, is challenging West Germany's position as the top exporter. The Japanese, initially lacking skills in precision machining, aimed first to build standard, low-cost, reliable products that could be used by almost any metalworking manufacturer or machine shop. In recent years such newly industrialized countries as South Korea, Taiwan, and Brazil have begun to displace Japan in low-cost lathes and drills; most recently these new entrants in the market have begun to switch more of their production to numerically controlled (NC) machines. The Japanese, meanwhile, have been moving toward higher precision with more advanced computer controls, and they are building highly integrated machining systems.

Recognizing the importance of overseas plants for marketing and supporting specialized equipment and systems, the Japanese and some European companies are building plants in the United States. Moreover, American machine-tool companies have entered into licensing and distribution agreements with Japanese firms to sell foreign-built machines in the American market, especially at the low end of the American manufacturers' lines. This strategy produces higher profits for the U.S. companies in the short run, but the long-term effect will be loss of the skills needed to design and build competitive low-cost machines.

Causes of the Decline

Several reasons have been cited for the decline of the American machine-tool industry, including its fragmentation, the family ownership of many firms, neglect by conglomerates that bought machine-tool builders, and vulnerability to cyclical capital spending. Although all of these factors played a part, they are not sufficient to explain the failures of the American industry. West Germany's industry also had many family firms, but it has been very successful. Conglomerates control many Japanese machine-tool builders, but rather than damaging the industry, they have helped Japan make significant gains in global markets. Business cycles are felt worldwide, but Japanese and West German firms have weathered them with less damage than American companies. In short, deeper reasons must be sought to explain why machine-tool makers in Japan and West Germany have prospered while those in the United States have suffered. It is necessary to answer such questions as: Why did offshore competitors find it so easy to take business from U.S. firms? Why have American factories lagged behind other nations in updating machinery? And why have machine-tool makers in the United States been slow to adopt innovations?

Many machine-tool firms in the United States were started by tinkerers who were excellent mechanics or designers. Because the companies were small and family-owned, however, they tended not to engage in long-term research efforts. Generations succeeding the founder were often not as close to the business and were therefore unwilling to make needed investments. Because of their geographic clustering around user markets, the small firms had a regional view of the business; they did not export, and they were not alert to developments in other countries. They were ill prepared to take advantage of advances in electronics, whether for product innovations or process changes.

There are a few outstanding exceptions to this pattern, such as Ingersoll Milling, where the founder's grandson is deeply involved in the business and where investments are made to keep both products and processes state-of-the-art. Thus, even though family ownership is often cited as a drawback, in some cases a private firm with strong management can move faster and deal with risk more effectively than most public companies. Kingsbury Tool is another American success story. This company was sold by the family and eventually bought by professional managers in a leveraged buy out. The new private owners made dramatic changes in product lines, invested millions in new equipment to control critical tolerances, and helped mechanically skilled employees to buy personal computers for home use and thereby to become more adept in electronics.

The trend toward conglomerate ownership during the 1960s and 1970s could potentially have helped the industry by providing capital for research and development and advanced machinery, which did happen in Japan and to some extent in Germany. The American conglomerates could also have rationalized product lines, manufacturing, and marketing, achieving greater economies of scale through higher volume and using modular designs to broaden product lines. And they could have helped overcome the parochialism of firms built around a single product line and aimed at a small group of regional customers.

Unfortunately, consolidation had the opposite effect. Conglomerates such as Textron, pushed by Wall Street for higher quarterly earnings, were attracted by the high profits of machine-tool makers in boom times. But the conglomerates had little commitment to the business. Rather than reinvesting, they used the profits to fund other ventures and for corporate overhead. Being "numbers-oriented," they tended to drop specialized machines, because it was hard to show a profit on each order. Instead, they concentrated on building high-volume products on steadily deteriorating equipment, eventually making the machine-tool producers vulnerable to commodity competition.

Many analysts and industry veterans believe that through such practices the conglomerates destroyed the American industry. But even though conglomerates did wreck certain firms and damaged the industry's long-term viability, there were deeper factors at work that would have led to the industry's decline in any case.

The large amplitude of business cycles in the industry also contributed to the weakness of U.S. machine-tool companies, but again, it was not the decisive factor. Sharp swings in profits discouraged long-term investment by the firms or their bankers. Employment that oscillated between 58,000 and 115,000 over the past two decades also deterred many capable workers from entering the industry. Since it takes four to five years to train a good machinist, the industry was often short of skilled workers when good times did arrive. The image of an old-fashioned industry with grubby, noisy shops also discouraged entry by those with engineering or management potential.

The industry's response to business cycles may have been even more damaging. Orders were backlogged during boom times and the backlog worked down as orders slowed so as to keep production and employment levels more stable over the course of a cycle. Customers often had to wait from 18 to 24 months for machine tools ordered during busy periods. Such long delays led to many cancellations if the economy subsequently slowed down. More significantly, this strategy made the domestic suppliers highly vulnerable to machines imported from Japan, which were offered at lower prices on quick delivery schedules. Once users had experience with the reliability and service offered by the Japanese, imports continued to rise even after domestic producers' backlogs dwindled.

Innovation lagged in U.S. machine tools for several reasons, including those stemming from the fragmented, family-firm structure of the industry and the limited exposure of American builders to international competition and markets. The inertia of the machine-tool industry might have been overcome by strong user demand for technological progress, but in fact such user-pull was weak in the United States. User firms had become complacent and assumed the superiority of U.S. manufacturing. While other nations went through a postwar reconstruction, American industry allowed its installed base of machinery to age. Under pressure for short-term results, industrial managers opted for proven technology rather than take risks with new technology. Major manufacturers like General Motors kept costs down by forcing tough price competition among their suppliers, a practice that discouraged innovation and investment by companies that made parts and equipment. There was little effort by the major manufacturing industries (such as autos, steel, consumer products, and textiles) to work with their equipment suppliers or to provide incentives to upgrade the state of the art.

This general malaise in manufacturing helps to explain why the United States was slow to adopt the most important advance in machine-tool technology in recent times: NC and CNC tools. There was another important barrier as well: a mismatch between the way the technology developed and the needs of most potential users. MIT's Servomechanisms Laboratory, under Air Force sponsorship, developed hardware and software suitable for precision aerospace manufacturing of very complex parts. These developments then became institutionalized through the efforts of the Aircraft Industry Association. The resulting hardware and software were much too costly for most industries and for smaller users. A program at the Illinois Institute of Technology Research Institute to propagate MIT's APT (Automatic Programmed Tools) software throughout industry failed to attract the interest of machine-tool builders. Scaled-down versions of the software suitable for such simple machines as lathes and drills, rather than complex contour-milling machines, did not become available, and the Air Force did not see its role as extending beyond the support of advanced aerospace manufacturing.

Some industrial firms did try to adopt NC technology, only to become bogged down in its complexity and discouraged by incompatibility and unreliability. The two largest American makers of controls for NC machines, General Electric and Allen-Bradley, built sophisticated controls requiring extensive engineering and support for each user, which drove up costs and impaired reliability. Since management in American industry generally did not consider manufacturing capability a strategic advantage, there was little demand by users that these problems be resolved. American control makers were also slow to make use of the flexibility of the microprocessor. Whereas Siemens in Germany and FANUC in Japan began to offer microprocessor controls in 1976, the U.S. companies waited until 1980, when they began to feel the pressure of foreign competition.

Other contributors to the decline of the American machine-tool industry included the engineering schools, the financial markets, and government. In the years after World War II, engineering schools adopted more science-oriented curricula that stressed mathematics and abstract concepts rather than the real world of manufacturing. Professors who did work with industry generally communicated with the R&D and engineering departments. Manufacturing research was less quantitative and more practice-oriented than methods for design and analysis and therefore did not fit as well into the new engineering curricula. In both industry and universities, manufacturing was considered a low-status field, whereas prestige and rewards went to the engineers who created and designed new products. Production managers tended to come from the shop floor, and even though they might have been bright, they did not have the breadth of knowledge and grounding in fundamentals that come from university engineering programs. They also were uncomfortable with newer technologies, particularly electronics. They generally did not see what role the new technologies would play in a competitive manufacturing strategy.

Even if companies did want to invest in advanced machine tools, pressures from the investment community worked against them. Costly machines could not satisfy one- or two-year payback formulas, and the uncertainties of new technology made such investments even harder to justify. If management did take risks, takeover specialists might move in, buying up firms and selling off pieces if stock prices fell.

With so many factors working against the machine-tool industry, it is doubtful that government could have prevented the decline. Unfortunately, government policies were in fact more often harmful than supportive. Antitrust laws helped prevent collaborative efforts that might have provided R&D support; frequent changes in tax policy discouraged long-term planning and investment by industry; and excessive regulation and paperwork discouraged exporting. American leaders failed to develop a vision of what was needed for maintaining the long-term strength of U.S. industry. There was little sense of the importance of leading-edge machine tools in keeping the tool-using industries globally competitive. There was almost no support for the country's manufacturing infrastructure, like generic research on process equipment or work on standards that could help propagate emerging technology throughout industry. What support industry did get was from the Department of Defense, and the requirements of the military are often quite different from those of the much broader commercial economy.

Reasons for the Success of Japan and West Germany

Europe and Japan faced many problems similar to those of the U.S. in the postwar period: a fragmented machine-tool industry with mostly family-owned firms, highly cyclic demand, and limited capital for investment. Added to this was the devastation of their industries by wartime bombing. The Europeans and the Japanese chose divergent paths to build up their machine-tool capabilities, but both approaches led to great success.

Japan. In the 1960s and 1970s the Japanese Ministry of International Trade and Industry (MITI) "encouraged" hundreds of small family firms to join stronger, larger companies. These larger enterprises then grew internally until the top 14 of about 70 machine-tool builders now account for nearly two-thirds of Japan's business. Whereas the largest American firms are generally loose aggregations of separate machine-tool manufacturers, Japanese giants operate as integral firms.

Japanese machine-tool builders were urged to develop modular, standard products suitable for a wide range of users. Simple modular designs that minimized parts counts also kept costs down and cut lead time. MITI pushed each builder to specialize in a particular type of machine. Firms such as Okuma and Yamazaki emphasized lathes and machining centers, while Okamoto got 90 percent of its revenues from grinders. These specializations helped achieve economies of scale. In the 1970s MITI pushed the use of simple NC and CNC machines before the Europeans adopted them and at a time when American NC vendors were still finding few buyers. NC-tool production rose from about 26 percent of Japanese machine tools in 1977 to 67 percent in 1984.

These policies were part of a bold and broad commercial vision. They were aimed at improving the performance of all Japanese manufacturers, especially smaller and midsized companies. NC and CNC machines brought flexible automation to small-lot, large-variety, just-in-time suppliers to the automotive, electronics, and machinery industries. In the United States sophisticated NC machines went predominantly to giant automobile and aircraft manufacturers, but in Japan small firms were major users of the new technology.

Japan also concentrated the design and manufacturing of NC controls into one company, FANUC. This not only led to economies of scale but also avoided the incompatibilities that plagued American users. FANUC gained 80 to 90 percent of the Japanese controls market during the 1970s and 40 to 50 percent of the world market by the early 1980s. Unlike American control makers, FANUC quickly adopted advanced solid-state technology and used a design-to-cost process to produce standard products at low cost. Where needed, technology was licensed, mostly from American firms, and in some cases it was simply copied.

By designing simple, reliable machines with low part counts and supplying good service and rapid delivery, the Japanese firms not only served their own downstream industries well but also positioned themselves for a strong export push. Japanese machine tools developed a market niche based on reliability, service, and low prices that contrasted with European strengths in leading-edge technology, precision, and high-performance machines.

From the mid-1970s, the Japanese concentrated on exporting CNC lathes and machining centers to the United States. Some firms also penetrated European markets, though more slowly because of trade barriers. In many cases Japanese marketers provided generous introductory offers and financing for American users, such as allowing 90-day trials at no cost. This allowed U.S. manufacturers to see how the equipment worked on their own production, rather than making them rely on the often misleading, nonstandardized performance data supplied by American vendors. The Japanese quickly gained a reputation for good service. Unlike most American companies, they listened to customers and responded to their requests, according to managers in companies that bought Japanese machines.

The Japanese government provided under-the-table subsidies to assist machine-tool builders in Japan's export push. First the companies were given lucrative sugar import licenses, but this practice was dropped after strong objections by the Europeans. Then MITI shifted to tapping pools of cash derived from gambling on bicycle and motorbike racing. When this ruse was exposed by an American attorney, MITI admitted that over $100 million per year was going to the industry from this source. It had originally claimed that the amount was only $500,000. Eventually documentation was found that placed the amount at close to $1 billion per year.

The strong Japanese position in low-cost machine tools is now being challenged by newly industrialized countries. In response, Japanese manufacturers are moving into new segments of the market and preparing for future changes in machine-tool technology. Users are demanding turnkey systems and more-customized machines. Japanese companies have been building plants in the United States to improve communications with customers and provide better engineering support. Japan is also developing capabilities in precision machining so as to challenge the European supremacy in those markets.

Another front on which the Japanese are advancing, aided by collaborative projects, is the flexible machining system (FMS). Japanese industry is ahead of the world in installing and using FMSs, and the machine-tool builders have taken the lead by putting the technology to work in their own factories. As machine-tool makers turn their own shops into flexibly automated factories, Japanese vendors will be able to turn out modular, specialized machines, building them to order on short lead times. They are accelerating the shift from competition based on product engineering to process capabilities. They are already beginning to offer integrated process solutions that use hardware produced via systems similar to those they are selling.

West Germany. West Germany's machine-tool industry consists of between 350 and 400 producers, predominantly midsized companies. Many of them grew from small family firms, and although most remain independent, an increasing number are affiliating with industrial conglomerates. The West German industrial groups treat their machine-tool subsidiaries quite differently, however, from American conglomerates. The parent is often an engineering group that integrates the toolmaker into its total business and makes the investments needed to retain technology leadership.

Historically, German trade associations encouraged a pattern of "cooperative specialization," in which each firm produced a limited range of sophisticated machine tools. A few firms within each sector competed fiercely based on technical excellence and innovation. This approach aided in exporting, because a single agent could represent many firms whose product lines did not overlap. The market niches dominated by German builders tended to be in high-end equipment. For example, the West Germans gained half of the world market in gear cutting, over a third in grinding, and a third in metal-forming. While the Germans continue to dominate the high-end markets, they are also beginning to feel the pressure from the Japanese in lower-end equipment such as lathes and machining centers, and they recognize that changes will be required to remain competitive.

The European user community, particularly in Germany, is technically proficient and helps drive innovation. Buyers tend to put technical performance at the top of their purchase criteria. Major customers are deeply involved in development efforts for new machines and show much more collaboration and trust than is evident in American industry. American industrial machine-tool users tend to take little responsibility for their equipment, expecting builders to identify their needs, specify requirements, design and install systems, train their people, and provide maintenance and service. German users are much more demanding when initial specifications are set; American buyers are more interested in delivery schedules and in how cost-effective the system will be in producing parts. The German approach not only stimulates process innovation but also facilitates rapid diffusion of new processes and methods.

Underlying the technical sophistication of the West Germans is a strong infrastructure of apprenticeships, polytechnic schools, universities, and technical institutes. This system generates manufacturing expertise at all levels of the enterprise, including skilled shop-floor workers, practical engineers who can make things work and solve real-world problems, and more research-minded engineers who push the limits of process technology. There is also an intricate web of communications among industry, trade associations, unions, and government helping to diffuse ideas and building consensus in such areas as collaborative research priorities.

Training is given a high priority in German companies, most of which provide three-year apprenticeships as well as various forms of continuing education. The technical institutes located at state-run universities, together with 34 Fraunhofer Institutes, are the focus of generic research, cooperative problem-solving, and advanced technical training. (The Fraunhofer Institutes complement the separate Max Planck Institutes, which support pure research.) About 20 of the university institutes and many of the Fraunhofer Institutes conduct work pertaining to machine tools. The institute at Aachen is widely considered to be the best machine-tool laboratory in the world, and others in Berlin, Hannover, and Stuttgart are also highly regarded. Although the programs remain fairly stable over time, close links with German industry help the institutes to keep up with changes in manufacturing.

The German federal government has not adopted the highly directive approach of the Japanese, but it does play a supportive, facilitative background role. It supports standardization efforts and does not allow antitrust concerns to retard collaborative research. State governments also fund a significant share of university and Fraunhofer Institute research. A recent study commissioned by the German machine-tool association concluded that German machine-tool manufacturers need more flexible automation but should also design more modular, standard units that can be produced in volume. The machine-tool makers are responding to these recommendations. Burkhardt + Weber, for example, has extensively modularized, so that 70 percent of the content of its machining centers now consists of standard modules, and all controls come from one maker (Siemens).

While there are many differences between the Japanese and the West German machine-tool industries—decision making is less centralized in Germany, for example—there are also strong similarities. Both nations see exporting as important not only to build volume but also to foster innovation and awareness of trends elsewhere. They both take a long-term view, making investments to keep up to date, accepting low-profit work if it will help them to gain experience, installing advanced systems in their own plants, and building plants overseas to get closer to customers even before sales justify the costs. Both nations compete through innovation and organize collaborative R&D projects. An emphasis on training encourages technical sophistication in user industries, and strong links between users and machine-tool suppliers ensure that products are designed to fit users' needs. And each nation has carved a niche in world markets that is based on what it does best.

The Outlook for the U.S. Industry

Without a coordinated, national effort the prospects for machine-tool builders in this country are not good. The United States has not established a global market niche as the Europeans, the Japanese, and more recently, even some of the newly industrialized countries have done. The funds needed to make the American machine-tool makers competitive again cannot be generated internally by this fragmented, cyclical industry. U.S. machine-tool companies are not export-oriented, and so they do not have the pressures to be innovative felt by their foreign competitors, and government controls discourage exporting. The status accorded to manufacturing by most managers and professionals remains low, and little has been done to make it an important part of engineering education.

Two recent efforts to help the industry catch up, both fostered by Department of Defense, fall far short of what is needed. The Air Force, through its Manufacturing Technology (ManTech) program, has encouraged research on manufacturing processes rather than products; the companion Technological Modernization (TechMod) program supplies seed money to get contractors to install advanced equipment. Recent studies have concluded, however, that the low funding of these programs and their focus on cost-reduction make them ineffective even for the strategic-defense needs of the United States. In any case, the defense and commercial marketplaces are quite different, and as the history of NC and CNC development illustrates, the Department of Defense is an inappropriate sponsor for a broad revitalization of U.S. manufacturing.

The second effort is the National Center for Manufacturing Sciences (NCMS), located in Ann Arbor, Michigan. More than 110 companies across a broad spectrum of machine-tool builders and users had joined by mid-1988. NCMS grew out of a 1985 meeting of machine-tool builders sponsored by the Department of Defense and held under the auspices of the Manufacturing Studies Board of the National Research Council. Initial funding for the center has come from the National Machine Tool Builders Association. NCMS aims to set a national agenda for manufacturing research and then promote the dissemination and commercialization of results. Research will be conducted by groups of members, sometimes in collaboration with universities or other research institutions. After a promising start, NCMS is working to build up funding to levels where it can become effective in upgrading American manufacturing.

Although these smali programs are encouraging, they are not nearly enough. Without a strong, commercially focused national policy, it is difficult to see how this critical industry can be turned around. And that does not bode well for American industry as a whole, since excellent machine tools are a key to the nation's manufacturing strength.

F

The Semiconductor, Computer, and Copier Industries

The semiconductor, computer, and copier industries are all products of American ingenuity. The semiconductor industry was born with the invention of the transistor at Bell Telephone laboratories in 1947. The birth of the computer cannot be dated quite so precisely, but there is little dispute that almost all of the steps in its early commercial development were taken in the United States. The modern xerographic copier is also an American invention, and its manufacture was virtually an American monopoly for more than a decade.

In world commerce, however, being the first to explore a territory gives a nation no permanent claim to sovereignty over it. All three of these areas once seemed to be secure American preserves, but all three are now under attack by overseas challengers. In semiconductors the effect of the competition has been ruinous; in computers and copiers the outcome is not yet clear.

Semiconductors

The U.S. semiconductor industry dominated world markets from the 1950s, when the transistor was first commercialized, through most of the 1970s. In the mid-1970s, when the American industry was at the height of its success, it held 60 percent of the world market, 95 percent of the domestic market, and half of the European market, but only a fourth of the Japanese market. Since then worldwide production has continued to grow (reaching about $30 billion in 1987), but the United States is no longer leading the

A summary report of the Commission's Semiconductor, Computer, and Copier Industries Working Group. A longer working paper by Don Clausing et al., "The U.S. Semiconductor, Computer, and Copier Industries," appears in *The Working Papers of the MIT Commission on Industrial Productivity*, 2 vols. (Cambridge: MIT Press, 1989).

growth. By 1987 the American share of the world market had shrunk to 40 percent. Europe too had fared poorly, with its share dwindling from about 15 percent to 10 percent in a decade. The big winners were the Japanese, whose global market share almost doubled in 10 years from 28 percent to 50 percent.

The erosion of the U.S. position is even worse than these figures suggest, because both the American decline and the Japanese progress are steepest in some of the most advanced and important semiconductor markets and technologies. Japanese firms now hold 40 percent of the world market for microprocessors, 65 percent for microcontrollers, and 40 percent for application-specific integrated circuits (ASICs), a high-growth market. The slippage is also severe in research and development for future technology. U.S. builders of capital equipment—the tools needed to make semiconductors—are fighting for survival, while Japanese competitors expanded their share of the market from 10 percent in the 1970s to 35 percent in 1987.

In 1987 Japanese semiconductor manufacturers supplied more than 90 percent of Japanese demand while taking over 25 percent of the American market. The United States is now a net importer of semiconductors, and 5 of the 10 largest semiconductor producers are Japanese. The semiconductor market is now bigger in Japan than in the United States.

Relative performance in research and development has also changed dramatically. The United States is still leading in many areas of theoretical research but trailing in applied research and development. With the help of national collaborative programs, the Japanese have moved ahead in a number of key technologies. These include X-ray lithography, which may be essential to the production of finer circuit patterns by the mid-1990s; gallium arsenide, a semiconductor with a more complex structure than silicon but with an intrinsic speed advantage (five times the electron mobility); superconducting devices, which also suggest a possible way to boost circuit speed, particularly in large computers; three-dimensional integrated circuits, which could help to increase circuit density and also have the potential for unique circuit functions; and integrated optoelectronics and solid-state lasers, which are increasingly important in advanced telecommunications and consumer electronics. A 1987 study by a Defense Science Board Task Force concluded that the United States continues to lead in only three of more than a dozen critical semiconductor technologies surveyed.

Japan has won more than 80 percent of world open-market sales of the most widely used integrated circuit in digital equipment, the dynamic random-access memory (DRAM). Invented by Intel in the United States and once made exclusively by several U.S. producers, DRAMs are now offered domestically only by Micron Technologies, a small Idaho firm, and Texas Instruments, which makes most of its devices in Japanese factories. (IBM and AT&T also make these chips, but only for their own use.) DRAMs have the densest circuitry of any integrated circuits, with simple cells that are replicated hundreds of thousands or millions of times. Thus, advances in fabricating these chips are at the leading edge of technology for integrated-circuit production. Manufacturers who successfully move to the next level of density in DRAMs can then apply similar fabrication techniques to other devices.

Another Japanese triumph is less widely known but is probably just as important: the Japanese have equaled or surpassed all world competition in many types of capital equipment, materials, and services important to the semiconductor industry. These areas include packaging, automated assembly equipment, various ultrapure materials, some categories of fabrication equipment, and such specialized procedures as the making of masks, the stencil-like patterns for chip fabrication. IBM's new semiconductor facility at East Fishkill, New York, was built with Shimizu as a construction consultant. Japanese firms supply nearly half of Intel's masks.

The loss of U.S. leadership across a wide range of semiconductor technologies in the short span of about a decade has enormous implications. Semiconductors are the basic building blocks for a rapidly expanding spectrum of high-growth, high-technology industries that touch every market sector: business, industry, consumer products, and defense. They are the most critical components for computers, telecommunications, factory automation and robotics, aerospace, radar, and many consumer products. They provide controls for still more products, including automobiles, appliances, machine tools, and military equipment.

In electronics, system capabilities are limited by device characteristics. The nation that produces the most advanced devices can produce the highest-performance systems and thus attain world leadership in huge downstream markets. The advantage is magnified if the latest chip developments are kept away from outsiders; this is already happening in Japan, where both semiconductor devices and the computers and other electronic systems built from them are generally made by the same huge, vertically integrated companies. The rapidity of the Japanese advance and the American retreat and the emphasis of the Japanese on those sectors with the greatest potential for the future suggest that without dramatic structural changes, the decline of the U.S. industry will not only continue but will accelerate.

It is tempting to attribute the entire turnabout to the Japanese government's assistance to this industry, its protection of the domestic market, and its encouragement of aggressive exporting. Undoubtedly these actions were critical to Japan's success, but other important factors must also be taken into account in any effort to halt or reverse the trend.

Many of the industries studied by the Commission are mature, concentrated, and unionized, made up of companies that tend to have rigid management strategies. The case of semiconductors demonstrates that American competitive difficulties extend to the dynamic, entrepreneurial, generally nonunionized high-technology sector as well. Indeed, the structure of the U.S. industry may be a major cause of its weakness.

Many innovations have come from smaller U.S. firms backed by venture capital. But as products have matured, these American companies, most of which make only semiconductors, have been competing against Japanese producers that are divisions of large, diversified conglomerates. These are stable firms that absorb a significant fraction of their semiconductor output internally and provide the financial strength needed to compete strongly in a volatile marketplace.

The Japanese competitors tend to be stronger than American open-market producers in such areas as product optimization, design for manufacturability, fabrication methods, and quality.

Some large U.S. firms do make semiconductors, but only for internal use (IBM, AT&T, and the Delco division of General Motors). The open-market segment of the American industry has not been rationalized either through consolidation or by mergers with large systems or equipment manufacturers.

Long-term strategies aimed at maximizing global market share are typical of Japanese firms, whereas American producers emphasize short-term profits. American companies frequently sell or swap advanced technology to boost profits, and they subcontract manufacturing to Japanese companies to reduce costs. Japanese companies also invest in innovative American start-ups, and thereby gain valuable new technology, while the Japanese government generally prohibits American investment in their firms.

Coordinated national R&D programs have enabled the Japanese to take the lead in important emerging technologies. The U.S. industry received heavy early support from the Department of Defense, but the Department's focus has shifted to strictly military needs, which have diverged from commercial requirements.

The structures of the U.S. and the Japanese semiconductor industries

The semiconductor industry has evolved very differently in the United States and Japan. The Japanese industry is a relatively stable oligopoly. Semiconductor production is dominated by large, diversified, vertically integrated firms such as NEC, Hitachi, Fujitsu and Toshiba, with semiconductors contributing only 10 to 25 percent of total revenues. These firms use roughly a fourth of their semiconductor production for their own systems and equipment, which range across the electronics spectrum from computers, communications, and robotics to consumer products. As a result, they constantly push their semiconductor affiliates to provide them with advanced devices that can enhance their competitive position.

The Japanese conglomerates are confederations of companies (*keiretsus*). The companies within a group have close alliances (including mutual stock ownership) with one another, with large Tokyo banks and other financial institutions, with their suppliers, and with the federal government. The Japanese government has protected the industry from foreign competition by helping to control imports and prohibiting most direct foreign investment. Personnel practices, including lifetime employment, keep turnover low. Semiconductor operations are almost always headed by engineers or scientists with strong technical backgrounds.

The Japanese providers of semiconductor capital equipment, materials, and services are also large, diversified firms. In some cases the semiconductor producers themselves participate in these markets; other suppliers are major companies with expertise in the relevant optical, chemical, or mechanical technologies. For example, automated photolithography systems are built by large camera companies, such as Canon and Nikon. NEC owns half of Ando, a maker of test equipment, and Fujitsu owns 22 percent of Advantest, another test-equipment manufacturer.

In the United States a two-part semiconductor industry has evolved consisting of "captives" and "merchants." The captives, such as IBM, General Motors (Delco), and AT&T, make semiconductor devices for internal use but mostly refrain from market competition. (AT&T has attempted some open-market sales of integrated circuits since deregulation of the telephone industry and has recently started taking production contracts for other large U.S. firms. IBM may be considering a similar move.) The open-market merchant industry, which once accounted for 70 percent of U.S. production and dominated the world market, is a structurally unstable, fragmented, highly entrepreneurial sector. Most American merchant producers are young, relatively small firms that often depend on semiconductor sales for all of their revenues. Market leadership, employee loyalties, and supplier relationships are transitory, and annual employee turnover has averaged 20 percent across the industry.

The capital equipment and service sectors in the United States parallel the semiconductor sector in its entrepreneurialism and fragmentation. There are a few stable, reasonably large equipment firms (such as Perkin-Elmer in photolithography and Teradyne in test equipment) along with hundreds of smaller firms, many of them start-ups. In 1986, 55 percent of the American firms supplying capital equipment and services to the semiconductor industry had sales of less than $5 million, and many of them were on the verge of failing.

Why the U.S. semiconductor industry remains fragmented
The emergence of many innovative start-up companies in the early phases of an industry is not unusual. The history of the automobile industry provides an illuminating example. In the youth of the industry at the turn of the century there were dozens of small, innovative automakers that dazzled both the public and the venture capitalists of the day. As it happens, most of these high-technology leaders were European firms. When the industry had matured, however, the successful companies were General Motors, Ford, and Chrysler. In spite of abundant dynamism, excitement, and famous names, the small European builders faded quietly from view.

The parallels with the present situation in the semiconductor industry hardly need to be pointed out. The entrepreneurial firms of the U.S. merchant industry have remained innovative, but they cannot keep up with their much larger Japanese rivals in other aspects of business practice: design for manufacturability, optimization of products and processes, and quality assurance. The Japanese producers also have the advantage of taking a longer, more strategic view of the industry, and of course they have far greater financial resources and marketing power.

The smaller American merchant firms have in the main neither consolidated by merging with one another nor joined with large equipment or systems firms to form vertically integrated producers. A few of the U.S. chip makers are older companies that have retained some other lines of business. Motorola makes communications equipment, but it sold its television operations to Matsushita in the 1970s. Texas Instruments still provides goods and services to the oil industry; it has also expanded downstream into computers and consumer products, but with limited success. Among firms founded as merchant producers of semiconductors, perhaps the clearest candidate for vertical integration is Intel. IBM made an investment in Intel, but more to ensure chip supply than to vertically integrate, and then sold off part of its stake during an industry slump. Intel on its own has also marketed a few downstream products, but on a very small scale.

Why hasn't the American industry been rationalized so as to more closely match the strengths of the formidable Japanese competition? To find an answer, it is instructive to examine the history of the industry in the United States.

The pattern for the American industry began to take shape in the 1950s, when AT&T, which had been the strongest force in the early semiconductor business, agreed as part of an antitrust settlement to license its patents and to refrain from open-market competition. To fill the void left by AT&T's departure, dozens of small firms sprang up, many headed by defectors from large, established companies, including AT&T itself. One of these start-ups was Shockley Semiconductor, formed in Northern California by William Shockley, a coinventor of the transistor. Shockley wanted the company to concentrate on a device known as the Shockley diode despite the opposition of bright young scientists on the staff. Eight of the disaffected younger men left Shockley to start Fairchild Semiconductor, which, over the years, spawned dozens of other start-up companies in the region south of San Francisco that came to be known as Silicon Valley. One of the other Fairchild founders was Robert Noyce, later coinventor of the integrated circuit. (The other coinventor was Jack Kilby of Texas Instruments.) Noyce eventually left Fairchild to help form Intel, and numerous firms were later spawned in turn by defectors from Intel.

Growth of the early industry was spurred by U.S. defense needs. The smaller thrust of American rockets compared with Russian boosters in the 1960s limited the weight that could be lofted, and so the Department of Defense pushed for the development of semiconductor and then integrated-circuit technology to reduce the weight of missiles and satellites. Defense procurement demanded technology more advanced than that for commercial uses and was not sensitive to costs. The military often paid for research and development and for early production experience and frequently demanded second-sourcing of new devices.

By the mid-1970s the military had ceased to provide substantial, commercially useful support through its R&D and procurement spending. Military demand declined from about 50 percent of U.S. semiconductor production in 1965 to about 15 percent a decade later, and the technology sought by the Department of Defense began to lag rather than lead commercial uses. Also, as a result of Congressional action, defense procurement policies shifted away from generic research and development toward strictly military technology. This shift reduced commercial spin-offs, while at the same time defense procurement remained insensitive to manufacturing costs.

Other government policies also probably contributed to the fragmentation of the industry. Antitrust policy discouraged industrywide cooperation. The tax treatment of capital gains and other tax policies gave small firms lower capital costs than large ones and allowed start-ups to offer higher effective compensation for key personnel (especially through stock options).

Another factor that helped to keep the industry fragmented was a strong venture-capital community, particularly in the San Francisco area. Regulatory changes in the early 1980s encouraged a surge in venture-capital flows just as the industry's growing stature and the need for large-scale investments made stability more important than ever. The larger, more mature firms (including Motorola, Fairchild, Intel, and AT&T) suffered major disruptions as entire advanced-development groups broke away to form new companies (a practice that gave rise to the term "vulture capitalism"). The new firms were often quite innovative at first, sometimes pioneering whole new sectors of the business. Then after two or three rounds of venture-capital financing, they would sell stock to the public, which made the founders overnight multimillionaires. Later the companies frequently languished and fell behind the fast-moving technology.

Such instability and high turnover encouraged the American companies to focus on short-term objectives. Technology leakage was seen as inevitable, both because of defections and also because it was easy to reverse engineer innovative products by etching away circuit patterns layer by layer and photographically copying them, a technique used with great success by Asian imitators. Personnel raiding was rampant, with some companies offering $1,000 to anyone bringing in an employee with needed skills. Every effort was made to cash in quickly on any technological advantage. The companies manufactured offshore in low-wage regions rather than make capital investments. They licensed technology to both domestic and overseas producers. (Since the Japanese market was effectively closed to American-made semiconductors, selling technology was seen as the only way to generate revenue there.) The business went through boom-and-bust cycles: periods of scarcity and rising prices were followed, often in only a few months, by glutted markets and dramatic downturns. Companies without the financing to tide them over hard times risked bankruptcy. Under these conditions of uncertainty, manufacturers cut back on research and development and avoided making long-term commitments to suppliers or customers. Massive layoffs were common, which undercut any feeling of loyalty to the firm. There was little training of employees, and the knowledge that is so important to being competitive in a high-technology industry was often lost through defections or layoffs.

The U.S. merchant industry tended to be parochial. Executives felt that they could rapidly generate new technology, while Japanese competitors tried to catch up using technology previously licensed to them. They failed to monitor Japanese progress and had excessive confidence in the collective dominance of the American industry.

The withdrawal of larger firms

For 20 years a pattern of instability, high mobility, and frenzied formation of new ventures has been considered critical to the industry's success. When, occasionally, small firms were acquired by large conglomerates (for example, Mostek by United Technologies and Zilog by Exxon), the results were usually disappointing. The common sentiment of those in the field was that such a highly creative, fast-paced industry requires the fervor and quick decision making of a start-up company. The careful planning, orderly structure, and financial and policy controls typical of large corporations were considered to be the route to failure.

America's major electronics companies did not simply ignore the semiconductor revolution in the 1950s and 1960s. Several vertically integrated manufacturers, including General Electric, RCA, Honeywell, and Sylvania, attempted to establish themselves in the merchant market. For one reason or another all of these efforts came to naught. Large firms that acquired semiconductor manufacturers also ran into difficulty. The new owners sometimes shuttled aside the engineers who managed the firms and installed management with financial expertise but with little knowledge of the technology or the business. This practice was very different from the Japanese approach, in which top management generally came up through the technical ranks.

One early example of a disastrous failure was the acquisition of Philco by Ford (circa 1960). Philco made television sets and appliances, had just entered the computer business, and had started a semiconductor operation, all in the Philadelphia area. A nearby R&D laboratory was developing new technology, including innovative semiconductor devices, large-scale computers, and optical readers for the postal system. Philco's vertically integrated structure, along with Ford's financial strength, provided a close parallel to the Japanese model that emerged later. Ford concentrated much of the decisionmaking for these businesses at its Detroit headquarters, however, where its emphasis was on strong financial controls. Under Ford's stewardship all of the businesses rapidly declined and were eventually sold off or abandoned. Ford shifted its high-technology efforts to the steadier, more lucrative military and aerospace sector (an option not available to the Japanese companies).

General Electric similarly had strong capabilities in semiconductors in the early 1960s and recognized the growing importance of the new technology for appliances, controls, electrical equipment, factory systems, and computers. At the time General Electric's laboratories rivaled the capabilities of such world leaders as AT&T's Bell Laboratories and IBM in developing new semiconductor technology. However, General Electric was then governed by a strong profit-center concept, under which every business unit had to justify itself economically. Operating on this imperative, General Electric eventually abandoned most of its semiconductor business (except for power devices) as well as computers (except for process-control systems). More recently General Electric reentered the integrated-circuit business with the acquisition of Intersil. On the other hand, when General Electric acquired RCA, most of RCA's semiconductor operations were sold, and RCA's innovative Princeton Research Laboratories (responsible for such important developments as the television camera tube and complementary metal-oxide-semiconductor [CMOS] integrated circuits, which are becoming the most widely used in the industry) were transferred to Stanford Research Institute (now SRI), a contract research firm. In late 1988 most of the remnants of General Electric's revived integrated-circuit business were sold to Harris Corporation.

The role of IBM in the American semiconductor industy has already been mentioned. While IBM remains the world leader in semiconductor production, it has chosen to produce devices only for its own use, a decision that remains controversial within the company. IBM's failure to participate in the open market robbed it of an opportunity to amortize capital equipment and research and development over a larger production volume. The decision also kept the company from sharpening its skills in the commercial marketplace. Another industry IBM chose not to enter was that for the equipment used in semiconductor fabrication. Although this equipment was simple in the early days of integrated circuits, it has become increasingly complex. Concern about the health of this industry in the United States has led IBM to take a very strong part in the recent formation of Sematech, a joint government-industry effort to upgrade U.S. production capabilities.

How Japan has overtaken the United States

Initially the United States provided the creative new product and fabrication technologies that drove the industry's progress in both Japan and the United States. Until the late 1970s Japanese firms imported American technology and capital equipment to serve their domestic market, while restricting both imports of chips and foreign investment. (A few investments were permitted, but generally through joint ventures; an exception was Texas Instruments, which was allowed to set up a wholly owned subsidiary in return for access to critical patents.) Japan generally refrained from exporting during this period. Many U.S. firms, both large and small, licensed technology to Japan; they acquiesced in market restrictions perhaps in part because they controlled the rest of the world market.

When the Japanese moved into the global market, they operated under a government-coordinated strategic program that encouraged exports, rewarded investments in future productivity, provided competition but discouraged unproductive distributional conflict, and continued protection of the domestic market. The earliest producers of solid-state devices, such as Sony, aimed primarily at the consumer-electronics market. In the 1970s, recognizing that Japan could not be strongly competitive in computers and other electronic systems when their integrated-circuit technology trailed that of world leaders by a year or two, the Japanese launched a successful national program to raise the technical capabilities of their giant electronics firms. Soon they matched the technological level of their American and European competitors, and more semiconductor innovations began to flow from the Japanese companies, particularly in manufacturing and process techniques.

The American decline began about a decade ago, when the industry started shifting from an emphasis on rapid innovation in the development of small-scale devices toward the manufacturing skills required to mass-produce the more elaborate chips exploiting very-large-scale integration (VLSI). The newer technology demanded large capital investments, expanded research and development, and huge product-development projects. This tilted the competitive advantage to large, stable, well-financed companies—most of which were in Japan—rather than the smaller American merchant firms. VLSI also required closer relationships between device suppliers and final systems producers, another advantage for the vertically integrated Japanese companies.

The United States continued to be strong in product innovation, and the Japanese continued to buy American technology from cash-strapped firms and to invest in pathfinding American firms. One example of the latter phenomenon is LSI Logic, the largest American maker of gate arrays (a form of custom integrated circuit) with 1986 revenues of $190 million. In 1981 LSI Logic licensed its technology for chip design to Toshiba, which now holds a larger share of the world gate-array market than LSI Logic does. More recently Kubota, a Japanese machinery manufacturer diversifying into high-technology markets, bought a 20 percent stake in MIPS Computer Systems for $25 million. MIPS was the first merchant vendor to offer an advanced microprocessor chip for reduced-instruction-set computing (RISC). (MIPS subcontracts manufacturing of the device to Matsushita.) In return for the

Kubota investment, MIPS agreed to share its technology with the Japanese firm.

Independent venture formation and mass defections are almost nonexistent in the Japanese semiconductor industry. Personnel raiding is rare and considered unethical. Salaries are controlled, and when companies invest in research and development and training, they are confident of receiving the benefit. Supplier relationships tend to be stable and long-term, with considerable technology transfer between buyer and seller. Since systems companies also have semiconductor affiliates, device prices in the merchant market have to be reasonable, or the buyer might switch to in-house production. The systems groups constantly demand advanced devices to keep their products competitive, and the semiconductor producers are also highly export-oriented. Also, the business is coordinated by the government to minimize wasteful duplication of effort: companies are encouraged to specialize in different market segments, and imports are controlled, remaining at a little over 10 percent in 1988.

The outlook for the semiconductor industry

The world semiconductor market is projected to grow from about $30 billion currently to perhaps $200 billion by the year 2000. This alone would be enough to make the decline of the industry in the United States of great concern. But semiconductors also play a vital role in many other important industries, including computers, instruments, communications, automobiles, machinery, and factory systems. Loss of the semiconductor business could contribute to the decline of other critical industries that depend on semiconductor devices for their competitive advantage.

The U.S. government has belatedly tried to deal with part of the problem. One well-meaning action was to impose import penalties on Japanese semiconductors (DRAMs in particular). Unfortunately, the trade restrictions have merely forced the Japanese to accept hundreds of millions of dollars in additional profit for DRAMs, and they have hurt American makers of computers and peripherals. The hoped-for reemergence of American DRAM production has been slow in coming because of the need for huge investments in fabrication facilities in a volatile marketplace. Another measure was the creation of Sematech, the joint effort by industry and the Department of Defense to help the United States maintain or regain leadership in fabrication technology, production techniques, quality control, test equipment, and related fields. Although some feel that Sematech's emphasis may be too strongly biased toward military needs, the prime sponsors assert that their intention is to make it a commercially oriented enterprise. To match the Japanese competition, American merchant suppliers will have to boost their skills in production, design optimization, and quality control as well as keep pace in fabrication methods.

The traditional structure and institutions of the U.S. industry appear to be inappropriate for meeting the challenge of the much stronger and better-organized Japanese competition. The merchant industry remains too fragmented, and the biggest producer, IBM, has not been selling in the open market. The technological edge that once enabled innovative American companies to excel despite their lack of financial and market clout has disappeared, and the Japanese have gained the lead. One promising development is the possible opening up of the big captive producers: AT&T and IBM are giving signs that they may be more willing to sell to other U.S. firms, even competitors. It remains to be seen if this will be a major factor in the future.

Without some dramatic realignment of the American merchant industry, its decline is likely not only to continue but to accelerate. The conventional economic prescriptions, such as tax credits, guaranteed procurement, import quotas, and industrywide R&D funding, are unlikely to have much success; in fact, they might impede structural rationalization by propping up the existing inefficient system. To be effective, policies must be aimed at correcting the industry's weaknesses. Incentives need to be shifted to encourage longer time horizons (including long-term relationships with suppliers and customers), to increase the profitability of productive investment compared with the gains available by liquidating assets, and to help ensure that developers can gain long-term benefits from proprietary technology. Policies should encourage structural rationalization, less personnel turnover, and more training. For example, R&D grants might be dispersed over a long period to firms with pension plans that encourage long-term employment. The grants could carry provisos to ensure that employees who remain with the firm will benefit from results of the research (perhaps through an employee stock plan). Imaginative new policy initiatives will be essential if the United States is to halt the decline of the merchant semiconductor industry.

The Computer Industry

In the early days of the computer industry American manufacturers accounted for a very large proportion of all the computers installed worldwide. Exports grew steadily, reaching $3.2 billion by 1977, while the United States imported no computers at all. During this period IBM was responsible for more than 40 percent of the industry's shipments, and its revenues were eight times those of its nearest competitor. Mainframe computers, by far the largest segment of the market, were made predominantly by IBM and the so-called BUNCH companies (Burroughs, Univac, NCR, Control Data, and Honeywell).

In the past decade or so the structure of the American industry has changed significantly, driven primarily by the steadily increasing capabilities of the semiconductor chips from which computers are built. The minicomputer enjoyed increasing popularity, fueling a large expansion by Digital Equipment Corporation (DEC) and vaulting it into the number-two spot behind IBM. The recent merger of Burroughs and Univac to form Unisys has altered this ranking. Newer sectors of the market that have grown rapidly include personal computers and powerful desktop workstations, along with microcomputer peripherals. The small but important supercomputer sector, led by Cray Research, has also grown fast, and supermicrocomputers have begun to move into the low end of this sector. IBM's steady growth has continued, but its mainframe competitors have not kept pace as this sector has matured, and there are signs of weakness in parts of the minicomputer sector as well.

The computer industry is one of the few remaining industries in which the United States continues to have a positive trade balance, but the trend is downward. The U.S. surplus in global computer trade peaked at $7 billion in 1981, fell to less than $3 billion in 1987, and is projected to be close to zero in 1988. (These figures exclude computers manufactured and sold abroad by such U.S. manufacturers as IBM and DEC; IBM World Trade alone has sales of some $25 billion, and much of this is produced abroad.) A major reason for the decline in the U.S. trade balance is the rapid rise of Japanese imports. Japan reached parity with the United States in bilateral computer trade in 1982, and it achieved a surplus of more than $4 billion by 1987. Meanwhile, the American share of the Japanese market has steadily declined. IBM's market share in Japan peaked at about 40 percent in the 1960s but has shrunk to less than 15 percent now. DEC holds only 1.6 percent of the Japanese market, compared with 6 percent of the world market.

Japanese penetration of the American market has been less dramatic in computers than in other industries, such as automobiles and consumer electronics. A factor that has stabilized the market, particularly for mainframe makers, is the incompatibility of competing lines of equipment. Cumulative investment by users in applications software, training, and vendor-specific peripherals have made switching to a competing system costly, time-consuming, and risky. Also buyers choose computers on the basis of the application software available for a machine, and the United States has been much stronger than Japan in software. Once a mainframe firm builds a customer base, it is difficult for other vendors with different architectures to penetrate it, even with superior performance or lower prices.

Still, Japan's excellence in manufacturing has enabled it to obtain contracts to build systems that are relabeled and sold by an expanding number of American and European computer vendors. Japan has also had greater success with peripherals, which are mostly electromechanical devices such as printers and disk drives that are much more interchangeable, particularly below the mainframe level. The value of the U.S. peripherals market is about equal to that for processors; the Japanese have captured perhaps 30 percent of the overall peripherals market and over 70 percent of the market for microcomputer peripherals.

The compatibility barrier has also been overcome in microcomputers. Because microcomputers use standard operating systems and readily available microprocessors, offshore competitors, particularly in Japan and other Asian nations, have been able to develop clones (especially those that conform to the IBM PC "standard") and sell fully compatible machines in the U.S. market. Even American-made computers now have a significant overseas content. American computer makers now obtain more than half of their semiconductors from Japan, buying most of them from the same diversified companies that are their competitors in the computer market.

Software exceeds both processors and peripherals in market size. The packaged-software industry sold about $30 billion worldwide in 1987, but this amount is dwarfed by the value of software developed within organizations. Estimates vary widely, but in the

United States alone the cost is probably in the area of $150 billion to $200 billion annually (including salaries and other costs for programming groups). American packaged software remains strong globally and has remained fairly invulnerable to import competition in the United States.

On balance, the U.S. computer industry is thriving. IBM continues to grow even though the mainframe market is maturing worldwide, and companies such as Sun, Apple and Compaq are riding the wave of popularity for workstations and personal computers. Some of the younger sectors, however, may be more vulnerable in the future, because they are made up predominantly of smaller, venture-capital-backed firms dependent on narrow product lines that are sold mostly in the United States. Peripheral makers already face strong import pressure, and most of them now manufacture offshore. Japanese competitors tend to be large, diversified, financially strong conglomerates that market globally (such as NEC in microcomputers, Canon and Toshiba in peripherals, and recently Matsushita and Sony in workstations).

The history of the U.S. computer industry

The computer industry began in the United States only a little over 35 years ago. IBM soon became so dominant that in the 1960s the industry was known as "IBM and the seven dwarfs." (The competition included RCA and General Electric as well as the BUNCH companies.) RCA tried to sell computers equivalent to IBM's at lower prices, but software and service were vital to buyers, and IBM invested far more than RCA in these areas. RCA finally abandoned the market in about 1970, writing off losses of some $300 million. General Electric had already withdrawn from all but its process-control computers, also taking large losses, when computer sales failed to reach financial objectives under its profit-center concept.

The U.S. government attempted through legal action to keep the early industry competitive. Although it might seem strange in today's environment of international competition, the Justice Department brought suit against IBM under antimonopoly statutes with the intention of breaking the company into pieces (a prospect that some competitors feared would create a set of "little" IBMs that might exercise even greater market domination). The suit cost many millions of dollars and lasted more than 10 years, only to be dropped in 1982 after the industry had gone through significant changes.

Even though the case was never resolved, government pressure did have some effect on the marketplace. For example, IBM modified its practice of "preannouncing" computers, which, it was alleged, had discouraged users from buying competitive systems already on the market. IBM was also forced to provide competitors with technical details of its new systems, because they so often set de facto standards in the marketplace. Probably the most important impact was the requirement that IBM unbundle software, selling it separately rather than making it part of the total cost of a system. This decision helped foster a competitive packaged-software industry in the United States, which later grew dramatically with the rise of the personal computer.

The government also provided R&D support for the industry, mainly through the Department of Defense. An early program to build the world's fastest computers in the late 1950s led to Univac's LARC and IBM's Stretch computers. Although IBM's entry was considered less successful, the project provided a test bed for many design concepts used in its highly successful commercial systems of the 360 and 370 generation. After Congress pressed the Department of Defense to fund only research and development aimed at strictly military needs, there was less opportunity for commercial spin-offs. Even so, as discussed in chapter 8, the Defense Advanced Research Projects Agency played a big role in such advances as time-sharing, computer networks, and artificial intelligence, and it continues to support advanced computer research mainly in university laboratories.

As the mainframe sector matured, competitors in the United States and Europe attempted to cut costs by turning to Japan to manufacture their systems; more recently they have increasingly marketed computers designed as well as built in Japan. Unisys, for example, buys mainframe components from Hitachi; Honeywell began by contracting with NEC only for manufacturing but now sells primarily NEC-designed computers; Amdahl markets IBM-compatible computers built by Fujitsu; and National Advanced Systems (a division of National Semiconductor) sells Hitachi computers. Japanese companies also build computers for such major European vendors as Siemens, BASF, and ICL.

In the past few years remarkable advances in VLSI have brought rapid changes in the computer industry. Following the rise of minicomputers came the explosive growth of microprocessors and personal computers based on them. Powerful desktop workstations emerged for computation-intensive tasks such as computer-aided design. Performance gains in supercomputers expanded their use in aerospace, scientific research, and weather forecasting. In R&D laboratories and companies backed by venture capital, multiprocessor computers are being readied to extend performance through architectural advances rather than simply by use of faster circuits. The industry is also putting more emphasis on distributed computing, with clusters of personal computers linked to one another and to nearby mainframes as well as to remote systems. This trend is increasing pressures by computer users for more standard interfaces and operating systems.

The mainframe sector now appears to be slowing down. Most of the newer fast-growth market sectors have been launched by start-ups, which later were joined by the major computer companies. The advanced-workstation market was pioneered by Apollo and Sun, and personal computers by Apple, with IBM and DEC making later entries. Tandem pioneered transaction-oriented, fault-tolerant computers, a market that IBM eventually joined by selling systems built by Stratus, a Tandem competitor. Convex launched the supermicrocomputer sector. And a number of start-up companies, such as Sequent, Encore, and Thinking Machines, are now offering systems based on new multiprocessor architectures.

The first generation of start-up ventures in the minicomputer field—such companies as Prime, Data General, and Wang—are beginning to display behavior similar to the stagnation in the mainframe arena: slow growth, occasional serious downturns with layoffs, defections of talented employees, increasing dependence on external suppliers, and low shares of newer markets.

The progress of the Japanese computer industry

Japan's early computer industry struggled into existence with the help of the government and Nippon Telegraph & Telephone (NTT), the domestic telephone monopoly (recently privatized). In the 1960s NTT's supplier "club" (*dendenkosha*) included giant firms like Fujitsu, NEC, and Hitachi, as well as a few others such as Oki. The suppliers made specialized machines for NTT's needs, using devices based on technologies a couple of years behind the Western state of the art.

A government-coordinated effort was started in 1965 for a Japanese system to supersede IBM's 360 line. Thereafter Japanese firms were urged by the Ministry of International Trade and Industry (MITI) to buy computers from domestic suppliers. A MITI

Vision of the Future issued in 1970 envisioned a shift to low-energy industries, because Japan was so vulnerable to cutoffs in energy supplies. Eventually this impetus led to the very successful VLSI circuit program of the late 1970s and early 1980s, which had the major objective of enabling Japanese computer makers to become world leaders. As a result, several major Japanese companies are now strong in both semiconductors and computers. The four largest computer producers—Fujitsu, NEC, Hitachi, and Toshiba— are also the largest semiconductor vendors.

Another MITI-coordinated project in the supercomputer field has led to very high performance supercomputers, but these machines have had little success in penetrating the U.S. market so far, partly because of software incompatibility but also owing to the efforts of the U.S. government.

Japanese firms trying to market microcomputers with proprietary operating systems in the United States ran into software-compatibility problems similar to those that slowed their penetration of mainframe processor markets. NEC, however, has had great success selling microcomputers in Japan (where it has gained over 70 percent of the personal computer market) and in the rest of Asia. Its approach was quite different from that typically taken by American firms in launching a new product line. Before entering the market, Koji Kobayashi, NEC's chairman, reportedly spent a year making personal contacts with software developers, retailers, resellers, and users and learning the marketplace. The strategy based on this firsthand knowledge was aimed at stimulating market growth, primarily through large demonstration centers featuring a wide range of NEC equipment. The Tokyo center at Hibiya cost $5 million, covers 30,000 to 40,000 square feet, and employs 44 people. Yet it sells no computers. Such centers allow potential customers to learn about NEC products and then buy them at low cost from discount stores, such as those in Tokyo's Akihabara district. This approach enables NEC to sell about half of its major personal-computer product (about 1.4 million units per year) through simple retail stores rather than higher-level outlets with computer-knowledgeable salespeople.

The Japanese computer companies have the advantages typical of other Japanese industries. Their strategies are focused on growth rather than short-term profits, and they pay out little in dividends to shareholders. Unlike American companies, which must finance growth primarily through retained earnings, the Japanese companies try to minimize book profits because of high corporate tax rates. Instead, they finance growth primarily through tax deductions (particularly for depreciation) and secondarily through loans and equity funds (generally from large financial institutions or other firms in their corporate families). Over a five-year period, for example, Fujitsu, the largest Japanese computer vendor, financed 34 percent of its growth from depreciation allowances, with only 17 percent from loans. Moreover, in 1986 Fujitsu paid 4.5 percent interest on loans, about half the rate paid by large American companies. Labor costs were also about half those for American computer companies, mainly due to lower salaries for professional and factory workers and dependence on a much younger labor force, particularly low-paid young women. This cost advantage has been reduced somewhat by the decline of the dollar.

By 1986, Fujitsu, Hitachi, and NEC together were spending more than double what IBM spent on research and development. Their investments in plant and equipment were also higher, with about 20 percent going for such productivity-enhancing equipment as factory automation, robotics, and material-handling systems. At the same time they were turning more to outside suppliers for subassemblies, peripherals, and the like. Combined sales of the Japanese computer companies reached $53.6 billion in 1987 (at 138 yen per U.S. $1), compared with worldwide revenues of $54.2 billion for IBM. Japanese computer sales are growing rapidly, while IBM's are leveling off.

Japan's fifth-generation program, started in the early 1980s, was another concerted effort to increase capabilities in advanced computer research, particularly artificial intelligence. Slated to cost some $500 million over seven years, the program had an ambitious goal: to develop the technology for intelligent machines that could solve complex problems, including automatic language translation, speech recognition, and pattern recognition. Although the program has fallen short of its technical goals, it has succeeded in what may have been its prime objective: to increase the number of leaders in advanced computer research and development in Japan from a handful to probably several hundred. The personnel were drawn from and returned to Japan's computer companies, which should become even more formidable competitors in tomorrow's markets as a result.

According to a MITI *Vision for the Year 2000*, the information industry will produce 21 percent of Japan's GNP by the turn of the century. (MITI includes within the information industry semiconductors, consumer electronics, data processing, and information and telecommunications equipment and services.) This plan envisions 2,000 new businesses and the creation of 2.5 million new jobs (44 percent of all new jobs in Japan over the period), with half of the jobs in the computer industry. In the past the Japanese have been quite successful in meeting the targets developed for such plans. The goal of achieving economic primacy in the worldwide information industry seems logical and strategically sound for a country like Japan, as it requires little in the way of raw materials and depends primarily on a good supply of intelligent, well-educated people.

The outlook for the U.S. computer industry
Although the U.S. computer industry remains strong, the outlook will not continue to be bright without strong initiatives. Computer builders in Japan, South Korea, and Taiwan are gaining the research and development, market-research services, and technical skills they need to be strong international competitors. Innovative start-up companies in the United States frequently sell their technology to their Asian competitors, and provide market knowledge and even direct assistance. (Larger American firms tend to be much more careful with proprietary information.) Many industry standards that evolve in the United States serve as virtual product specifications for imitative competitors with lower manufacturing costs and shorter development times. American universities conduct nonsecret research and development and are educating a growing cadre of Asian engineers. All this openness is an essential cost of leadership and the free-enterprise system. We do not advocate that American universities and laboratories should shut the door on basic research, but some greater protection of American advances as they get closer to products may be in order.

In the long run, the U.S. computer industry must take some steps to ensure that it remains competitive as challengers gain strength. Production capabilities need to be retained and upgraded, particularly in view of Japan's growing investments in productivity-enhancing equipment and its reputation for high-quality production of both electromechanical and electronic equipment. The recent decision of Matsushita to have Tandy produce its Panasonic microcomputers in its Fort Worth plant may be the first sign of a reversal of the trend toward offshore manufacturing. U.S. computer makers must also work cooperatively with domestic chip suppliers to ensure that they will continue to have access to the latest microcircuit technologies, which are crucial to the performance of their systems. Software leadership is another important requirement, especially as Japan develops "software factories" and improves the programming tools that can make software development faster and more efficient.

The Copier Industry and the Case of Xerox

The copier industry grew from a single product in 1959 (the Xerox 914) to a business with $22 billion worth of shipments worldwide in 1987. Out of this total Xerox (exclusive of Fuji Xerox) has retained about a third, $7.5 billion. Xerox pioneered the market for xerographic copiers based on inventions purchased from Chester Carlson, an independent inventor. The company had no competition until 1970; then IBM entered the market, to be joined by Kodak in 1975.

During the 1970s the Japanese also entered the U.S. market, competing for sales of the least-expensive machines, those capable of making 30 copies per minute or less. Xerox's share of this market segment fell dramatically, from about 80 percent in 1975 to a low of 8.6 percent in 1984. Initially Xerox did not respond to the Japanese challenge in this low–profit segment of the market. By 1979, however, the company had begun a program to lower manufacturing costs and to raise quality, which has since enabled it to retake some of the low-end market (its share rose to 11.2 percent in 1986). It has also sought to protect its dominant position in the high end.

Why did this strong, pioneering American company allow Japanese competitors to take over a major segment of its market? How did it then shift its strategy to regain some of the lost market and to protect against further encroachment? The history of the Xerox case is an important one, because it provides a view of a prototypical U.S. company, hugely successful in its early days when it pioneered a rapid-growth market and then faltering as the market matured and as manufacturing costs, product differentiation, and customer satisfaction became crucial in a highly competitive marketplace. What makes the Xerox case particularly interesting is the company's success in reversing its decline.

How Xerox lost the low end of the copier market

Haloid Corporation, the tiny Rochester, New York company that became Xerox, risked all in taking Carlson's xerographic inventions from the laboratory to the marketplace, almost going bankrupt before introducing the 914 in 1959. But the machine created a new market that grew far beyond the fondest hopes of the early backers.

Engineers working on the 914 and its successors considered the complex xerography process to be somewhat like black magic, and they concentrated on designing a machine that would just work rather than rationalizing their designs to maximize quality and reduce manufacturing costs. Without competition, there was no pressure to go back to refine the design. Instead, the company's entire development effort was focused on expanding into larger and faster copiers, which were perceived to be more profitable. By 1970 Xerox had extended copying speed up to 60 per minute.

When IBM entered the market in 1970, Xerox was busy pushing the speed of its large copiers toward 120 copies per minute, and the competition did not evoke any change in strategy. In 1974, when the 120-copy-per-minute 9200 was introduced, Xerox's machines still were very big, were very expensive, had a tremendous number of parts, and were not noted for quality or trouble-free operation.

Then in 1975 Kodak entered a very profitable part of Xerox's business, the upper-middle-speed range, with its Ektaprint copier. Kodak's expertise in chemistry enabled it to achieve superior copy quality. Furthermore, its first machine featured a completely automatic recirculating document handler, a product Xerox had been planning for some time. Xerox shifted a major portion of its development resources toward meeting these challenges from Kodak.

During the 1970s Xerox was also trying to expand into computers and office systems, using the copier business as the cash cow to finance this thrust. Scientific Data Systems, a computer company, had been acquired in 1969 for $900 million with hopes of getting into the mainframe-computer business. Later Xerox's Palo Alto Research Center (PARC) developed a wide range of innovative technologies for microcomputers, networking, and allied areas, but the company failed to convert this unique, advanced technology into commercially successful products.

While Xerox management was diverted by domestic competition at the high end of the copier market and by its ventures beyond copiers, Japanese companies were penetrating the low end of the copier market in the United States with high-quality, low-cost products. Xerox executives knew that their low-end machines were not competitive with models from Canon, Minolta, Ricoh, and several other Japanese companies. They got an early warning from their own overseas affiliates: Rank Xerox in Europe, a little more than half owned by Xerox, and Fuji Xerox in Japan, owned half by Fuji Photo Film Company and half by Rank Xerox. Fuji Xerox operated fairly independently, taking Xerox designs and converting them into products for Japan with slight modifications (such as those for different electric service and paper sizes). By 1975 Fuji Xerox was losing market share in Japan because of intense competition led by the Japanese camera companies. To continue to compete, Fuji Xerox had to stop depending on the basic Xerox designs and instead develop its own products, and it needed to launch a company-wide quality-control program. This effort proved to be a great success for Fuji Xerox, leading to a resurgence of profits. Even today most of the low-end Xerox copiers sold in the United States come from Fuji Xerox.

These events were a clear signal to Xerox management that its products were not competitive with the better Japanese models. Yet as the Japanese invaded the low-end marketplace throughout the 1970s, Xerox offered no response. It was not until 1979 that the company finally awakened to the seriousness of the Japanese challenge. Although the low end of the business was not very profitable, the Japanese could use positions established there as beachheads to expand into more profitable areas. Moreover, the success of the new product designs produced by Fuji Xerox showed that some worthwhile advances were taking place in Japan. As a result, in 1979 Xerox began sending study missions to Japan to analyze Fuji Xerox and other Japanese companies.

Xerox was jolted by the findings of these missions. The Japanese could produce copiers at half the production cost, with a development schedule that was half as long and with only half as many people on the development team! The quality of Japanese copiers was also far superior. When measured by the number of defective parts on the assembly line, Japanese quality was 10 to 30 times better than Xerox's performance in the United States. These dramatic findings led to a resurgence in Xerox that is still going on. In retrospect, it is clear that management had enough information in 1975 to recognize the threat and could have launched a response years earlier than it did.

Why Xerox was vulnerable to Japanese competition

With its great success in creating a fast-growth market based on patented xerographic technology, Xerox had little incentive to reduce manufacturing costs, improve quality, or become more responsive to customers. With no competition, quality was not considered a serious problem; in fact, there was even some thought in the company that a large service business was a contributor to profits.

The product-development process was chaotic: it stretched development time, lowered quality, and sometimes raised manufacturing costs. There was excessive reliance on trial and error, which led to the creation of many prototypes. As a result, development laboratories were swamped with prototype hardware, and this made it difficult to improve designs through systematic experiments. There were similar failures to optimize in the development of production processes. Other American companies shared these weaknesses in product and process development. In fact, Xerox was considered a leader in some development methods, even though its approach was clearly inferior to the best Japanese practice.

Xerox designs called for large numbers of parts, they were not well suited to manufacture, and they did not adequately meet to customer needs. Initial concepts were often selected without adequate consideration of alternatives, and often design proceeded with no consideration of production requirements. Although there was an Advanced Manufacturing Engineering liaison organization to link design with production, it served more as an added layer of people between designers and the factory rather than as an effective interface group. Also, suppliers were not brought into the early design process.

Production operations also had weaknesses. There was excessive dependence on inspection to sort out bad units after production—indeed, after many faulty units may have been produced—rather than using on-line quality control to spot and fix problems immediately. Large inventories were maintained to prevent shortages from stopping production, and Xerox had a large supplier base with multiple sources for most parts.

A severe problem in the company was the large gulf between important functional organizations. Three key product groups (planning, design and development, and production operations) needed to collaborate, yet they did not meet in the corporate structure until the top levels at corporate headquarters. Thus, a product plan was "thrown over the wall" to the design-and-development specialists, who, in turn, prepared their design and "threw it over the wall" to production operations. In many cases the resulting design was difficult to manufacture. Systematic rigidity and a lack of cooperation between groups seriously hindered the company's progress. The lack of cooperation extended to suppliers, which were treated as production houses that made parts in accordance with Xerox designs, often in an adversarial relationship; there was little effort to take advantage of, or to build on, their competence.

There also appear to have been cultural factors that limited the company's ability to cope with change. David Kearns, the chairman of Xerox, complained publicly of the high cost and long training periods needed to change attitudes within the company and to establish new measures of individual and corporate performance. Another factor that may have limited the response to competition in the copier market is the high dividends paid out by Xerox and other American corporations in comparison with Japanese firms. Xerox paid $300 million in dividends for 1986, nearly 65 percent of that year's net earnings. A comparable example is IBM, which paid 43 percent of its 1985 earnings as shareholder dividends. Big Japanese companies pay little or no dividends, which gives them much more internal capital for research and development and for modernizing factories. In an interview with *Electronic Business* magazine in November 1986, Kearns agreed that the Xerox dividend was quite high in relation to profits, but he said that the company was on a growth track that would justify the dividend. He granted that Japanese competitors have some advantages in their financial structure, but he did not see those differences as a major cause of the company's problems. "Excluding the economy, our destiny is in our hands, not someone else's," he commented.

The resurgence of Xerox

Once Xerox management understood the powerful challenge being mounted by Japanese competitors, strong actions were taken starting in 1979 to improve the company's operations. The steps taken included the following:

- Copier development and production were reorganized. New management was brought in from other parts of the company, and the planning, development, and production functions were more closely integrated. A Design For Assembly program was created.

- There was increased emphasis on competitive benchmarking, including comparison tests between Xerox machines and competitive models and also comparisons of Xerox methods with those of world leaders in important activities.

- Employee involvement was greatly increased.

- Leadership Through Quality, a company-wide quality-control effort, was introduced in 1984. In this program 70,000 of 100,000 Xerox employees worldwide were trained over the following three years. Statistical process-control methods were adopted for the factory and for evaluating parts from suppliers.

- Suppliers were brought into the early stages of product design.

- Inventories were greatly reduced, as was the number of suppliers.

- Customer satisfaction received much greater emphasis.

This huge, costly undertaking has brought considerable success. The company cut both its production costs and the number of people in manufacturing by half, and it improved quality (measured in terms of defective parts on the assembly line) by factors of 10 to 30. As a result, the Japanese intrusion into the more profitable part of the copier business has been slowed down. As noted above, Xerox raised its share of the low end of the market to 11.2 percent in 1986 (although it sells primarily Fuji Xerox copiers in this range). Xerox boasts that it is the only American company that has lost market share to Japanese competition and reversed the trend without receiving government assistance. The company's 10 series of copiers, which started with the 1075 in 1982, has been a big success in the marketplace.

The outlook for the industry

Xerox's strong response to Japanese competition should help the company continue to regain lost market share in the United States and should also help make it more competitive in world markets. The Japanese can be expected to continue improving productivity, so Xerox cannot afford to gloat over its recent success.

Xerox remains ambivalent about personal copiers, which have emerged recently in the low-end sector. Kearns has stated that

Xerox has not figured out how to make money on this type of product and that the company will not enter the market unless it can make it a profitable venture. At the same time, he admits that there are internal debates within the company about the wisdom of not being represented in this sector. If personal copiers achieve high quality at low prices, the great convenience of such products could eventually erode the use of central copiers, where Xerox is strong.

Xerox is a contender in the fast-growing desktop publishing market, but it has very strong competition from microcomputer companies such as Apple Computer and the vendors of popular software packages. Facsimile is another area that could eventually have an impact on the copier market. Facsimile transmission was widely adopted sooner in Japan than in the United States or Europe, so that Japanese manufacturers now make about 95 percent of the world's fax machines. The market is now doubling each year in the United States and in Europe, whereas it has leveled off in Japan. Although Xerox sells Fuji Xerox equipment in the United States, Xerox is not a major player in this market.

Fax machines use technology similar to copiers, and some are being used to make copies as well as to send documents over telephone lines. Although current models are not suitable for volume copying, it is possible that business workstations of the future may use the same equipment for personal copying and facsimile transmission, as well as for printing out computer displays. Japanese companies such as Canon are leaders in the laser mechanisms that may be favored for such machines.

Another sector of the copier market that may get a push from the evolution of facsimile machines is color copying. Up to now this has been a small segment with large, very costly machines. Over the next few years the telephone network will go to direct digital transmission, based on the worldwide Integrated Services Digital Network (ISDN) standards now taking shape. High-bandwidth transmission over such lines will make it feasible to send color fax images. Major facsimile producers like Canon in Japan feel that the market success of this service will depend on the wider acceptance of color copying at the same time. Hence, Canon is now pushing a marketing of quality color copying. If this effort succeeds, there may be much greater demand for color copiers at the high end of the market, Xerox's present stronghold.

Xerox is moving to position itself for such future shifts in the marketplace. In recent years, however, it has been Japanese companies in such fields as consumer electronics that have been willing to take the major risks involved in pioneering new market sectors. Their present willingness to absorb losses to establish a personal copier market may be a harbinger of events to come.

G

The Steel Industry

The American steel industry was once the largest, most modern, and most efficient in the world. From 1975 to 1985, however, it suffered declining demand for its products, loss of market share at home, falling production and employment, and low or negative earnings. By 1986 imports had risen to 37 percent of domestic consumption, with the trend accentuated by the strength of the U.S. dollar. (A little more than half of the imports came in the form of steel itself; the rest consisted of steel in automobiles and other products.) Many plants were shut down, and nearly two-thirds of the jobs in the industry were lost. From world leader in steelmaking capacity 25 years ago, the U.S. industry has dropped to third place behind the Soviet Union and Japan.

Even with the recent decline, steel remains a major industry in the United States, with annual sales of $50 to $60 billion, assets of $30 to $40 billion, and employment of more than 200,000 workers. The fate of the industry has serious ramifications for the national economy, because steel is the primary material for such major manufacturing sectors as automobiles, consumer durables, and construction. Steel is also critical to national defense. Almost every piece of military hardware contains steel.

The domestic steel industry has two major segments, the integrated producers and the minimills, which have had different histories and now have different outlooks. The integrated producers are large companies that operate blast furnaces, coke ovens, and complete facilities for making steel from iron ore. The minimills are smaller producers that make carbon steels and low-alloy

A summary of the report of the Commission's Steel Industry Working Group. A longer working paper by Merton Flemings et al., "The Future of the U.S. Steel Industry in the International Marketplace," appears in *The Working Papers of the MIT Commission on Industrial Productivity*, 2 vols. (Cambridge: MIT Press, 1989).

steels in electric furnaces, using scrap as a raw material. The minimills have prospered, on the whole, during the past 15 to 20 years, and they continue to do well today. It is the integrated steelmaking firms that have suffered the most severe economic setbacks.

And yet just when most analysts were about to lay the integrated sector of the industry to rest, many firms reported significant profits in 1987. For the first time since 1974 the industry as a whole surpassed the average financial rate of return for all manufacturing industries, and even exports increased. Through 1988 integrated steel mills and iron-ore mines operated near capacity (albeit a capacity that had been much reduced). Does this represent a fundamental reversal, or is it a temporary change based on such fluctuating factors as currency exchange rates? The answer will depend on how well America's integrated steelmakers adjust to the global marketplace. Examining the causes of the earlier decline provides insight useful in setting future policy directions.

A number of factors were responsible for the economic difficulties experienced by the integrated producers in the early 1980s. Some of these factors were outside the control of the steel industry, including foreign competition, relatively high labor costs, unconstructive government interference, and a shortage of capital to invest in more efficient equipment. Other factors, including a lack of technological foresight, continued operation of inefficient plants, poor labor-management relations, and a lack of cooperation with customers, were the responsibility of domestic industry.

Technology

In the postwar decades the domestic integrated producers lost their technological lead. They failed to adopt quickly the newest technologies, such as the basic oxygen furnace (BOF), continuous casting, and computer controls, as they became available in other parts of the world. And when the advantages of the new technologies became apparent, their adoption was delayed by financial commitments to existing plants and a shortage of investment capital. When cash did become available, other investments often proved more attractive.

Some of the smaller U.S. firms were among the first to adopt the BOF and continuous casting, but most U.S. integrated firms lagged behind foreign producers, in particular the Japanese, in their willingness to adopt new technologies (see figure G.1). Early on,

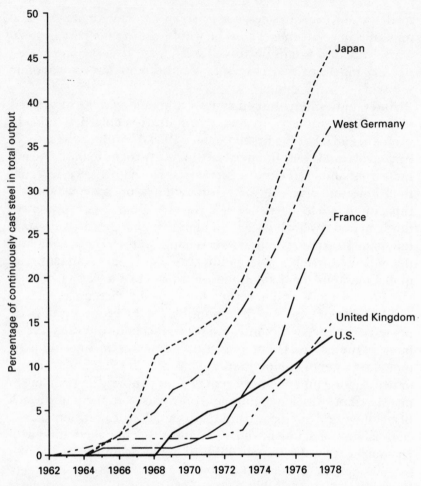

Figure G.1   Implementation of continuous casting
Source: U.S.Congress, Office of Technology Assessment, *Technology and Steel Industry Competitiveness* (Washington D.C.: U.S. Government Printing Office, 1980), p. 131.

this reluctance was not due to a lack of capital or to unwillingness to invest in steel processing. In fact, between 1960 and 1980 the United States and Japan made roughly equal investments in steelmaking. The Japanese, of course, had the advantage of an expanding steel industry, and their steel companies did not have to suffer the financial consequences of premature write-offs of existing plants. But even when investments were made in the United States, a number of modernization programs were stopped short of completion in the face of market uncertainties. Rising costs for labor and capital, together with prices depressed by import competition and overcapacity, made alternative investments more attractive than further spending on steelmaking facilities. Integrated producers chose to diversify into such industries as oil and chemicals instead of upgrading steel plants. As a result, numerous U.S. plants were only partially modernized, which created imbalances in the production stream.

In Japan, by contrast, the Ministry of International Trade and Industry (MITI) coordinated efforts to improve the industry's productivity. The major firms and government representatives met frequently to agree on plans and pricing. To pressure the firms to improve their operations, MITI limited its investments to those firms that could meet certain productivity levels. This policy led to modern, fully automated, well-balanced steelmaking facilities. Because of the resulting technology gap, American integrated mills could not, until recently, match the quality of the newer mills in Japan in some market segments.

The inability of U.S. firms to make needed technological changes has been attributed to the lack of an international perspective and to the mature, relatively inflexible organizational structure and management of the integrated firms. The Japanese steelmakers, on the other hand, scoured the world to find the best technology available. Japan's NKK was helped by an American firm, Kaiser Engineers, when it designed a BOF plant, and both Yawata and NKK sent engineers to Austria for training two or three years before opening their BOF facilities. Japanese engineers and other employees are rotated through assignments in marketing, factory work, basic research, finance, and new product and process development. As they move into management posts, this experience gives them a broad knowledge of the firm's technical and manufacturing capabilities.

The late development of the steel industry in Japan accelerated the adoption of new process technologies by the integrated steelmakers there. Moreover, the uniformity of operations, the structure of the industry, and government-industry cooperation facilitated the transfer of information among companies and plants. The product mix was kept narrow, and the largest of the six Japanese steel firms had no more than four times the capacity of the smallest.

The Role of Government

Through MITI the Japanese government actively promoted the international competitive position of its steel industry. The firms were able to improve their performance by jointly purchasing raw materials and by coordinating the production and sale of steel in the international market through trading companies.

In contrast, the U.S. steel industry had troubled relations with the federal government. In the opinion of many observers, the confrontation between President Kennedy and the U.S. Steel Company in 1962 established de facto price controls on steel for more than a decade. The industry was unable to raise prices during periods of high demand, and this constraint limited profits and hence the amount of capital available for modernization.

Interfirm cooperative efforts to economize were thwarted by inconsistencies in federal antitrust policy. The Department of Justice worried that consolidated operations might unfairly restrict competition in the domestic market, and so American companies were not able to work together as were the Japanese companies. More recently the Department of Justice and the Federal Trade Commission have become more receptive to mergers and joint research projects by steel firms, but the industry remains uneasy, because this policy could be discontinued at any time.

Capital Investment

The American steel industry had difficulty generating the capital needed to deploy the most modern technology. Only twice since 1960 has the rate of return of the U.S. steel industry exceeded the average of all manufacturing industries. When investments were made in U.S. steel plants, the equipment frequently took longer to get into operation and tended to be more costly than in other countries. It takes four or five years to plan, design, and build a new blast furnace in the United States, in comparison with three years in Japan and two years in Korea. And in the United States, construction costs average $1,700 per ton of finished capacity, whereas the range is from $700 to $1,500 in other countries. One reason for these differences is that labor agreements in the United States discourage construction for more than 8 to 10 hours a day, while building usually continues 24 hours a day in other countries.

Coordination between capital-equipment suppliers and the steel companies is much better in other countries than it is in the United States. The nature of the problem is illustrated by the basic oxygen furnace and the special refractory brick needed for its lining. Refractory makers in the United States tend to be small firms with little R&D capacity. For the most part, the big steel companies refused to share information on their steelmaking techniques with them. In Japan, by contrast, MITI led an effort to upgrade the quality of refractory materials and the facilities necessary to produce them, and the major steel firms worked closely with these suppliers to develop and produce superior products. American producers of capital goods have frequently been unable to supply the domestic industry with state-of-the-art equipment. Instead, the steel industry has had to go offshore to obtain competitive facilities.

Another consequence of the economic difficulties experienced by U.S. integrated producers is their diminishing ability or willingness to support activities with long-term payoffs. American steel companies have been cutting back on research, spending less than 0.5 percent of sales on research and development in recent years. Meanwhile, Japanese steel companies have been increasing their R&D efforts in spite of waning sales to the United States (due to the dramatic shift in exchange rates) and the loss of most shipbuilding to South Korea. Kawasaki Steel recently opened a large high-technology laboratory in Chiba, for example. The American companies' failure to compete in research and development today will make it more difficult for them to compete in production methods and products in the next decade.

Technology Management

As in other industries, the effectiveness of the American management style has been called into question by comparisons of the U.S. integrated producers with their Japanese counterparts. American companies tend to make problem solving a specialist function, with troubleshooters from a central location being made available to deal with production problems. The Japanese steelmakers (and the U.S. minimills) rely much more on operating personnel to solve production problems as they arise. On the other hand, research departments in many U.S. steel companies in the 1960s and 1970s lost interest in processes and process development because those areas were considered the province of operating personnel. It was just those neglected areas that were to prove crucial in the competitive race of the 1980s.

In recent years a number of integrated companies have formed joint ventures with Japanese firms, especially to produce cold-rolled sheet or galvanized sheet for the auto industry. At National Steel, which is partially owned by Japan's NKK, the Japanese partner has set up technical teams of its own people and put them in National's plants, even though both firms have their own research centers. Groups at each plant handle research, engineering, and production planning for that plant, a practice that replaced the former practice of sending in a traveling "fire fighting" team whenever trouble arose. This policy is at least partly responsible for the recent turnaround at National: the company's steel-making productivity has increased 40 percent, output of prime product has risen 20 percent, and downtime has decreased 50 percent.

Customer Relations

In comparison with Japanese practices, cooperation between American integrated steel producers and their customers has been weak. For example, the steel and auto industries have not been able to agree on standardized tests and marking systems for steel products. Steel companies complain that auto companies do not have effective supplier-rating systems. Just-in-time delivery has proved difficult to implement because American auto companies vacillate in their demands for steel.

Vigorous efforts are now being made to improve cooperative relations, particularly with the largest consumer of steel, the auto industry. Steel suppliers have also organized Product Application Centers (PACs) to help auto companies in developing prototypes of new parts, and automakers have agreed to buy steel from the firms providing the support.

Labor-Management Relations

A major burden for the American steel industry has been the antagonistic tone of labor-management relations. Until 1982 labor unions won major concessions from the steel industry in wages, benefits, and work rules. The financial consequences of these concessions, especially those resulting from the terms of the Experimental Negotiation Agreement of 1973, contributed to the erosion of U.S. competitiveness. In exchange for a no-strike pledge, the agreement guaranteed a minimum annual real-wage increase of 3 percent and a cost-of-living adjustment clause as a standard feature of future contracts. The resulting rise in labor costs has been blamed for increased imports from nations where producers paid less for labor per ton of steel.

The recent financial distress of the steel industry has limited union demands. Labor has accepted reduced hourly rates and greater flexibility in work rules and manning requirements. In addition, layoffs of both blue-collar and white-collar workers, the closing of the older, inefficient plants, and a shift in exchange rates have favored U.S. producers and made their labor costs competitive with those in all but the developing countries.

Specialty-Steel Producers and Minimills

The structure of the U.S. steel industry has changed dramatically over the past 20 years. Although the actors remain the same, the roles and market shares of the integrated firms, minimills, and imports have been transformed. Integrated producers are losing market share both to domestic minimills and to imports.

Another segment of the U.S. steel industry that has taken on new prominence is made up of producers of specialty steels like stainless steel. Although specialty steels account for only about 1.5 percent of the market, they generate about 10 percent of the profits because they are higher value-added products. The specialty steel firms have benefited from U.S. import quotas on stainless sheet and strip, and they expect to maintain growth of about 2.2 percent per year between 1985 and 2000.

Technological development has been faster in the specialty-steel segment than among the large integrated producers. In the 1960s the United States pioneered a state-of-the-art specialty steelmaking process, the argon-oxygen decarburization process. Various forms of this process are currently used in virtually all stainless-steel processing, and the method has future implications for the processing of low-carbon steels. The specialty segment also led the industry in energy-saving measures (such as the use of off-peak power and natural gas direct from the wellhead) and in statistical process control. Such specialty firms as Universal-Cyclops and Allegheny Ludlum have been highly market conscious. For example, Allegheny tracks and analyzes the detailed production costs of even small amounts of custom grades of stainless steel.

Minimills have also been aggressive in adopting new technology. Advances in electric-arc-furnace technology during the 1970s helped minimill operators to move into markets for many low-grade steels, like small structural and bar products. Subsequently the more aggressive minimills have started to compete directly with the integrated producers for a share of the higher-quality end of the market. The minimills have developed a formula for success that relies on constant marketing updates and customer contact, weekly production schedules to ensure synchrony with market changes, changes in the production mix to match the market, and substantial sales to steel service centers, which provide reliable information about changes in the needs of customers.

The typical minimill has taken advantage of the inherent flexibilities of electric furnaces, continuous casting, and modern rolling facilities, which allow for fast changeovers from one product to another. Incremental improvements in process technology are more easily made under the minimill regime of simple sequential production of a limited number of products than in a complex integrated system. Minimills conduct little research on their own, but they search worldwide for the best steelmaking technology before investing in new equipment.

The Outlook for the Industry

Most long-term forecasts of the consumption of steel anticipate decreases or stagnation in developed countries, but demand for all types of steel products should grow in developing countries, particularly Taiwan, China, India, Korea, and Brazil. It is unlikely that American integrated firms will develop a long-term export position in the growing markets of developing countries. If the dollar remains weak, however, U.S. firms could expect some temporary increase in exports to these markets.

Foreign producers continue to hold a significant share of the market for carbon-steel products that could be produced by the U.S. integrated firms, like bars, structural components, rail, and pipe. The American firms have responded to this situation by shifting their product mix to increased output of high-value-added sheet products, which are produced only in small quantities by the steel industries of most developing countries. Another significant trend is seen in the growth of joint ventures between U.S. producers and steelmakers from other industrialized countries.

Minimills can be expected to increase their penetration of markets now held by the integrated firms, including those for such products as semifinished slabs, cold-finished bars, plates, rails, tubes, pipes, and sheets. Some steel-industry analysts anticipate that minimills could produce half the steel in the United States by the year 2000. This estimate seems overly optimistic, however. Several factors are already slowing the growth of this sector of the industry, including use of the minimill concept by integrated companies, a flattening of market growth, imports from foreign minimills, limited availability of high-grade scrap, and a lack of investment capital for the advanced equipment needed to tap new markets.

In the years since 1982 the integrated carbon-steel industry has undergone a painful restructuring but in the process has greatly improved its competitive position. Labor productivity and average product quality have been improved by closing a number of outdated and high-cost facilities, by the adoption of new work rules, and by the introduction of new technology. The integrated steel industry is to be applauded for the great strides it has made, although a number of problems remain. These include product quality at some plants, production efficiency, labor-management relations, and capital cost. The ability of the integrated producers to make improvements in these areas will determine their long-term competitive position with respect to both foreign producers and the domestic minimills.

H

The Textile Industry

The U.S. textile industry, one of the oldest and largest sectors of the nation's industrial economy, has experienced upheaval in recent years. Imports have captured more than half of the market for apparel in the United States, and they seriously threaten other large segments of the industry. In the first half of the 1980s, 282,000 jobs were lost in the industry's two biggest sectors: apparel (employment down 11 percent) and textile mill products (down 15 percent). With the emergence of dynamic, export-oriented textile and apparel industries in newly industrialized areas such as Hong Kong and Korea, and with the prospect of a huge, modernized Chinese textile industry, many analysts fear that the casualties of the past decade may be only a prelude to more severe losses.

The competitive weakness in the textile industry will not be remedied simply by increasing conventional labor productivity. In fact, textile and apparel firms have been among the U.S. leaders in productivity gains during the past 15 years. Between 1975 and 1985 textile-mill productivity increased an average of 5.6 percent per year, more than any other manufacturing industry. In apparel, productivity growth for the decade was a reasonably healthy 2.7 percent per year. For these industries, investment in labor-saving equipment can be only part of a strategy for improved competitiveness in domestic and international markets.

The question of what should be done for the textile and apparel industry has been hotly debated in recent years. One view holds that this sort of labor-intensive, "sunset" industry should be allowed to wither away as resources and capital are shifted to more prom-

A summary report of the Commission's Textile Industry Working Group. A longer working paper by Suzanne Berger et al., "The U.S. Textile Industry: Challenges and Opportunities in an Era of International Competition," appears in *The Working Papers of the MIT Commission on Industrial Productivity*, 2 vols. (Cambridge: MIT Press, 1989).

ising "sunrise" industries. The opposition view recommends that trade barriers be strengthened to protect the industry while it automates some production operations and shifts others offshore. Both views hinge on the belief that a labor-intensive industry cannot survive in a high-wage country in the face of market competition from aggressive low-wage producers.

The Commission's research has revealed serious flaws in these popular views of the causes of the decline and the options for the future. Although some parts of the industry do appear to be irretrievably lost (particularly the manufacture of low-cost, low-quality, labor-intensive products), the rest of the industry does not have to share this fate. In fact, contrary to either of the commonly cited options, the Commission's Textile Industry Working Group concluded that the potential exists for a revitalized, albeit restructured, domestic textile industry. And if broad segments of even this aging, labor-intensive industry can be revived by adjusting structure, strategies, and technology, this has important implications for the entire industrial economy.

The Structure of the Industry

The textile-industry complex can be divided into four main sectors: fibers, textile-mill products, apparel and other end uses, and associated industries (such as textile machinery and chemicals). The fiber sector was once dominated by natural fibers (primarily cotton), but now synthetics make up about 75 percent of the American market. The United States is the largest supplier of synthetic fiber in the world, and 90 percent of U.S. output is generated by 10 multinational firms (led by Du Pont, Celanese, and Monsanto). This high degree of industrial concentration is due to the capital-intensive nature of synthetic-fiber production.

The textile-mill-product sector—which includes all operations involved in converting fiber to fabric as well as products such as sheets, towels, floor coverings, tire cordage and rope—is much less concentrated. A little more than a fourth of U.S. sales come from the 12 largest producers, led by Burlington Industries, Milliken, and J. P. Stevens. The other three-fourths of textile-mill production comes from small and medium-size firms and plants. For example, there are about 450 weaving, 500 knitting, and between 300 and 400 tufting mills in the United States, most of them in the Southeast. Overall, there are more than 6,000 firms producing textile-mill products. These firms fight for their shares of a low-growth market, battling one another as well as foreign producers to maintain output, sales, and profits.

Textile-mill products have three major uses: they are incorporated into apparel, home furnishings, and industrial and specialty products. Historically, apparel producers dominated, but this is no longer the case, as home furnishings have increased their share of fiber consumption in recent years. Industrial uses are also multiplying. Apparel is made primarily in small firms: some 15,000 firms, over 70 percent of them employing fewer than 50 workers, operate about 21,000 plants.

There are a number of other industries closely associated with these three major sectors, the most important of them being textile machinery. The United States once had one of the largest textile-machinery industries, but in the 1970s many of the oldest and largest firms closed their doors or were forced to restructure and reduce their scale. About 500 American firms still produce textile machinery. Only one claims to provide a full line of machines. Most produce specialized products or parts and accessories. Only in controls and finishing equipment do American firms hold a dominant share of the domestic market.

Performance of Industry Sectors

The American fiber industry has been a strong performer, with large American firms holding powerful positions in the global synthetics market. U.S. production of synthetics nearly doubled between 1970 and 1984. At the same time, however, the American share of the global market was actually declining: it fell from 32.5 percent in 1970 to 24.9 percent in the mid-1980s because of an explosion in worldwide capacity and increasing competition from Japan and several newly industrialized nations. The American fiber industry (both natural and synthetics) has traditionally competed by producing standard products at high efficiency and low cost, a strategy now threatened not only by foreign competition but also by changes in production technology and by market pressures for greater flexibility.

Textile-mill products have fared much worse than fibers: the U.S. trade balance plummeted from a $43 million surplus in 1974 to a deficit of nearly $2.5 billion in 1984. During that period imports of cotton fabrics climbed from 267 million to 463 million pounds, while U.S. exports dropped 70 percent (to 65 million pounds). Imports of synthetic fabrics just about doubled in the same period (to 159 million pounds), while exports declined by 17 percent.

Similarly, in apparel the market share claimed by imports more than doubled between 1974 and 1985, reaching 48 percent of the U.S. market (in square yardage). The rate of market erosion shows no sign of diminishing. Exports have done little to compensate for the trend: at their peak in 1980 they amounted to only 3 percent of U.S. apparel production.

Among associated industries, applications of nonwoven fiber materials for medical, industrial, and other uses are growing. The textile-machinery sector, on the other hand, has declined precipitously, sinking from 93 percent of the domestic market in 1963 to 55 percent in 1987. American builders of textile machinery have fallen far behind the state of the art. For example, they produce none of the shuttleless looms that have revolutionized weaving. More than 92 percent of the export sales of U.S. textile-machinery producers are replacement parts for machines sold years ago rather than new machines.

Market Protection, Wages, and Regulation

The relatively poor performance of the textile industry in the United States is commonly attributed to inadequate levels of trade protection, higher wages, and tougher regulation in such areas as safety and pollution. There is abundant evidence, however, that these have not been decisive.

Protection. During the past two decades industrialized nations have made varied efforts to limit the importation of textiles and apparel. For example, the European Economic Community (EEC) moved only slowly to implement the first Multi-Fiber Arrangement (MFA), regulating the international textile trade; a subsequent surge in imports cost the EEC nations an estimated 430,000 jobs between 1971 and 1978. During those years imports into the United States grew at a much lower rate, partly because of the speed with which this country moved to sign bilateral agreements with major exporting countries. By the early 1980s the EEC nations reached a consensus on MFA implementation, and in successive rounds of MFA negotiations they pressed for restrictions to protect the European market for certain textile and apparel products.

European quotas focus on eight broad categories that encompass a majority of textile and apparel imports (cotton yarn, cotton fabrics, synthetic fabrics, T-shirts and knit shirts, jerseys and pullovers, trousers, blouses, and men's woven shirts). In the U.S. quota system these products fall into 75 separate categories. While the U.S. system of narrow categories allows for more effective targeting of quotas, it also has a serious disadvantage. An aggressive exporting nation can quickly shift its export mix away from products with tight quotas into new products not yet subject to quotas. For example, the Hong Kong apparel industry, confronted with quota barriers for its conventional product lines in the late 1970s, "discovered" ramie, a rough linenlike fiber seldom used in apparel and therefore not yet under quota. Suddenly the U.S. market was flooded with ramie-blend imports from the Far East as producers and retailers promoted ramie as a new high-fashion fiber.

Between 1981 and 1986 Europe gained some control over the rate of growth in imports of textiles and apparel. Imports to the EEC from dominant suppliers declined by 5 percent overall and by more than 7 percent in the eight key categories. At the same time the dam burst in the United States. Imports of most quota items rose at a rate of more than 6 percent per year, and total import levels increased at an average annual rate of 15 percent.

The different MFA systems of protection in Europe and the United States are no doubt partly responsible for the different trends in imports. Another important factor is the role of the State Department and of foreign-policy considerations in American trade policy for textiles. In the case of some countries, such as China, the Soviet Union, and the Philippines, trade considerations have generally taken a back seat to geopolitical calculations.

Japan provides another contrast to the United States. In Japan imports have risen significantly in recent years; last year for the first time Japan became a net importer of textiles. Through the 1970s and most of the 1980s, however, Japan has been more successful than European nations and the United States in slowing the tide of imports. Moreover, that success has been achieved without resorting to protective legislation. Import duties on textiles and clothing are low (about 8 percent versus 20 to 25 percent in the United States); there are no import quotas (except on raw silk and silk thread); nor is there legislation regulating the country of origin of imports. What protects the market is a network of informal but tight links among the various segments of the Japanese industry that

make it difficult for foreigners to penetrate the market. Bureaucratic barriers, such as tough customs inspections, also work to
reduce imports. These mechanisms are beginning to break down
as Asian yarn, fabric, and apparel producers are improving quality
and becoming more sophisticated. More than 40 percent of Japan's
sweaters are now imported, and knitwear penetration is already 80
percent. But during the chaotic 1970s and 1980s, the "hidden"
barriers to imports served Japan well.

Since the Europeans and the Japanese appear to have had more
success than the United States in restricting imports, does it follow
that better strategies to keep out imports would save the American
textile and apparel industry? The Textile Industry Working Group
concluded that the answer is no. Many of the industrial nations that
have been most successful in maintaining a strong and competitive
textile and apparel complex are countries with the least effective
protection. Moreover, in the product lines in which the Japanese
and the Europeans are dominant, competition from lower-wage,
lower-quality rivals is not a significant factor.

The textile industry of the United Kingdom, with perhaps the
most elaborate protectionist arrangements in Europe, has been
among the least successful of European textile industries. West
Germany, in contrast, has been the European nation most resistant
to protectionism and most committed to free trade. Import penetration of the West German market is high; indeed, Germany is the
second largest importer of textiles and apparel (after the United
States), and on a per capita basis it is the largest, importing about
twice as much as Britain and France and four times as much as the
United States. Yet West German exports have risen from 11 percent
of production in 1960 to 48 percent in 1984. West Germany is now
the third largest textile exporter (after Italy and Hong Kong).

The firms responsible for the export successes of the European
and Japanese textile industries operate in market niches where
they appear to experience little competition from low-cost producers; the protection afforded by import quotas are therefore hardly
relevant. These niches are typically higher value-added products,
in which considerations of design, quality, and rapid adjustment to
changing trends play a major role. Italy, for example, restricts
imports from Hong Kong and Korea (but not from neighboring
low-wage countries such as Portugal, Greece, and Turkey). But
Italy's strength as an exporter is in high-quality, high-fashion
knitwear, woolens, and other apparel, not in lower-quality, mass-
market goods.

Similar examples can be found in Japan and several other nations. Protection is not the key to success and appears only to buy time. Firms that adjust their strategies so they can compete even without trade barriers can be quite successful; those that do not adjust either fail or are eventually forced to adapt.

Wages and Regulation. In the past, there was some truth to the charge that lower wages and less regulation in other developed nations put the U.S. textile industry at a disadvantage. Today, however, the prosperity of the textile industries in those countries is based on market strategies, technology and sound labor policies rather than on the exploitation of human and natural resources. For example, districts in northern Italy, where low-wage workers once operated their own machines in garages and spare rooms, now have thriving industries that are highly unionized. Management has adjusted its strategies to remain competitive despite higher labor costs. In contrast, companies that fled south to lower-wage areas have done poorly because they could not keep up with the steadily rising quality and service standards of international markets.

West Germany and Japan have similarly abandoned the practice of trying to wring the maximum amount of work from the smallest possible wage. In West Germany textile firms responded to growing import pressure in the 1970s by moving abroad for cheaper labor. German firms bought finished goods in low-wage countries and sold them under German labels; they invested directly in foreign firms; and they developed offshore processing arrangements so that they could contract out the labor-intensive parts of production to low-wage producers and retain the skill- and capital-intensive tasks. In the 1980s, however, the firms shifted their strategy, focusing on higher-quality and higher-priced goods and abandoning much of the offshore production of the previous decade.

In Japan a high proportion of firms in the textile business are small-scale family enterprises that can survive periods of economic downturn through self-sacrifices by owners and employees. However, low and flexible labor costs have not been the dominant component of the sector's competitive strategy. Japanese producers have been moving out of those segments of the industry where labor costs are the sole basis for competitive advantage. Their strength derives from other factors: small producers join together in cooperatives and have links to big firms and to trading companies, from which they receive information, orders, and financial assistance. Government assistance to small businesses, along with incentives for restructuring, have also helped the Japanese textile and apparel industry to remain an important factor in the economy, generating almost 6 percent of manufacturing value added.

Neither low wages nor other forms of backwardness (like low levels of environmental and workplace protection) explain the comparative success of the European and Japanese textile industries. Environmental regulation in Europe and Japan is as stringent as it is in the United States, and if regulatory actions impose greater costs on American firms because of the greater age of the American industrial plant, as some argue, there is no consensus that the difference has had any adverse affect on competitiveness. The inflexibilities that higher levels of unionization and more restrictive labor legislation impose on European firms are more constraining than any comparable U.S. practices. In Italy and France, for example, layoffs and plant closings over the past 15 years have been highly regulated and require collective bargaining with unions. The organization of shift work and weekend operations, working conditions on the shop floor, subcontracting, and training, all of which are generally within the realm of managerial discretion in the United States, are subject to negotiation and bargaining in most European countries.

In sum, in industrialized nations with relatively healthy textile and apparel industries, success can no longer be attributed to rapacious exploitation of human or natural resources. Low wages or weak regulation may explain the capital accumulation of earlier periods, but today the success stories must be explained by other factors.

Critical Factors for Success

In the textile and apparel complex of industries, labor-saving capital investment is a necessary condition for competitiveness, but not a sufficient condition. A high-investment strategy may fail because investments are made in less than optimal production technologies. Moreover, certain factors not reflected in conventional productivity statistics appear to be crucial to long-term success. These include the appropriateness of a firm's market strategy and the density of interfirm and interindustry linkages. The Commission has found that in the case of fiber, textiles, and apparel, these "invisible factors," as they have been called by some researchers, can help explain why certain national industries, and certain firms within those industries, are more successful than others.

Automation Strategies. One strategy for competitive success in the global market for textile and apparel, particularly in the large U.S. market, is based on automation and capital investment. For this strategy to succeed, however, a high rate of capital investment must be coupled with an emphasis on technological innovation, a commitment to research and development, and mechanisms for rapid and sophisticated technology transfer. Investment alone will not suffice, because companies from lower-wage areas can purchase new technology (little of which originates in the United States) as easily as American firms can.

Successful firms both in this country and abroad tend to accept longer payback periods and see innovative investment as part of their competitive edge. Although textile and apparel firms have traditionally rejected investments with an expected payback period longer than six months or a year, some industry leaders use a different calculus. The Milliken Corporation often makes investments with three-year payback. As one manager put it, "Roger Milliken doesn't do anything for today's gain because he doesn't need today's gain." The Russell Corporation, an integrated manufacturer of sweat suits and sports uniforms, spends more than 10 percent of sales on capital equipment and claims that it does not even calculate payback periods. A recent $25 million investment in automated ring-spinning machinery was justified not in terms of return on investment but in terms of the jump the firm would get on the competition in the production of high-quality combed cotton yarn.

Expenditures on research and development are traditionally low in the textile industry; in 1985 the industry average was only 0.5 percent of sales. However, in many of the most successful large firms a key element of competitive strategy is a commitment to new product and process development through research and development. Milliken channels about 2 percent of sales revenue into research and development, focusing on innovations that will give the company first-entry and proprietary rights. Large Japanese firms also tend to commit significant resources to research and development, including research with very long lead times. The menswear firm Melbo has worked with K. Kawabata of Kyoto University for 15 years to develop a system for evaluating the "touch" of a fabric. Melbo and other Japanese apparel producers now use Kawabata's system in making purchasing decisions for fabric and machinery.

If a firm wants to compete in the world market primarily through an automation strategy, it must be able to develop and maintain a technological edge over its competitors. Just as an emphasis on innovation and research and development can provide that edge for larger firms, information can be critical to the success of smaller firms, particularly information about advanced technology. In this area American firms appear to be at a distinct disadvantage. In Japan small producers have access to information on technology through a network of regional textile-research institutes and industry cooperatives. The research institutes provide advice, assistance, and fashion-trend information to small firms that cannot afford their own R&D staffs. For example, the Osaka Research Institute has been working on a computer program to make punch cards for jacquard looms, an innovation that would reduce pattern-preparation time for smaller firms. The cooperatives provide technical assistance, financial guidance, and advice to small and medium-size firms. For example, the Nishiwaki Weavers' Cooperative, consisting of 716 member companies, helps local weavers keep up with new technologies and also promotes rationalization of the fragmented local weaving industry. Institutions of this type have not evolved in the more competitive, less cooperative U.S. industry.

Niche Production Strategies. In the United States, where mass production has triumphed more completely than in any other nation, the textile industry has generally pursued a strategy of long-run production of standard goods for the mass market. To keep production costs low, firms have pushed for higher and higher productivity by installing faster looms and using synthetic fibers or inexpensive, high-production yarns. A narrow focus on keeping wages low and fighting unionization has also been central to competitive strategy.

This strategy paid off handsomely for decades, until imports began to threaten the dominance of American textile and apparel firms in their own domestic market. But endeavoring to be the lowest-cost producer of standardized goods in competition with less-developed nations where wage rates are far lower became a less and less viable business plan. Successful German and Italian firms made the transition away from mass production to a strategy based on identifying a segment of the market, a niche, in which they could compete on the basis of quality, style, originality, or prestige, and not solely on the basis of cost. American firms have been slow to make the transition, and this sluggishness has cost many firms significant market share and resulted in the loss of many jobs.

The success of small Italian firms operating in specialized markets has been widely publicized in the United States. But large firms have also contributed to the Italian success in textiles and apparel by shifting production from relatively undifferentiated goods for large markets to smaller runs of higher-quality goods. For example, Lanificio Ferla, a woolens producer in the Biella area, went through a major restructuring in the 1970s and began specializing in higher-quality fabrics, developing closer contacts with designers and clients, and paying more attention to fashion trends. Throughout Biella the firms that emerged as strong competitive enterprises were those that moved away from integrated production to concentrate on segments of the production process where they had special strengths. Similarly, in Turin, GFT (Gruppo Finaziario Tessile), a large garment manufacturer that had modeled itself after American mass producers, responded to competitive pressures in the 1960s by making shorter runs, producing for more targeted market segments, and creating a highly skilled design and production work force. GFT is now beginning to produce in the United States for the American market.

Parts of the Japanese textile and apparel industry have always been made up of smaller, specialized firms. Among these firms, weaving is broken down into several discrete activities, each carried out by very small firms connected through a complex system of contractual arrangements. Production runs are small: weavers typically produce in lot sizes of 3,000 yards for export and 1,000 yards for domestic consumption. (In comparison, lot sizes as small as 3,000 yards have only recently become available from American manufacturers. A few years ago the average lot size at Milliken was 20,000 yards, and at Dan River 10,000 to 12,000 yards.)

Larger Japanese firms have also pursued a production strategy based on specialization and differentiation. Melbo, the large menswear manufacturer, has used state-of-the-art technology to devise a unit-production system that allows it to make one suit at a time and keep inventory down. Melbo is planning for the day when customers will be able to submit special orders by computer, specifying the fabric, size, style, and delivery date for a suit.

Melbo's use of advanced technology to increase production flexibility, though fairly typical of the way automation is applied in Europe and Japan, is in marked contrast to the American experience. American firms have generally chosen to incorporate new technology into inflexible mass-production systems designed to squeeze out labor content and produce large runs. This has been the case, for example, with unit-production systems and computerized marking and grading. National programs in the United States and Japan to automate apparel sewing illustrate the divergent strategies. The Textile/Clothing Technology Corporation in the United States is focused on automating individual operations performed separately on garments with long production runs. The Japanese automated-sewing project is aimed at more flexible sewing systems, such as development of moving sewing heads that operate in three dimensions.

Why has the United States been so slow to adopt flexible production methods and to seek niche markets? One factor may be the very success of mass production in this country before the late 1960s. Mass merchandising of high-volume products had worked so well for so long that in comparison with Europe and Japan there were fewer specialized producers to emulate and fewer institutional arrangements in place that could promote successful niche strategies.

There have also been major barriers to information flow in the multitiered complex of American textile and apparel firms. Many textile-mill managers, for example, have no contact at all with the apparel firms that use their fabrics. One textile-firm manager related a chance meeting with an executive from Hartmarx, a major menswear manufacturer, who expressed astonishment at the mill's low prices and then indicated a willingness to pay more for special services and features. The sales agent who had been representing the mill to Hartmarx had never discussed the mill's production options with the apparel giant because he thought he could sell more by keeping prices down. Apart from failures to communicate, there is the problem of adversarial relationships. Strong firms in the United States have used their market power to demand price concessions from their suppliers. In Europe and Japan long-term collaborative arrangements with a few suppliers have been more common.

American firms appear to have focused on the wrong issues. While European firms were coming to understand the need for major shifts in their mode of operation and were modernizing and reorganizing to support new strategies based on quality and flexibility, U.S. textile manufacturers continued narrowly to focus on labor costs. They had two goals: protection against imports from low-wage countries and the maintenance of relatively low wages at home by avoiding unions and producing offshore. Neither strategy helped American firms make the changes that would enable them to remain competitive.

Moreover, the single-minded pursuit of low labor costs has led American firms to underestimate the importance of education and professional training. Not one of the U.S. industry representatives interviewed by the Commission considered the educational qualifications of workers a significant factor in firm productivity. In contrast, European and Japanese textile and apparel executives told of process and product innovations that would not have been possible without a high level of worker skill, initiative, responsibility, and general education. One Japanese firm said its workers submit about 6,000 suggestions per year for improvements in manufacturing processes. In France and Italy managers described interactions between designers and weavers that are rare in the United States.

An overemphasis on mass production puts American firms at a disadvantage in competition with other high-wage regions that have developed alternative strategies. It limits flexibility in adopting new technology, the effectiveness of human resources, and the ability to respond rapidly to market shifts. Apparel manufacturers blame much of the import surge on the inflexibility of the American textile industry. For example, one dressmaking firm known for whimsical print patterns makes only 300 of any dress design in a particular color or pattern, using about 1,000 yards of fabric. Although this firm does about 70 percent of its dressmaking domestically, its managers complain that they must import fabric to get the high quality and small batches they need. Makers of men's shirts make the same complaint.

Interfirm linkages. One of the strengths of Japanese industry, including the textile industry, is an intricate network of interfirm and interindustry linkages. In Germany and Italy, too, informal and contractual relationships between firms at different points in the textile complex provide a competitive advantage to all those participating. Linkages between suppliers and customers can reduce inventories and order times, provide feedback about consumer preferences, and lead to product and process innovations. Bottlenecks can be eliminated and production can be rationalized.

In the United States, where competition has always been strong and cooperation limited both by law and by custom, such linkages between firms have been much weaker. When price was all, firms preferred to make short-term arrangements based on price rather than enter into long-term relationships with suppliers and customers. Today some of the most successful firms in the industry have begun to pay more attention to the productivity gains that can be achieved through such relationships. The recent emergence of interindustry linkages is among the most promising developments in American textile production.

Greenwood Mills, for example, recently halved the number of fiber producers with whom it does business, opting for long-term, trusting relations with just two fiber producers. Greenwood has also helped its major customer, Levi Strauss, cut inventory from four weeks to three days by prescreening color shades for consistency and by loading fabric on trucks in the sequence in which it would be used. For another customer, Lee Jeans, Greenwood coordinates loading and delivery to eliminate warehousing altogether.

Apparel, textile, and fiber firms and retailers have recently joined to launch the Quick Response Program, designed to improve information flow, standardize recording systems, and improve turnaround time throughout the system. In effect, Quick Response proposes to create in the United States the kind of efficient linkages that are fostered in Japan by the big trading companies and in Germany by cartels. The program could be an important boon to productivity and competitiveness. Advocates hope that Quick Response will cut the 66-week cycle from fiber to retail in the United States to 21 weeks and thus lower costs and make many imports less appealing. Will Quick Response succeed? According to industry experts, that depends on whether it diffuses down to the high-fashion, quick-turnaround segments of the industry or, like much new technology in this industry, is adapted to suit the needs of firms still committed to mass production.

The Outlook for the Industry

There are signs that the American textile industry is beginning to respond to changes in the global marketplace. Dan River, for example, has reduced its production runs, which were once 10,000 to 12,000 yards per pattern, to the range of 3,000 to 4,000 yards. Finer yarn sizes, up to 80/1, were recently added to the Dan River line, and 5 to 7 percent of shirting is now woven with yarns as fine as 50/1. Dying is also done in smaller lots: more than half the lots are under 1,000 yards.

Specialization is spreading through the industry, even in the older firms. Dan River expanded its line after acquiring the fine-fabric division of J. P. Stevens, which also sold off a number of other divisions so that it could concentrate on household applications. Companies are narrowing the range of products they make but broadening the options within each category. Greenwood has focused on denim production by buying the denim divisions of both Dan River and Pepperell. Springs has become the major producer of piece-dyed broadcloth.

There is evidence of progress in each of the areas identified by the Industry Working Group as associated with superior economic performance in textiles: a shift to niche-production strategies, effective use of new technologies to achieve more flexible production, decentralization and specialization in large firms, and interfirm and interindustry linkages. But the Working Group also observed serious obstacles to broader diffusion of these advances that remain a part of the culture of the American fiber, textile, and apparel industry: short time horizons, weak or hostile interfirm relations, inadequate attention to human resources, and the general dominance of mass production. How the industries adjust depends in large part on the ability of industry leaders and company managers to encourage broad diffusion of successful practices. The external environment is not benign: global capabilities are likely to increase in both developed and industrializing nations, which would make competition even tougher. However, if progress is made quickly in overcoming the identified obstacles, the textile industry complex can be highly productive and profitable with a relatively stable share of domestic and world markets.

Appendix I

Policy Recommendations Presented in Related Studies

The principal purpose of this appendix is to provide a brief summary of the policy recommendations advanced in other recent studies of productivity and competitiveness.

The issue of U.S. competitiveness has received extraordinary attention in recent years. In view of the large volume of literature, primary emphasis here is placed on recent major studies prepared by various groups or committees, including a number of national commissions or councils. Most of the studies covered cut across many industries or economic sectors, consider a fairly broad range of questions, and not only analyze the underlying problems but also offer policy recommendations. Individual contributions, including recent results of academic research, are also cited, where appropriate, both to sharpen and to challenge the basic findings and policy remedies offered by the major studies under review.

The policy recommendations advanced by these studies are varied and far ranging and reflect the diversity of perspectives on the nature of the problem. It is helpful to organize these recommendations into seven broad areas:

- Macroeconomic policies
- Institutional and regulatory reforms
- Science and technology policies
- Capital formation
- Education and training
- Management strategies
- International economic policies

Prepared by Kirkor Bozdogan for the MIT Commission on Industrial Productivity.

Recommendations in these seven areas are summarized below. An effort has been made to provide a fairly representative sample within each area, but the survey is not exhaustive. Sources are cited in the notes.

Macroeconomic Policies

What are the macroeconomic policies appropriate for improving American productivity and international competitiveness? The general answer seems to be to reduce the federal budget deficit and the U.S. balance-of-payments deficit and to increase savings and investment through stable fiscal and monetary policies.

There is a virtually unanimous call for a reduction in the large federal budget deficit. Although many cite the various benefits of such an action, few offer specific recommendations as to how to attain the goal. The Business Roundtable urges that Gramm-Rudman-Hollings targets for mandatory annual budget reductions be respected because they discipline federal spending. Beyond this, the Business Roundtable does not favor any increases in corporate taxes, recommends that spending cuts be broadened to include defense, agriculture, Social Security, and other non-means-tested programs, and urges that "real deficit reduction be the task at hand, not budget process reform and creative accounting."[1]

Observing that the first step in a long-term plan for reducing the federal budget deficit should be a "scrutiny of military spending," the Cuomo Commission goes further and recommends a number of measures to contain federal spending increases. These include fully taxing Social Security benefits for those with incomes above a certain level, taking steps to control the cost of health care (such as requiring doctors and hospitals to limit charges for each patient), and reducing certain farm subsidies that primarily benefit large producers.

In addition, the Cuomo Commission favors a tighter fiscal policy accompanied by a more flexible monetary policy in order to lower interest rates while reducing the budget deficit. To allay fears of inflation, the Commission also urges such measures as voluntary wage and price restraints and energy conservation; the recommended actions on health-care costs would also contribute to this end.[2] Meanwhile, the President's Commission on Industrial Competitiveness urges a "stable" monetary policy to help lower the cost of capital.[3]

After noting that the most potent and sure way to increase national savings is to reduce the federal budget deficit, Dornbusch, Poterba, and Summers urge tax measures that do not impede competitiveness by interfering with incentives to save or invest. They recommend a broad value-added tax, as well as piecemeal reforms that raise taxes on socially costly activities (higher taxes on cigarettes and distilled spirits, an increase in the gasoline excise tax, etc.).[4] The Cuomo Commission too recommends the adoption of a value-added tax and favors an extra tax on gasoline and diesel fuel, probably in the form of an oil import fee.[5] Although the importance of increasing private savings is noted, few specific recommendations are offered. The Cuomo Commission, in defense of its recommendation of a value-added tax, notes that it has the advantage of raising a lot of revenue as well as creating incentives for saving more and consuming less.[6]

Institutional and Regulatory Reforms

Among high-priority imperatives, reforming U.S. antitrust regulations receives an almost unanimous call. The President's Commission on Industrial Competitiveness recommends modifying section 7 of the Clayton Act and other antitrust statutes to recognize the potential efficiency gains resulting from business combinations and to provide antitrust exemptions for certain types of mergers and other types of business relationships that promote national objectives. The Commission also favors restricting triple damage liability to cases of business behavior explicitly prohibited by law. Under still another Commission proposal, the Department of Justice and various other government agencies would meet periodically to set antitrust policy.[7]

The Business Roundtable similarly recommends reforming U.S. antitrust law, including amending section 7 of the Clayton Act to codify the 1984 merger guidelines issued by the Department of Justice, which draw no distinction between domestic and foreign producers in defining specific markets.[8] More broadly, the Business Roundtable urges a less confrontational relationship between business and government on antitrust issues.

The Business Roundtable further recommends a reform of U.S. product-liability law by adopting a fault-based system of liability with limitations on recovery for misuse of a product and negligent conduct, by limiting liability for noneconomic damages, by awarding punitive damages only in cases of malicious conduct, by reducing liability awards based on other benefits received for the same injury, such as workers' compensation, and by limiting the liability of those who merely sell a product rather than make it.[9]

Regulatory reform also includes the further deregulation of certain industries, such as public utilities, advocated by the Committee for Economic Development.[10] The Committee also suggests that regulations meant to achieve social aims be judged by benefit-cost criteria and advocates a number of actions to reduce the costs of meeting environmental, health, and safety regulations while permitting more effective use of market incentives.[11] The National Research Council recommends that a reexamination of regulatory policies include consideration of the effects of such policies on the capacity of American industries to innovate and to compete internationally.[12]

Finally, there has been a general call for the creation of new institutional mechanisms to address a variety of problems associated with U.S. competitiveness, as well as for closer and more effective dialogue and collaboration between government, industry, labor, and academia. The proposed new institutional mechanisms include a department of science and technology and a department of trade, recommended by the President's Commission on Industrial Competitiveness.[13] Earlier the Business–Higher Education Forum had recommended the appointment of a presidential adviser on economic competitiveness, the establishment of an information center on international competitiveness within the Department of Commerce, and the creation of a National Commission on Industrial Competitiveness, which in fact was formed.[14]

Science and Technology Policies

There is an overwhelming consensus that science and technology policies should be accorded high priority in rejuvenating U.S. international competitiveness. This consensus grows out of the general belief that strengthening scientific and technological enterprise is crucial both to the nation's economic well-being and to its military security. The policy challenge facing the United States is pointedly expressed by the Business–Higher Education Forum, which emphasizes that "a principal objective of public policy should be to increase the effectiveness of technological innovation as a contributor to industrial productivity and international competitiveness."[15]

The National Research Council defines the policy challenge more broadly. While maintaining a world-class research structure is essential in the effort to expand technological frontiers, the Council urges that research be seen as part of a complex, interwoven process ranging from basic research to commercialization of new products. The process is presently carried out by a system of interlocking institutions, both public and private, engaged in fostering and disseminating technological advances. To keep the system strong throughout will require farsighted government action, technologically sophisticated managers, quality research personnel, and a technically competent labor force. The system also requires a healthy supply of capital, the economies that come with large-scale production, a global view of markets to support subsequent rounds of technological advance, and a general business climate that is conducive to entrepreneurial risk taking and spawning new enterprises.[16]

Many recommendations focus on various means for fostering long-term research and development and innovation. The suggestions include a higher R&D tax credit. Another idea is regulatory reform to do away with air pollution standards that mandate a particular control technology, which would thereby encourage the development of new solutions. Other proposals concern the protection of intellectual property rights, cooperative research and development, aid to basic research (for example, by upgrading scientific equipment and instruments in universities), and technology transfer and commercialization.[17] Similarly, the President's Commission on Industrial Competitiveness argues in favor of R&D policies and programs that emphasize competitiveness as a central goal, greater incentives for private-sector research and development, streamlined regulatory systems that enhance rather than inhibit innovation and commercialization, increased government support of university research, and improved management of federal laboratories.

As mentioned above, the President's Commission also recommends the creation of a cabinet-level department of science and technology to replace the current fragmented policymaking apparatus and provide an integrated, focused, institutional framework for guiding the nation's science and technology policies. The new department would also create a better cooperative relationship between government, industry, and universities and would provide a high-level adviser to the president on matters of science and technology policy.[18]

The National Academy of Engineering stresses the rapidly changing role of the federal government in stimulating and supporting the conversion of new technology into commercial products and processes. It also draws attention to the fact that the government is redefining the role of the federal laboratories to be more supportive of technical developments in industry while also encouraging wider collaboration between government, industry, and universities. The Engineering Research Center program of the National Science Foundation is specifically cited as an important university-based engineering research effort that relates to industrial competitiveness.[19]

The National Academy of Engineering further underlines the importance of evolving new technological alliances within the U.S. economy.[20] These include such joint R&D efforts as Sematech, a federally supported consortium of U.S. firms that proposes to develop manufacturing technology for a new generation of integrated circuits. Another collaborative R&D program, the National Center for Manufacturing Sciences, has been established under the National Cooperative Research Act of 1984; its mission is to fund research that will develop technologies aimed at improving manufacturing processes and materials and to implement such technologies in its member companies in order to enhance their international competitiveness.

State governments have taken the initiative in launching many other collaborative programs aimed at developing technology and industry, often in joint efforts with private firms and universities. Finally, the federal government, through the Stevenson-Wydler Act of 1980 and several subsequent legislative actions, has started assuming a greater role in facilitating the transfer of federally funded technology to private industry. The Federal Technology Transfer Act of 1986 provides for the creation of a federal laboratory consortium for technology transfer and has made it easier for American companies to work with federal laboratories to develop new and improved products, systems, and services.[21]

Capital Formation

An increase in the nation's fixed capital stock through investment in new plant and equipment is vital for growth in productivity and international competitiveness. Through capital investment the results of new technology are brought into the production process, which lowers costs and improves product quality. Countries that invest more also tend to have higher rates of growth in productivity. Previous studies are unanimous in recommending that the nation's fixed capital stock be modernized and increased.

The President's Commission on Industrial Competitiveness focuses on three specific areas: the supply of capital, its cost to American industry, and mechanisms to ensure that capital flows to its most productive uses.[22] The issue of the supply of capital reverts back to the problems of the large federal budget deficit and the low savings rate in the United States. On the question of how to mobilize greater private savings in the U.S. economy, there appears to be a general dearth of ideas. The Tax Reform Act of 1986, which was intended to increase savings and investment, is considered by some to have failed in accomplishing this objective. In this view, the tax reform legislation "did more to stimulate consumption than investment, and constituted a step backwards in this respect."[23] Until the U.S. savings rate improves, it seems unlikely that much will be done about the high cost of capital.

The allocation of capital to its most productive uses is another issue that remains largely unsettled. Some observers believe that the Tax Reform Act of 1986 has improved the chances for an efficient allocation of capital by correcting some distortions, particularly the uneven cost of funds across sectors. Others argue that the present tax system still has features that impair the performance of U.S. firms in world markets. For example, the 1986 act reduced the share of company R&D expenditures that can be allocated to domestic-source income, reduced the temporary R&D tax credit, and disallowed deductions of dividend income.

The importance of improving and expanding the nation's public infrastructure seems to have received spotty attention at best. Among those studies that address the subject, the Cuomo Commission asserts that "no nation can retain its posture as an economic leader if its spine is collapsing," and proposes a 10-year program to rebuild and expand the infrastructure.[24]

Education and Training

Recommendations pertaining to education and training generally cover five specific areas: elementary and secondary education, higher education (with a focus on engineering and business education), continuous training of workers, retraining displaced workers, and education and training of disadvantaged workers and segments of society.

Elementary and secondary education. Considerable policy attention has been focused on improving the quality of the nation's elementary and secondary educational system. The President's Commission on Industrial Competitiveness favors more rigorous educational standards coupled with strengthened efforts to address the dropout problem and measures aimed at greater computer literacy. The Commission urges the establishment of public-private partnerships to provide coordinated services in the school setting, citing as examples such programs as Cities in Schools and Adopt-A-School.[25]

The Business Roundtable emphasizes the acquisition of basic skills for jobs and careers in the twenty-first century. According to this vision, children should read, write, and compute in the early grades. By high school graduation, students should have had a minimum of four years of English, three years of mathematics, three years of science, and three years of social science; they should also be proficient in the use of computers.[26] The White House Conference on Productivity has stressed the importance of improving education at all levels, with particular emphasis on making students more familiar with technology and computers. Greater emphasis should also be placed on meeting the needs of gifted and talented students, as well as those in need of special assistance.[27]

The Cuomo Commission calls for a "renewal" of the nation's primary and secondary education, for which the federal government must assume the financial burden. The failure to undertake such a renewal would mean perpetuating and expanding America's underclass, which in turn would put the U.S. economy at a continuing disadvantage in competition with other major industrial nations. Accordingly, the Commission urges the establishment of more rigorous standards of educational achievement, such as some form of "exit testing" comparable to the baccalaureate examination in France and the A-level and O-level examinations in Britain. A longer school year and greater emphasis on team effort, cooperation, and group achievement are also favored.

The Cuomo Commission believes teachers are the key to educational reform and would like to see higher pay for all teachers, as well as additional incentives to attract teachers in such subject areas as mathematics and science, where there is a shortage. The Commission also urges the federal government to consider an investment program to rebuild the nation's educational infrastructure in the same way that the federal government earlier took responsibility for building highways and dams.[28]

Higher education. The nation's higher educational system has also been the subject of policy attention. The Business–Higher Education Forum would like to see university initiatives in teaching and research place greater emphasis on such areas as foreign languages, cultures, and sociopolitical institutions and on comparative international studies of management practices.[29] The Forum also calls for a reemphasis on manufacturing engineering and expanded teaching and research in business schools on the management of research and development, technological innovation, productivity, and quality improvements.[30]

In the area of science and engineering education, key policy objectives are to alleviate the faculty shortage, update the research equipment and instrumentation of universities, and address the issue of declining enrollments by American students in science, engineering, and other technical fields. For business education the chief policy concern has been a systematic reevaluation of business school curricula to ensure that they adequately reflect fundamental changes in technology and the global economy.[31]

On the needs of business schools the President's Commission on Industrial Competitiveness endorses the views of the Business–Higher Education Forum, but in considering the education of engineers the Commission makes several recommendations of its own. For example, the Commission calls on the federal government to provide stipends that would encourage the best students to pursue graduate study in engineering. Other recommendations include an increase in funding for engineering research, expansion of the National Science Foundation's cross-disciplinary engineering research centers, and a tax credit for companies that fund university research or donate equipment.[32]

The National Academy of Engineering draws attention to the emerging emphasis on manufacturing engineering and to new research programs and organizations (such as the engineering research centers sponsored by the National Science Foundation and many new state-sponsored technology programs involving universities and industry). The Academy would provide colleges and universities with the resources they need to establish new programs and curricula that will contribute to U.S. industrial competitiveness.[33] The Academy also urges the federal government to develop an incentive program to encourage more U.S. citizens to pursue advanced technical degrees in fields that are increasingly dominated by foreign nationals. A related proposal suggests modifying laws and regulations so that foreign nationals who receive an advanced degree in science and engineering at an American university could stay and work in the United States if they chose to.[34]

Continuous training of workers. Many studies recognize that continuous training of workers is essential in an economy marked by rapid economic, technological, and structural change. The National Academy of Engineering notes that continuous education is essential to increasing national productivity and is particularly important for the technical work force. The Academy believes, therefore, that institutional and individual commitment to lifelong education should be encouraged and strengthened. Although the primary responsibility to undertake such education lies with the individual, industry and government should provide opportunities and support for worker participation.[35]

The President's Commission on Industrial Competitiveness is more specific. It urges that the U.S. tax code not further bias employers against funding employee training, that future changes in tax law seek a balanced treatment of investments in physical and human capital, and that employer-financed tuition be permanently exempted from personal income tax. In addition, the Commission advocates strengthening the ability of vocational and community colleges to provide industrially relevant training. To this end the federal government should offer increased funding; technical committees should be established under the Vocational Training Act to provide curriculum-related information to the schools; and the states should create equipment pools to alleviate shortages and to facilitate the sharing of scarce resources.[36]

The Business–Higher Education Forum also favors tax incentives to stimulate additional industry investment in the education and training and retraining of workers, including apprenticeship programs. It further recommends certain incentives for individuals to save for their own training and retraining in the form of an individual training account similar in concept to the individual retirement account.[37]

The Cuomo Commission draws attention to extensive efforts in worker training and retraining at the state and local level that could well serve as a model for the nation as a whole. For example, in California and Delaware, business, labor, and state government have created partnerships to develop training programs, tying funding to results. In Iowa the state has been instrumental in helping community colleges to create training programs to meet the needs of specific companies. Massachusetts, Florida, Kentucky, Minnesota, and Washington have formed "skills corporations," which are semipublic organizations designed to foster partnerships between business and educational institutions for worker training and retraining. The Massachusetts Bay State Skills Corporation, established in 1980, has served as a model for many similar efforts across the country.[38]

Retraining displaced workers. Displaced workers are generally skilled or semiskilled blue-collar workers who have been steadily employed (mostly in smokestack industries) but who in midcareer face involuntary unemployment of long duration. They need very specialized training or retraining, and some of them also need remedial help with basic skills before acquiring new technical skills.

The need to provide such specialized training for displaced workers is widely recognized. The White House Conference on Productivity offers three guiding principles in this area. First, job-search assistance and training should be made available to workers as soon as it is known that they are facing unemployment, and the assistance should be tailored to each worker's aptitudes and interests. Second, public efforts should augment, rather than serve as a substitute for, private efforts. National programs should be sensitive to the ongoing activities of displaced workers, as should businesses; in this respect, the Private Industry Councils provided for in the Job Training and Partnership Act of 1982 could be tapped to provide useful assistance. Third, training and job-search assistance should have a formal link with the unemployment-insurance system.[39]

The Business–Higher Education Forum recommends the development of a coherent and comprehensive national program for displaced workers modeled on the G.I. Bill. The program would provide educational vouchers to individual displaced workers financed jointly by employers, employees, and the federal government.[40] The Business Roundtable recommends replacing current targeted retraining programs of the Job Training Partnership Act and the Trade Adjustment Assistance program with a comprehensive displaced-worker program. There would be greater public-sector participation in the new program, including adequate public resources to facilitate a quick response to the needs of the unemployed and fast delivery of assistance.[41]

Again, initiatives at the state level might serve as models for future policy directions. A number of states, including New York, Ohio, Michigan, Iowa, New Jersey, Massachusetts, and Vermont, have developed programs to provide assistance with the training and employment of workers displaced by plant closings.[42]

Education of disadvantaged workers. Previous studies have placed little emphasis on the education and training of disadvantaged workers and other disadvantaged people who are not currently participating in the work force. Many of these are people whose disadvantages are their very lack of education, namely, the adult illiterate population. Among the very few offering policy suggestions in this area, the Business Roundtable believes that the persistence of such disadvantaged workers and groups represents a social problem that cannot be tolerated and should be solved through shared responsibility by government, the private sector, and the disadvantaged individuals themselves.

More specifically, the Business Roundtable urges increased private-sector participation, particularly at the local level, in the creation of training programs and job opportunities. It also endorses present efforts that specifically target the needs of disadvantaged workers and groups (for example, Title II of the Joint Training Partnership Act, elements of the Primary and Secondary Education Act, the Vocational Education Act, and Aid to Families with Dependent Children). In addition, it encourages innovative new programs for disadvantaged workers and programs designed to help families get off welfare through gainful employment.[43]

Management Strategies

The President's Commission on Industrial Competitiveness observes, "American ability to compete lies primarily within the private sector."[44] Thus, the Commission believes, business has a responsibility to establish world leadership in the commercialization of product and process technology, to increase investment in both physical and human capital, to develop new ways of reaching consensuses on goals within companies, and to broaden its vision by taking a global view of markets and accepting the certainty of global competition.[45] The Commission urges management and labor to forge a new relationship based on trust and cooperation through a new commitment to equity, consistency, candor, and problem solving. Further, new compensation plans like profit sharing and employee stock-purchase programs should be considered to boost employee incentives and dedication.[46]

The National Academy of Engineering underscores the crucial importance of creating innovative products and services and making continuous improvements in existing technologies, and it urges U.S. industry to adopt new ways of designing, developing, and manufacturing products. The first step is for firms to recognize the importance of the production activity and to follow the approach of designing for manufacture or designing for assembly. All elements of the organization must participate in creating an effective product, which cannot happen within the traditional compartmental and linear system of production.[47] Drawing on the recent experience of Hewlett-Packard,[48] the Academy stresses the importance of breaking down traditional organizational barriers, improving manufacturing, maintaining better quality control, and establishing communication between engineers and workers and between the design and manufacturing arms of the company.

The National Research Council notes that as the capabilities and advantages of new manufacturing technologies are demonstrated, they will become increasingly important to future management strategies for improving competitiveness. As new manufacturing technologies are more widely adopted in the years ahead, the most important factors in improving responsiveness, flexibility, costs, and quality will be the effectiveness of management practices, of organizational design, and of decision-making criteria.[49]

International Economic Policies

Recommendations in the area of international trade policies are addressed to a variety of issues: improving trade policies and the policy-making apparatus within the United States, promoting American exports to the rest of the world, responding to "trade-distorting" policies of other countries, reforming the international trading system through the current negotiations on the General

Agreement on Tariffs and Trade (GATT), coordinating international policies on currency exchange rates and macroeconomic issues, and resolving the third-world debt problem.

Much of the attention to domestic trade policy concerns the policy-making apparatus, which has been highly splintered in the past. Various studies also discuss the problems of industries threatened by severe import penetration and the appropriate balance between national security and export controls on high-technology products. For example, the President's Commission on Industrial Competitiveness recommends establishing a new department of trade to improve the policy-making process. Next, changes in U.S. antitrust law are recommended to remove legal obstacles that hamper the ability of American firms to compete internationally. Also, U.S. export controls based on national-security interests should be made consistent with those agreed on by the 15 allied members of the Coordinating Committee for Multilateral Export Controls. Such controls should be used only when all diplomatic sanctions have been exhausted, should be applied multilaterally, should respect prior contractual obligations, and should not be binding on foreign subsidiaries of U.S. firms.[50]

Recommendations for more effective promotion of U.S. exports argue for greater government support of exports and increased export financing. Other measures would remove many legal hurdles facing exporters and provide more and better information on foreign markets to American exporters. (Government agencies routinely collect such information, but they fail to communicate it effectively to American companies.[51])

A most difficult area has been how the United States should respond to the trade-distorting policies of other countries. The aim is to deter, offset, or eliminate trade barriers and unfair trade practices in such areas as agricultural products, textiles, and aircraft. Foreign governments have been criticized for paying subsidies to their domestic industries, while protecting home markets through both tariff and nontariff trade barriers. Another important source of concern in this area is continuing dissatisfaction with the GATT rules and procedures for resolving disputes.

To deal with these problems directly, some analysts recommend that the United States adopt a "tailored trade" approach to trade problems with specific countries. This would mean developing free-trade arrangements with free-trade economies, managed-trade agreements with managed-trade economies, and mixed agreements with those economic systems somewhere in between. At the same time, trade policy would also have to address certain issues that cut across all these categories, such as the protection of intellectual property rights.[52]

The task of modernizing GATT is given a high priority. The main objectives include improving current trading rules in such areas as agricultural products, broadening GATT's coverage to include services and investments, emphasizing the protection of intellectual property rights, dealing with the issue of government subsidies of domestic industries, and streamlining and enhancing GATT's procedures for settling disputes. Other areas of interest include countertrade (barter) and international tax practices.[53] The current Uruguay Round of negotiations to modernize GATT comes at a critical time in international trade relations. After four decades the trade liberalization ushered in by GATT has shown signs of breaking down. There is, therefore, considerable urgency to preserve and renew confidence in GATT before present difficulties escalate into a global trade war.[54]

It is feared that U.S. efforts to reduce the trade deficit may dampen demand in the world economy. If growth in demand is sluggish and such countries as Japan and West Germany fail to adopt stimulative macroeconomic policies while the United States is dealing with its budget deficit, the result could be a recession overseas. This danger argues for closer international coordination of macroeconomic policies, as well as for efforts to reduce the volatility of foreign-exchange fluctuations.[55]

Finally, resolving the third-world debt problem has increasingly occupied worldwide attention. Recently the major policy thrust has been to shift the debtor countries from austerity to growth. Debt-service payments by the less-developed countries and their ensuing macroeconomic austerity measures have harmed their ability to absorb exports from the rest of the world, including the United States. The debt problem in the third world has therefore been an important impediment to worldwide economic growth. Hence, there is a growing emphasis on resolving the debt problem through such methods as "equity conversion" of existing debts, stretching-out repayment schedules, and the development of a secondary market that discounts the value of the loans. Also, some have suggested that Japan, with its ample trade surplus, launch the equivalent of a Marshall Plan for less-developed countries.[56]

Select Bibliography

Baily, Martin Neil, and Alok K. Chakrabarti. *Innovation and the Productivity Crisis.* Washington, D.C.: The Brookings Institution, 1988.

Business–Higher Education Forum. *America's Competitive Challenge: The Need for a National Response.* A Report to the President. Washington, D.C.: The Business–Higher Education Forum, 1983.

Business–Higher Education Forum. *America's Competitive Challenge: The Need for a National Response.* The Report in Brief. Washington, D.C.: The Business–Higher Education Forum, 1983.

Business Roundtable. *American Excellence in a World Economy.* New York: The Business Roundtable, 1987.

Business Roundtable. *American Excellence in a World Economy.* A Summary of the Report. New York: The Business Roundtable, 1987.

Business Roundtable. *Strategy for a Vital U.S. Economy.* New York: The Business Roundtable, 1984.

Choate, Pat, and Juyne Linger. "Tailored Trade: Dealing with the World As It Is." *Harvard Business Review,* January–February 1988, pp. 86–93.

Committee for Economic Development (CED). *Productivity Policy: Key to the Nation's Economic Future.* New York: CED, 1983.

Committee for Economic Development (CED). *Strategy for U.S. Industrial Competitiveness.* New York: CED, 1984.

Congress of the United States, Congressional Budget Office. *The GATT Negotiations and U.S. Trade Policy.* Washington, D.C.: U.S. Government Printing Office, 1987.

Congress of the United States, Congressional Budget Office. *Has Trade Protection Revitalized Domestic Industries?* Washington, D.C.: U.S. Government Printing Office, 1986.

Council on Competitiveness. *America's Competitive Crisis: Confronting the New Reality.* Washington, D.C.: Council on Competitiveness, 1987.

The Cuomo Commission on Trade and Competitiveness. *The Cuomo Commission Report.* New York: Simon and Schuster, 1988.

Dornbusch, Rudiger, James Poterba, and Lawrence Summers. *The Case for Manufacturing in America's Future.* Rev. ed. Rochester, N.Y.: Eastman Kodak Company, 1988.

Krugman, Paul R. "Introduction: New Thinking about Trade Policy." In Paul R. Krugman, ed., *Strategic Trade Policy and the New International Economics,* pp. 1–21. Cambridge: MIT Press, 1986.

Krugman, Paul R. "Targeted Industrial Policies: Theory and Evidence." In *Industrial Change and Public Policy,* pp. 123–155. Kansas City: Federal Reserve Bank of Kansas City, 1983.

Krugman, Paul R. "The U.S. Response to Foreign Industrial Targeting." *Brookings Papers on Economic Activity* 1 (1984): 77–131.

Landau, Ralph. "U.S. Economic Growth." *Scientific American,* June 1988, pp. 44–52.

Lawrence, Robert Z. *Can America Compete?* Washington, D.C.: The Brookings Institution, 1984.

Lodge, George C., and William C. Crum. "The Pursuit of Remedies." In Bruce R. Scott and George C. Lodge, eds., *U.S. Competitiveness in the World Economy*, pp. 479–502. Boston: Harvard Business School Press, 1985.

National Academy of Engineering. *The Technological Dimensions of International Competitiveness.* A report to the Council of the National Academy of Engineering prepared by the Committee on Technology Issues That Impact International Competitiveness. Washington, D.C.: National Academy of Engineering, 1988.

National Research Council. *International Competition in Advanced Technology: Decisions for America.* Prepared by the Panel on Advanced Technology Competition and the Industrialized Allies, Office of International Affairs, National Research Council. Washington, D.C.: National Academy Press, 1983.

National Research Council. *Toward a New Era in U.S. Manufacturing: The Need for a National Vision.* Washington, D.C.: National Academy Press, 1986.

Norton, R. D. "Industrial Policy and American Renewal." *Journal of Economic Literature* 24 (1986): 1–40.

Poterba, James M. "Tax Policy and Corporate Saving." *Brookings Papers on Economic Activity* 2 (1987): 455–513.

President's Commission on Industrial Competitiveness. *Global Competition: The New Reality.* Vols. 1 and 2. Washington, D.C.: U.S. Government Printing Office, 1985.

Reich, Robert B. *The Next American Frontier.* New York: Times Books, 1983.

Scott, Bruce R. "National Strategies: Key to International Competition." In Bruce R. Scott and George C. Lodge, eds., *U.S. Competitiveness in the World Economy*, pp. 71–143. Boston: Harvard Business School Press, 1985.

Scott, Bruce R. "National Strategy for Stronger U.S. Competitiveness." *Harvard Business Review*, March–April 1984, pp. 77–91.

Scott, Bruce R. "A Vision of Competitive United States." Unpublished paper. Harvard Business School, 1987.

Thurow, Lester C. *The Zero-Sum Solution.* New York: Simon and Schuster, 1985.

White House Conference on Productivity. *Productivity Growth: A Better Life for America.* Report to the President of the United States. Washington, D.C.: U.S. Department of Commerce, National Technical Information Service, 1984.

Young, John A. "Technology and Competitiveness." *Science* 241 (1988): 313–316.

Zysman, John, and Laura Tyson, eds. *American Industry in International Competition: Government Policies and Corporate Strategies.* Ithaca, N.Y.: Cornell University Press, 1983.

Appendix II

The MIT Commission on Industrial Productivity

Commission Members

Chairman
Professor Michael L. Dertouzos
Department of Electrical Engineering and Computer Science
Director of the Laboratory for Computer Science

Vice-Chairman
Professor Robert M. Solow
Institute Professor
Department of Economics

Executive Director
Professor Richard K. Lester
Department of Nuclear Engineering

Members
Professor Suzanne Berger
Head of the Department of Political Science

Professor David Botstein
Department of Biology
(left MIT in January 1988)

Professor H. Kent Bowen
Department of Materials Science and Engineering
Codirector of the Leaders for Manufacturing Program

Professor Don P. Clausing
Department of Electrical Engineering and Computer Science

Professor Eugene E. Covert
Head of the Department of Aeronautics and Astronautics

Professor John M. Deutch
Provost of the Institute

Professor Merton C. Flemings
Head of the Department of Materials Science and Engineering

Professor Howard W. Johnson
Special Faculty Professor of Management, Emeritus
President, Emeritus
Honorary Chairman of the MIT Corporation

Professor Thomas A. Kochan
Sloan School of Management

Professor Daniel Roos
Department of Civil Engineering
Director of the Center for Technology, Policy, and Industrial
Development

Professor David H. Staelin
Department of Electrical Engineering and Computer Science

Professor Lester C. Thurow
Dean of the Sloan School of Management

Professor James Wei
Head of the Department of Chemical Engineering

Professor Gerald L. Wilson
Dean of the School of Engineering

Commission Staff

Executive Director
Richard K. Lester

Deputy Director
Kirkor Bozdogan

Administrative Coordinator
Virginia L. Sherbs

Research staff
Charles H. Ferguson

Richard F. Kazis

Artemis March

Cathie Jo Martin

James Womack

Rapporteur
Teresa L. Hill

Staff writer
Robert C. Haavind

Research assistants
John S. Berg

Thomas Berger

Hans-Georg Betz

Elizabeth A. Downie

Christopher L. Erickson

Stephen F. Filippone

Laura Hastings

Steven Kamin

Louisa Koch

John F. Krafcik

John S. Lin

Aileen Liu

Richard M. Locke

Barbara A. Masi

Michael J. Massimino

Mark J. McCabe

Yiorgos L. Mylonadis

Wayne Nelson

James J. Pastoriza, Jr.

Subramanian Rangan

Brian K. Sliker

Thomas Turner

Commission Working Groups

The Commission organized itself three times into different structures best suited to the successive phases of its work. The Commission first formed eight industry working groups and a special working group on education and training and augmented these groups with members drawn from the MIT community. The Commission then reorganized itself into two working groups charged with examining longer-term trends with broad implications for future productive performance. The two groups addressed these trends from the perspective of internal operations and the general business environment, respectively. Finally, the Commission reorganized into two working groups, one charged with developing recommendations for education and training and the other with developing general recommendations for industry, government, and labor. The membership of these groups is listed below.

Automobile industry

Professor Daniel Roos (group chairman)
Department of Civil Engineering
Director of the Center for Technology, Policy, and Industrial Development

Professor Joel P. Clark
Department of Materials Science and Engineering

Professor Don P. Clausing
Department of Electrical Engineering and Computer Science

Professor Michael A. Cusumano
Sloan School of Management

Professor John B. Heywood
Department of Mechanical Engineering

Professor Thomas A. Kochan
Sloan School of Management

Professor Charles F. Sabel
Department of Political Science

Professor Robert M. Solow
Department of Economics

Dr. James Womack (staff)
Center for Technology, Policy, and Industrial Development

Mr. John F. Krafcik (research assistant)
Center for Technology, Policy, and Industrial Development

Chemical industry
Professor James Wei (group chairman)
Department of Chemical Engineering

Professor David Botstein
Department of Biology

Professor Charles L. Cooney
Department of Chemical Engineering

Professor John M. Deutch
Provost of the Institute

Professor Henry D. Jacoby
Sloan School of Management

Professor Howard W. Johnson
President, Emeritus
Honorary Chairman of the MIT Corporation

Professor Eric Lander
Department of Biology

Professor Richard K. Lester
Department of Nuclear Engineering

Professor Phillip A. Sharp
Department of Biology

Professor Kenneth A. Smith
Associate Provost and Vice President for Research

Professor Christopher Walsh
Department of Chemistry

Dr. Kirkor Bozdogan (staff)
Commission on Industrial Productivity

Mr. Yiorgos Mylonadis (research assistant)
Sloan School of Management

Commercial-aircraft industry
Professor Eugene E. Covert (group chairman)
Department of Aeronautics and Astronautics

Professor Thomas A. Kochan
Sloan School of Management

Dr. Artemis March (staff)
Commission on Industrial Productivity

Ms. Elizabeth A. Downie (research assistant)
Sloan School of Management

Consumer-electronics industry
Professor David H. Staelin (group chairman)
Department of Electrical Engineering and Computer Science

Professor Michael A. Cusumano
Sloan School of Management

Professor J. Francis Reintjes
Department of Electrical Engineering and Computer Science

Professor Richard S. Rosenbloom
Harvard Business School

Professor Robert M. Solow
Department of Economics

Dr. John E. Ward
Department of Electrical Engineering and Computer Science
(retired)

Dr. Kirkor Bozdogan (staff)
Commission on Industrial Productivity

Mr. Stephen F. Filippone (research assistant)
Department of Electrical Engineering and Computer Science

Machine-tool industry
Professor Kent H. Bowen (group chairman)
Department of Materials Science and Engineering

Professor Dimitri A. Antoniadis
Department of Electrical Engineering and Computer Science

Professor Gabriel R. Bitran
Sloan School of Management

Professor George Chryssolouris
Department of Mechanical Engineering

Professor David E. Hardt
Department of Mechanical Engineering

Professor Ronald M. Latanision
Department of Materials Science and Engineering

Professor Lester C. Thurow
Dean of the Sloan School of Management

Professor Eric A. Von Hippel
Sloan School of Management

Dr. Artemis March (staff)
Commission on Industrial Productivity

Mr. John S. Lin (research assistant)
Sloan School of Management

Semiconductor, computer, and copier industries
Professor Don P. Clausing (group chairman)
Department of Electrical Engineering and Computer Science

Professor Jonathan Allen
Department of Electrical Engineering and Computer Science

Professor Michael L. Dertouzos
Department of Electrical Engineering and Computer Science

Professor Joel Moses
Department of Electrical Engineering and Computer Science

Professor Paul L. Penfield, Jr.
Department of Electrical Engineering and Computer Science

Dr. Charles H. Ferguson (staff)
Center for Technology, Policy, and Industrial Development

Mr. John S. Berg (research assistant)
Department of Mechanical Engineering

Steel industry
Professor Merton C. Flemings (group chairman)
Department of Materials Science and Engineering

Professor Joel P. Clark
Department of Materials Science and Engineering

Professor Morris Cohen
Department of Materials Science and Engineering

Professor Thomas W. Eagar
Department of Materials Science and Engineering

Professor John F. Elliott
Department of Materials Science and Engineering

Professor Timothy G. P. Gutowski
Department of Mechanical Engineering

Dr. David Ragone
Department of Materials Science and Engineering

Professor Lester C. Thurow
Dean of the Sloan School of Management

Professor Harry L. Tuller
Department of Materials Science and Engineering

Ms. Barbara Masi (research assistant)
Department of Materials Science and Engineering

Textiles industry
Professor Suzanne Berger (group chairman)
Department of Political Science

Professor Stanley Backer
Department of Mechanical Engineering

Professor Michael J. Piore
Department of Economics

Dr. Cathie Jo Martin (staff)
Commission on Industrial Productivity

Mr. Christopher L. Erickson (research assistant)
Department of Economics

Mr. Richard F. Kazis (research assistant)
Department of Political Science

Mr. Richard M. Locke (research assistant)
Department of Political Science

Mr. Wayne Nelson (research assistant)
Department of Political Science

Working Group on Education and Training
Professor Suzanne Berger (group chairman)
Department of Political Science

Mr. Richard F. Kazis (research assistant)
Department of Political Science

Dr. Cathie Jo Martin (staff)
Commission on Industrial Productivity

Mr. Thomas Berger (research assistant)
Department of Political Science

Mr. Hans-George Betz (research assistant)
Department of Political Science

Dr. Artemis March (staff)
Commission on Industrial Productivity

Ms. Laura Hastings (research assistant)
Department of Political Science

Professor Richard K. Lester
Department of Nuclear Engineering

Working Group on Longer-Term Trends within the Firm
Professor Merton C. Flemings (group chairman)
Department of Materials Science and Engineering

Professor H. Kent Bowen
Department of Materials Science and Engineering

Professor Don P. Clausing
Department of Electrical Engineering and Computer Science

Professor Eugene E. Covert
Department of Aeronautics and Astronautics

Professor Michael L. Dertouzos
Department of Electrical Engineering and Computer Science

Professor Thomas A. Kochan
Sloan School of Management

Dr. David Ragone
Department of Materials Science and Engineering

Professor Gerald L. Wilson
Dean of the School of Engineering

Working Group on Longer-Term Trends in the Business Environment
Professor Robert M. Solow (group chairman)
Department of Economics

Professor Suzanne Berger
Department of Political Science

Professor John Deutch
Provost of the Institute

Professor Howard W. Johnson
President, Emeritus
Honorary Chairman of the MIT Corporation

Professor Richard K. Lester
Department of Nuclear Engineering

Professor Daniel Roos
Department of Civil Engineering

Professor David H. Staelin
Department of Electrical Engineering and Computer Science

Professor Lester C. Thurow
Dean of the Sloan School of Management

Professor James Wei
Department of Chemical Engineering

Dr. Kirkor Bozdogan (staff)
Commission on Industrial Productivity

Working Group on Education and Training Recommendations
Professor Michael L. Dertouzos (group chairman)
Department of Electrical Engineering and Computer Science

Professor Suzanne Berger
Department of Political Science

Professor H. Kent Bowen
Department of Materials Science and Engineering

Professor Merton C. Flemings
Department of Materials Science and Engineering

Professor Howard W. Johnson
President, Emeritus
Honorary Chairman of the MIT Corporation

Professor Richard K. Lester
Department of Nuclear Engineering

Professor Lester C. Thurow
Dean of the Sloan School of Management

Professor Gerald L. Wilson
Dean of the School of Engineering

Working Group on Recommendations to Business, Government, and Labor

Professor Richard K. Lester (group chairman)
Department of Nuclear Engineering

Professor Eugene E. Covert
Department of Aeronautics and Astronautics

Professor Don P. Clausing
Department of Electrical Engineering and Computer Science

Professor John M. Deutch
Provost of the Institute

Professor Thomas A. Kochan
Sloan School of Management

Professor Daniel Roos
Department of Civil Engineering

Professor Robert M. Solow
Department of Economics

Professor David H. Staelin
Department of Electrical Engineering and Computer Science

Professor James Wei
Department of Chemical Engineering

Mr. Richard F. Kazis (research assistant)
Department of Political Science

Notes

Chapter 1
1. The papers are as follows: James P. Womack, "The U.S. Automobile Industry in an Era of International Competition: Performance and Prospects"; Kirkor Bozdogan, "The Transformation of the U.S. Chemicals Industry"; Artemis March, "The U.S. Commercial Aircraft Industry and Its Foreign Competitors"; Don P. Clausing et al., "The U.S. Semiconductor, Computer, and Copier Industries"; David H. Staelin et al., "The Decline of U.S. Consumer Electronics Manufacturing: History, Hypotheses, and Remedies"; Artemis March, "The U.S. Machine Tool Industry and Its Foreign Competitors"; Merton Flemings et al., "The Future of the U.S. Steel Industry in the International Marketplace"; Suzanne Berger et al., "The U.S. Textile Industry: Challenges and Opportunities in an Era of International Competition"; Richard Kazis, "Education and Training in the United States." All appear in *The Working Papers of the MIT Commission on Industrial Productivity*, 2 vols. (Cambridge: MIT Press, 1989).

Chapter 2
1. Martin N. Baily and Alok K. Chakrabarti, *Innovation and the Productivity Crisis* (Washington, D.C.: Brookings Institution, 1988). The dispute over whether growth has been negative or merely slow hinges on how wage rates are adjusted for inflation and on whether or not fringe benefits are included in the calculation.

2. For a summary of the causes of the productivity slowdown in the OECD countries, see Organization for Economic Cooperation and Development, *OECD Economic Outlook*, no. 42 (Paris: OECD, 1987), pp. 39–48.

3. Computation based on data presented in U.S. Department of Commerce, Bureau of Economic Analysis, *The National Income and Product Accounts of the United States, 1929–1982, Statistical Tables* (Washington, D.C.: U.S. Government Printing Office, 1986), table 6.2 and table 6.7B; *Survey of Current Business*, July 1988, table 6.2 and table 6.7B.

4. "Gross Product by Industry: Comments on Recent Criticisms," *Survey of Current Business*, July 1988, pp. 132–133.

5. U.S. Department of Commerce, International Trade Administration, *United States Trade: Performance in 1987* (Washington, D.C.: U.S. Government Printing Office, 1988), p. 6.

6. George N. Hatsopoulos, Paul R. Krugman, and Lawrence H. Summers, "U.S. Competitiveness: Beyond the Trade Deficit," *Science* 241 (1988): 299–307.

332 Notes

7. Martin N. Baily and Alok K. Chakrabarti, *Innovation and the Productivity Crisis* (Washington, D.C.: Brookings Institution, 1988.)

8. Data obtained from U.S. Department of Commerce, Bureau of Economic Analysis, *The National Income and Product Accounts of the United States, 1929–1982* (Washington, D.C.: U.S. Government Printing Office, 1986); and *Survey of Current Business*, July 1988. As a share of total U.S. spending of all kinds, purchases of manufactured goods other than food and fuel remained roughly constant between 1960 and 1986.

9. U.S. Congress, Office of Technology Assessment, *Paying the Bill: Manufacturing and America's Trade Deficit*, report no. OTA-ITE-390 (Washington, D.C.: U.S. Government Printing Office, 1988), p. 55.

10. National Science Board, *Science and Engineering Indicators—1987* (Washington, D.C.: National Science Foundation, 1987), p. 105.

11. R. B. Costello, *Bolstering Defense Industrial Competitiveness: Report to the Secretary of Defense by the Under Secretary of Defense (Acquisition)* (Washington, D.C.: Office of the Under Secretary of Defense for Acquisitions, Department of Defense, 1988.)

Chapter 3

1. Michael J. Piore and Charles F. Sabel, *The Second Industrial Divide: Possibilities for Prosperity* (New York: Basic Books, 1984), especially chapters 6 and 9.

2 . Antony Sheriff, "The Competitive Product Position of Automobile Manufacturers: Performance and Strategies," MIT International Motor Vehicle Program International Policy Forum, Villa d'Este, Lago di Como, Italy, May 1988.

3. The Kawabata system for evaluating the feel (the "hand") of a fabric was developed by K. Kawabata of Kyoto University during a fifteen-year research program funded by Melbo Apparel Company, one of the major manufacturers of men's clothing in Japan.

Chapter 4

1. James C. Abegglen and George Stalk, Jr., *Kaisha: The Japanese Corporation* (New York: Basic Books, 1985), p.56.

2. G. N. Hatsopoulos and S. H. Brooks, "The cost of capital in the United States and Japan," paper presented at the International Conference on the Cost of Capital, John F. Kennedy School of Government, Harvard University, November 19–21, 1987.

3. See, for example, G. N. Hatsopoulos, P. R. Krugman, and L. H. Summers, "U.S. Competitiveness: Beyond the Trade Deficit," *Science* 241 (1988): 299–307.

4. For a discussion of the ownership structure of Japanese firms and the financial relationships among them, see Michael Gerlach, "Alliances and the Social Organization of Japanese Business," unpublished Ph.D. dissertation, Yale University, 1987; and W. Karl Kester, "Capital and Ownership Structure: A Comparison of United States and Japanese Manufacturing Corporations," *Financial Management*, spring 1986, pp. 5–16.

5. Robert H. Hayes and William J. Abernathy, "Managing Our Way to Economic Decline," *Harvard Business Review* 58 (1980): 67–77.

6. Stewart C. Myers, "Finance Theory and Financial Strategy," *Interfaces* 14 (1984): 126–137.

Chapter 5

1. "A dialogue on competitiveness," *Issues in Science and Technology*, Summer 1988.

2. John Krafcik, "European Manufacturing Practice in a World Perspective," MIT International Motor Vehicle Program Policy Forum, Lake Como, Italy, May 1988.

3. Kim B. Clark, W. Bruce Chew, and Takahiro Fujimoto, "Product Development in the World Auto Industry: Strategy, Organization, and Performance," *Brookings Papers on Economic Activity* 3 (1987): 729–781.

4. K. Clark and T. Fujimoto, "Product Development as Problem Solving—The Case of the Automobile Industry," a paper presented to the Seminar on Productivity, Technology, and Operations Management, Harvard Business School, May 5, 1986.

5. See, for example, Stephen S. Cohen and John Zysman, *Manufacturing Matters: The Myth of the Post-Industrial Economy* (New York: Basic Books, 1987); Rudiger Dornbusch, James Poterba, and Lawrence Summers, *The Case for Manufacturing in America's Future* (Rochester, N.Y.: Eastman Kodak Company, 1987); Robert H. Hayes and Steven C. Wheelwright, *Restoring Our Competitive Edge: Competing through Manufacturing* (New York: John Wiley and Sons, 1984); National Research Council, Manufacturing Studies Board, Commission on Engineering and Technical Systems, *Toward a New Era in U.S. Manufacturing: The Need for a National Vision* (Washington, D.C.: National Academy Press, 1986).

6. Edwin Mansfield, "Industrial R&D in Japan and the United States: A Comparative Study, " *American Economic Review* 78 (1988): 223.

7. L. M. Branscomb, "Towards a National Policy on Research and Development," a conference sponsored by the Council on Research and Technology (CORE-TECH) and the Conference Board, MIT, October 8, 1987.

8. Roland W. Schmitt and Ralph E. Gomory, "Competition from Japan," *MIT Report*, December 1988–January 1989, p. 3.

9. Edwin Mansfield, "Industrial Innovation in Japan and the United States," *Science* 241 (1988): 1771, table 4 .

10. R. Jaikumar, "Postindustrial Manufacturing," *Harvard Business Review*, November–December 1986.

Chapter 6

1. Comparative studies of achievement are reported in William K. Cummings, "Japan's Science and Engineering Pipeline: Structure, Policies, and Trends," a paper prepared for the Office of Technology Assessment, October 23, 1987; and in "Engineering: The Great Educational Gap," *Far Eastern Economic Review*, December 22, 1983. Results of the most recent tests of science achievement for students in 17 countries are summarized in John Walsh, "U.S. Science Students near Foot of Class," *Science*, March 11, 1988.

2. International Association for the Evaluation of Educational Achievement, *Science Achievement in Seventeen Countries: A Preliminary Report* (New York: Pergamon Press, 1988).

3. "Preliminary Report: Second International Mathematics Study," University of Illinois, 1984.

4. Electronic Industries Association, *Engineering Education: Supply/Demand and Job*

Opportunities (Washington, D.C.: Electronic Industries Association, 1982).

5. Crispin Campbell, "What in the World Do We Know?" *Boston Globe,* July 28, 1988, p. 2.

6. Frank Newman, *Higher Education and the American Resurgence* (Princeton: The Carnegie Foundation for the Advancement of Teaching, 1985); U.S. Office of Technology Assessment, *Educating Scientists and Engineers: Grade School to Grad School* (Washington, D.C.: U.S. Government Printing Office, 1988).

7. Survey cited in "Swedish Schools," *The Economist,* November 12, 1988, p. 18.

8. The Commission's research on West German education and productivity was carried out by Hans Betz and reported in his working paper, "Meeting the Challenge: Vocational Education and Training in the Federal Republic of Germany," March 3, 1988.

9. The description of Sanyo training is drawn from an interview with Hiroyasu Kawai, managing director of the Sanyo Corporate Educational Training Center, Kobe, February 2, 1988. Commission interviews at Nippon Steel, Seiko Instruments, Kyocera, NEC, and Tokyo Electric Power showed very similar patterns. On the importance of rotation in the careers of Japanese engineers, see D. Eleanor Westney and Kiyonori Sakakibara, "Comparative Study of the Training, Careers, and Organization of Engineers in the Computer Industry in Japan and the United States," a working paper of the MIT-Japan Science and Technology Program, Cambridge, Mass., 1985. On-the-job training for workers is analyzed in Robert E. Cole, *Work, Mobility, and Participation: A Comparative Study of American and Japanese Industry* (Berkeley and Los Angeles: University of California Press, 1980); and Ronald Dore and Mari Sako, *Educating the Japanese for Work* (Stanford: Stanford University Press, 1988).

10. Wolfgang Streeck, "Skills and the Limits of Neo-Liberalism: The Enterprise of the Future as a Place of Learning," a paper presented to the Conference on Changes in Work and Social Transformation, Universitario di Studi Europei, Turin, Italy, November 27–29, 1987, p. 21.

11. Arndt Sorge and Malcolm Warner, "Manpower Training, Manufacturing Organization, and Workplace Relations in Great Britain and West Germany," *British Journal of Industrial Relations* 18 (1980): 318–333; and Arndt Sorge, Gert Hartmann, Malcolm Warner, and Ian Nicholas, *Microelectronics and Manpower in Manufacturing: Applications of Computer Numerical Control in Great Britain and West Germany* (Aldershot, England: Gover, 1985). See also the research of S. J. Prais in *Productivity and Industrial Structure* (Cambridge: Cambridge University Press, 1981); "Vocational Qualifications of the Labor Force in Britain and Germany," *National Institute Economic Review,* November 1981; and S. J. Prais and Karin Wagner, "Some Practical Aspects of Human Capital Investment: Training Standards in Five Occupations in Britain and Germany," *National Institute Economic Review,* August 1983.

12. Ramchandran Jaikumar, "Postindustrial Manufacturing," *Harvard Business Review,* November–December 1986.

13. These issues are addressed in the Prais research cited previously; see also Rainer Schultz-Wild and Christoph Koehler, "Introducing New Manufacturing Technology: Manpower Problems and Policies," *Human Systems Management* 5 (1985): 231–243.

14. Westney and Sakakibara, "Comparative Study of Engineers."

15. See, for example, Thierry Noyelle, *Beyond Industrial Dualism: Market and Job Segmentation in the New Economy* (Boulder, Col.: Westview Press, 1987). See also Barbara Baran and Carol Parsons, "Technology and Skill: A Literature Review," Berkeley Roundtable on the International Economy, prepared for the Carnegie Forum on Education and the Economy, January 1986.

16. Dore and Sako, *Educating the Japanese for Work*, p. 58.

17. Though this point has been challenged for Japan, the research reported in Masanori Hashimoto and John Raisian, "Employment Tenure and Earnings Profiles in Japan and the United States," *American Economic Review* 75 (1985): 721–735, seems to establish it clearly.

18. Bernard Casey, "The Dual Apprenticeship System and the Recruitment and Retention of Young Persons in West Germany," *British Journal of Industrial Relations* 24 (1986): 63–81.

Chapter 7

1. Robert Hayes and Kim Clark, "Explaining Observed Productivity Differentials Between Plants: Implications for Operations Research," *Interfaces* 15 (1985): 13.

2. Robert Thomas, "Technological Choice: Obstacles and Opportunities for Union-Management Consultation on New Technology," Sloan working paper 1987–88, Sloan School of Management, MIT, 1987.

3. *The Economist*, July 2, 1988.

4. Thomas A. Kochan, Robert B. McKersie, and Henry C. Katz, *The Transformation of American Industrial Relations* (New York: Basic Books, 1986).

5. Haruo Shimada and John Paul MacDuffie, "Industrial Relations and Humanware," working paper, Sloan School of Management, MIT, 1987.

6. Eric von Hippel, *The Sources of Innovation* (New York: Oxford University Press, 1988), p. 4, table 1-1.

7. Based on interviews with USX and Chrysler executives.

8. Mansfield, "Industrial Innovation in Japan and the United States," *Science* 241 (1988): 1771.

9. Stephen K. Yoder, "If Japan Poses Threat in Superconductors, Shoji Tanaka is Why," *New York Times*, April 29, 1988, pp. 1, 24. The membership of the consortium includes Hitachi, Mitsubishi Electric Corporation, NEC, and Sumitomo Electric Industries.

10. U.S. Congress, Office of Technology Assessment, *Commercializing High-Temperature Superconductivity*, OTA-ITE-388 (Washington, D.C.: U.S. Government Printing Office, 1988).

11. J. Markoff, "Experts Warn of U.S. Lag in Vital Chip Technology," *New York Times*, 1988, p. 1.

12. See M. E. Brenton, "The Role of Standardization in Telecommunications," in Organization for Economic Cooperation and Development (OECD), *Trends of Change in Telecommunications Policy*, Information, Computer, Communications Policy (ICCP) Series, no. 13 (Paris: OECD, 1987), pp. 159–167.

Chapter 8

1. See, for example, William J. Adams, *Restructuring and the French Economy: Government and the Rise of Market Competition since World War II* (Washington, D.C.: Brookings Institution, forthcoming); Richard J. Samuels, *The Business of the Japanese State* (Ithaca, N.Y.: Cornell University Press, 1987).

2. See Edward F. Denison, *Trends in American Economic Growth, 1929–1982* (Washington, D.C.: Brookings Institution, 1985); G. B. Christainsen and R. H. Haveman, "Public Regulations and the Slowdown in Productivity Growth," *American Economic Review* 71 (1981): 320–325; Robert W. Crandall, "Pollution Controls and Productivity Growth in Basic Industries," in T. G. Cowing and R. E. Stevenson, eds., *Productivity Measurement in Regulated Industries* (New York: Academic Press, 1981), pp. 347–368.

3. Congress of the United States, Congressional Budget Office, *Environmental Regulation and Economic Efficiency* (Washington, D.C.: U.S. Government Printing Office, 1985).

4. Joseph P. Kalt, "The Impact of Domestic Environmental Regulatory Policies on U.S. International Competitiveness," in A. Michael Spence and Heather A. Hazard, eds., *International Competitiveness,* (Cambridge, Mass.: Ballinger, 1988), pp. 221–262.

5. Catherine Morrison, E. Patrick McGuire, and Mary Ann Clarke, *Keys to U.S. Competitiveness,* Conference Board Report No. 907 (New York: The Conference Board, 1988).

6. Council on Competitiveness, *Picking Up the Pace: The Commercial Challenge to American Innovation* (Washington, D.C., 1988).

7. Council on Competitiveness, *Picking Up the Pace,* p. 3.

8. U.S. Arms Control and Disarmament Agency, *World Military Expenditures and Arms Transfers, 1987* (Washington, D.C.: U.S. Government Printing Office, 1988), p. 57.

9. National Science Board, *Science and Engineering Indicators—1987* (Washington, D.C.: U.S. Government Printing Office, 1987), appendix tables 4-4 and 4-37.

10. The President's Blue Ribbon Commission on Defense Management, *A Formula for Action: A Report to the President on Defense Acquisition* (Washington, D.C.: U.S. Government Printing Office, 1986). Also known as the "Packard Report."

11. National Research Council, *The National Challenge in Computer Science and Technology* (Washington, D.C.: National Academy Press, 1988). The GNP fraction includes internally developed software as well as commercial software and hardware.

12. For a detailed discussion of the evolution of the U.S. computer industry with an emphasis on the relationship between the U.S. federal government and key developments in computing technology, see Barbara G. Katz and Almarin Phillips, "The Computer Industry," in Richard R. Nelson, ed., *Government and Technical Progress* (New York: Pergamon Press, 1982), pp. 162–232. Also, for a discussion of parallel processing, see Geoffrey C. Fox and Paul C. Messina, "Advanced Computer Architectures," *Scientific American,* October 1987 (special issue, The Next Revolution in Computers), pp. 67–74.

Chapter 9
1. See, for example, Eleanor Westney, "Designing for Designers," *Technology Review*, April 1986, pp. 26–39; Marcie J. Tyre, "Technological Change and Problem Solving in the Production Process," working paper, MIT Sloan School of Management, 1988; Deborah G. Ancona and David Caldwell, "Beyond Task and Maintenance: Defining External Functions in Groups," forthcoming in *Group and Organizational Studies*; and John C. Henderson, "Involvement as a Predictor of Performance in I/S Planning Design," working paper, MIT Sloan School of Management, Management in the 1990s Project, 1988.

Chapter 12
1. This effort was led by the MIT Commission on Engineering Undergraduate Education.

Study C
1. This study excluded general aviation and helicopters, which total 10 to 15 percent of airframe sales. It also excluded military aircraft because the Commission's focus was on commercial competition and productivity. "Aircraft" thus refers to large commercial transports, their engines, and parts. The report is based on information current in the winter of 1987–1988.

2. Office of Science and Technology Policy, "National Aeronautical R&D Goals: Technology for America's Future," Washington, D.C., March 1985.

3. Wolfgang H. Demisch, Christopher C. Demisch, and Theresa L. Concert, "The Jetliner Business," The First Boston Corporation, October 5, 1984. At that time only the 707 and 727 had shown a cumulative profit; since then, the 747, the 737-300, and possibly the MD-80 have moved into the black. These analysts assert that it requires cumulative sales of at least 600 units to achieve profitability.

4. Validation is a lengthy and costly process that is essential before new technology can be confidently incorporated into new aircraft. It gives designers an understanding of performance limits and risks under actual or simulated operating conditions. Validation of new generic systems or subsystems was a particularly vital benefit of military programs. Because of the divergence of military and commercial needs and fewer military-program starts, military funding is now supporting much less validation of commercial technology.

5. John Newhouse captures the flavor of "the sporty game" in his book by that name (New York: Alfred A. Knopf, 1982).

6. Legally, Airbus is a Groupement d'Interet Economique, or a "pooling of common interests," which allows multiple partners to band together for a well-defined corporate interest. Airbus itself has no capital, but it is backed by the full financial resources of its partners (Deutsch Airbus, 37.9 percent; Aerospatiale, 37.9 percent; British Aerospace, 20 percent; and CASA, 4.2 percent). Airbus handles overall program management, marketing, coordination, and product support.

7. Richard J. Samuels and Benjamin C. Whipple, "Defense Production and Industrial Development: The Case of Japanese Aircraft," in Chalmers Johnson et al., eds., *Politics and Productivity: How Governments Create Advantage in World Markets* (Cambridge: Ballinger Books, forthcoming).

Appendix I

1. The Business Roundtable, *American Excellence in a World Economy* (New York: The Business Roundtable, 1987), pp. 21–24.

2. The Cuomo Commission on Trade and Competitiveness, *The Cuomo Commission Report* (New York: Simon and Schuster, 1988), pp. 114–115.

3. The President's Commission on Industrial Competitiveness, *Global Competition: The New Reality* (Washington, D.C.: U.S. Government Printing Office, 1985), vol. 1, pp. 25–29.

4. Rudiger Dornbusch, James Poterba, and Lawrence Summers, *The Case for Manufacturing in America's Future*, rev. ed. (Rochester, N.Y.: Eastman Kodak Company, 1988), pp. 16–17.

5. The Cuomo Commission on Trade and Competitiveness, *The Cuomo Commission Report*, pp. 112–113.

6. The Cuomo Commission on Trade and Competitiveness, *The Cuomo Commission Report*, p. 113.

7. The President's Commission on Industrial Competitiveness, *Global Competition*, vol. 2, pp. 192–193.

8. The Business Roundtable, *American Excellence in a World Economy*, pp. 45–47.

9. The Business Roundtable, *American Excellence in a World Economy*, pp. 44–45.

10. Committee for Economic Development (CED), *Productivity Policy: Key to the Nation's Economic Future* (New York: CED, 1983), p. 64.

11. Committee for Economic Development, *Productivity Policy*, p. 65.

12. National Research Council, *International Competition in Advanced Technology: Decisions for America*, prepared by the Panel on Advanced Technology Competition and the Industrialized Allies, Office of International Affairs, National Research Council (Washington, D.C.: National Academy Press, 1983), p. 44.

13. The President's Commission on Industrial Competitiveness, *Global Competition*, vol. 1, pp. 22, 41.

14. Business–Higher Education Forum, *America's Competitive Challenge: The Need for a National Response*, The Report in Brief (Washington, D.C.: The Business–Higher Education Forum, 1983), p. 8.

15. Business–Higher Education Forum, *America's Competitive Challenge: The Need for a National Response*, A Report to the President (Washington, D.C.: The Business–Higher Education Forum, 1983), p. 7.

16. National Research Council, *International Competition in Advanced Technology*, p. 4.

17. Business–Higher Education Forum, *America's Competitive Challenge*, A Report to the President, pp. 7–11.

18. The President's Commission on Industrial Competitiveness, *Global Competition*, vol. 1. pp. 18–25.

19. National Academy of Engineering, *The Technological Dimensions of International Competitiveness*, a report to the Council of the National Academy of Engineering prepared by the Committee on Technology Issues That Impact International Competitiveness (Washington, D.C.: National Academy of Engineering, 1988), p. 39.

20. National Academy of Engineering, *The Technological Dimensions of International Competitiveness,* pp. 40–41.

21. National Academy of Engineering, *The Technological Dimensions of International Competitiveness,* p. 41.

22. The President's Commission on Industrial Competitiveness, *Global Competition,* vol. 1, pp. 25–26.

23. Dornbusch, Poterba, and Summers, *The Case for Manufacturing in America's Future,* p. 6.

24. The Cuomo Commission on Trade and Competitiveness, *The Cuomo Commission Report,* p. 114.

25. The President's Commission on Industrial Competitiveness, *Global Competition,* vol. 1, p. 37.

26. The Business Roundtable, *American Excellence in a World Economy,* pp. 26–27.

27. White House Conference on Productivity, *Productivity Growth: A Better Life for America,* report to the President (Washington, D.C.: U.S. Department of Commerce, National Technical Information Service, 1984), p. 22.

28. The Cuomo Commission on Trade and Competitiveness, *The Cuomo Commission Report,* pp. 122–126.

29. Business–Higher Education Forum, *America's Competitive Challenge: The Need for a National Response,* The Report in Brief, p. 12.

30. Business–Higher Education Forum, *America's Competitive Challenge: The Need for a National Response,* The Report in Brief, p. 13.

31. The Business Roundtable, *American Excellence in a World Economy,* p. 37.

32. The President's Commission on Industrial Competitiveness, *Global Competition,* vol. 1, pp. 36–37.

33. National Academy of Engineering, *The Technological Dimensions of International Competitiveness,* pp. 59–60.

34. National Academy of Engineering, *The Technological Dimensions of International Competitiveness,* p. 63.

35. National Academy of Engineering, *The Technological Dimensions of International Competitiveness,* pp. 66–67.

36. The President's Commission on Industrial Competitiveness, *Global Competition,* vol. 1, pp. 35–36.

37. Business–Higher Education Forum. *America's Competitive Challenge: The Need for a National Response,* The Report in Brief, p. 11.

38. The Cuomo Commission on Trade and Competitiveness, *The Cuomo Commission Report,* pp. 106–107.

39. White House Conference on Productivity, *Productivity Growth,* p. 23.

40. Business–Higher Education Forum, *America's Competitive Challenge, The Report in Brief,* p. 11.

41. The Business Roundtable, *American Excellence in a World Economy,* p. 29.

42. The Cuomo Commission on Trade and Competitiveness, *The Cuomo Commission Report,* p. 107.

43. The Business Roundtable, *American Excellence in a World Economy*, pp. 29–30.

44. The President's Commission on Industrial Competitiveness, *Global Competition*, vol. 1, p. 2.

45. The President's Commission on Industrial Competitiveness, *Global Competition*, vol. 1, p. 2.

46. The President's Commission on Industrial Competitiveness, *Global Competition*, vol. 1, pp. 34–35.

47. National Academy of Engineering, *The Technological Dimensions of International Competitiveness*, pp. 27–29.

48. John A. Young, "Technology and Competitiveness," *Science* 241 (1988): 315.

49. National Research Council, *Toward a New Era in U.S. Manufacturing: The Need for a National Vision* (Washington, D.C.: National Academy Press, 1986), p. 47.

50. The President's Commission on Industrial Competitiveness, *Global Competition*, vol. 1, pp. 40–41.

51. The President's Commission on Industrial Competitiveness, *Global Competition*, vol. 1, p. 41.

52. Pat Choate and Juyne Linger, "Tailored Trade: Dealing with the World As It Is," *Harvard Business Review,* January–February 1988, p. 91.

53. The Business Roundtable, *American Excellence in a World Economy*, pp. 49–55; the President's Commission on Industrial Competitiveness, *Global Competition*, vol. 1, pp. 41, 44.

54. Congress of the United States, Congressional Budget Office, *The GATT Negotiations and U.S. Trade Policy* (Washington, D.C.: U.S. Government Printing Office, 1987), p. ix.

55. The Business Roundtable, *American Excellence in a World Economy*, pp. 22–23.

56. The Business Roundtable, *American Excellence in a World Economy*, p. 23.

Index

Aerospace, 96
Airbus Industrie, 12, 109, 202, 204–213
Aircraft industry, 11–12
  customer relations, 204–205
  deregulation, 215–216
  foreign, 210–214
  and government support, 206–207
  market share, 209
  research and development, 214–215
  sales, 207–208
  structure, 202–204
  trade balances, 208
  vertical linkages in, 104–105
Ampex, 13, 56, 73, 226
Antitrust restrictions, 106
Armco Steel, 15, 52
AT&T, 10, 63, 229, 250, 251, 253–255,
  257, 261
Automobile industry, 18–20
  comparisons, 182–186
  European, 179
  future prospects, 186
  Japanese, 171–173, 179–182
  sales, 172
  structure of, 174–175
  trade balances, 172
  U.S., 175–178
  vertical linkages in, 100–101

BASF, 16, 190, 265
Basic research, 67–68, 153
Bayer, 16, 190
Benchmarking, 52, 119, 142, 150
Best practice, 118, 126, 132, 147, 150
Boeing, 12, 208
Bottom-up approach, 3–9
Branscomb, Lewis, 74
British Steel Corporation, 96

Capital costs, 36, 53, 59, 61, 145, 152
Capital formation, 37, 308
Capital investment, 37
Chaparral Steel, 14, 76, 81, 97, 118, 122
Chemical industry, 15–16
  decline of, 192–195
  foreign restructuring, 197–198
  outlook for, 200
  productivity, 190–192
  structure, 189–190
  trade balances, 191
  U.S. restructuring, 195–200
Clark, Kim, 70–71, 95, 183
Collective goods, 105, 145
Company size, 63
Competitiveness measures, 26
Computer-aided tomography, 56
Computer industry, 10–11, 131
  history of, 264–266
  Japanese progress, 266–269
  outlook for, 269–270
  overview of, 261–264
Computer networking, 107
Consumer electronics industry, 12–14
  demise of, 217–228
  Japanese, 228–229
  outlook for, 230–231
  structure of, 221
  trade balances, 218
Continuous improvement, 74–77, 127,
  134, 148
Cooperation, 45, 56, 94
  and competition, 94, 138–139
  and rotation, 98
  and specialization, 97–98
  teamwork, 158
Cooperation and flatter organizations, 139
Coordination with suppliers, 120
Copier industry, 11

Copier industry (*continued*)
  low-end market, 271–272
  outlook for, 275–277
  overview of, 270
  Xerox, 273–275
Cost of capital, 59, 61
Craft production, 47
Customer feedback, 75, 119–120
Customer service, 32, 142
Customized products, 133

Defense, 41, 67
  reduced benefits of, 116
  and technology, 114–116
Defense practices in the private sector,
  115
Deficit
  federal, 152
  trade, 33–35
Design, 69–70
  of manufacturing processes, 78–80
  for quality, 128
Design/build teams, 123
Diversification, 55
Dore, Ronald, 91
Du Pont, 16, 120, 189–190, 199, 200, 289
Dynamic random-access memory chips
  (DRAMs), 9

Economic policy, 315
Economy of scale, 23
Education, 21–22, 24, 35, 81–92, 136,
  143–165, 309, 314
  attitudes in, 77
  depth and breadth, 160
  higher, 85–86
  learning at work versus learning in
    school, 83–89, 91
  math achievement, 84
  and productivity, 83
  science achievement, 84
  and sense of crisis, 92
Educational institutions, productivity
  problems of, 165
Employee breadth, 137
Employee participation, 137–138, 141, 149
Employer care and productivity, 135
Employment, 31
Equal access to foreign markets, 152
Executives' priorities, 62

Failures to adapt, 38
Flatter organizations, 122–124, 149
  and cooperation, 139

Flexibility, 32, 149
  total, 131–133
Flexible manufacturing systems, 19–20,
  76, 89, 149, 182
Ford, 52, 117, 119, 121–125, 175–179, 183,
  199, 253, 257

General Electric, 199–200, 203–204,
  210–211, 227, 240, 257–258, 264
Government policy, 127, 134
  economic policy, 145
  macroeconomic, 152
  and risk taking, 61
Governmental indifference to
  commercialization, 77
Greenwood Mills, 120

Hayes, Robert, 64, 95
Hoechst, 16, 190, 192, 200
Honda, 103–104, 173–174, 183
Horizontal linkages and antitrust, 105
Human resources, underestimation of, 82
Human Resources Center, 125
Hurdle rate, 61

IBM, 9–11, 63, 67, 69–70, 92, 107, 122,
  123, 125, 139, 199, 250–254, 257–258,
  261–266, 268, 270–271, 274
ICI, 16, 190, 196
Information infrastructure, 146
Inland Steel, 15, 103–104
Innovation, continuous, 74–77, 127, 134,
  148
Institutional reforms, 305
Interfirm relations, 139
International awareness, 150
International monitoring, 142
Investment, 35–36, 67
  long-term, 144
  and optimism, 36
Investors, nature of, 62

Jaikumar, Ramchandran, 76, 89
Job security, 125, 138
Just-in-time (JIT) production system, 95,
  128

Labor
  commitment of, 124
  cooperation with, 150
  as promoters of innovation, 151
Labor-management cooperation, 153
Labor-management relations, 98

Labor productivity, 26–27
Long-term goals, 66

Machine-tool industry, 20–21, 73–74
  collapse of, 232–234
  Japanese, 241–243
  outlook for, 246–247
  performance of, 234–236
  reasons for decline, 236–241
  sales, 235
  structure of, 234
  West German, 243–246
Macroeconomics, 35, 304
Management, 314
  hands-on, 161
Mansfield, Edwin, 72, 75, 104
Mass production, as an outmoded model, 47
McDonnell Douglas, 12, 201–202, 208–209, 212
Microelectronics, 9, 10
Milliken, 17, 121, 289, 296, 298
Ministry of International Trade and Industry (MITI), 20, 102, 106, 224
Multifactor productivity, 27

National Cooperative Research Act, 106
National Steel, 76, 284
Nippon Steel, 91
NUMMI plant, 20, 81, 137

Organization and cooperation, 97
Organizational forms, 38
Organizational rigidities, 166

Parochialism
  and innovation, 50
  and sales, 50
Pratt & Whitney, 203–204, 210, 232–233
Private sector, limits of, 112
Process design, 72
Producer-supplier relations, 57
Product development, 32, 70–72
  Japanese organization of, 70–71
Product variety, 149
Productive performance, 33
  measures of, 133
  problem in, 166
Productivity, 26, 32
  growth, 26, 27–32
  labor, 26–27
  long-term, 147
  measures of, 26–32, 148
  multifactor, 27

outlook, 166–167
research, 165

Quality, 32
Quality before costs, 132
Quick Response Program, 17, 121

RCA, 74, 227–229, 257–258, 264
Regulation
  adversarial nature of, 111
  costs of, 110
  reforms in, 305
Research, basic, 67–68, 153
Research and development, 36, 57
Response time, 32
Retraining, 90–92
Robust manufacturing systems, 82

Sakakibara, Kiyonori, 90
Sako, Mari, 91
Savings, 37, 60
Science and Technology Policies, 306
Self-reliance, 45
Sematech consortium, 10–11, 77, 258, 260–261, 308
Semiconductor industry, 9–10
  fragmentary nature of, 253–256
  Japanese successes, 258–260
  outlook for, 260–261
  overview of, 248–252
  structure of, 252–253
  withdrawal of larger firms, 256–258
Services, 39
Short time horizons, 39
Simultaneous engineering, 123
Sorge, Arndt, 89
Standards, 107, 140
  and economies of scale, 105
Steel industry, 14–15
  capital investment in, 282–283
  customer relations, 284
  and government, 282
  labor-management relations, 285
  minimills, 285–286, 287
  outlook for, 286
  overview of, 278–279
  technology, 279–281
  technology management, 283–284
  vertical linkages in, 102
Strategic sectors, 33
Streeck, Wolfgang, 89
Subcontractors, relations with, 48
Superconductivity, 107

Suppliers, cooperation with, 150
Systemic rigidities, 45

Technology, 23
  cost effective, 121
  effective use of, 133
  and government, 112
  integrating into the organization, 122
Textile industry, 16–18
  automation of, 296
  interfirm linkages, 300–301
  niche production, 297–300
  outlook for, 301–302
  performance of, 290–291
  protection of, 291–294
  structure of, 289–290
  as a sunset industry, 288–289
  vertical linkages in, 101–102, 104
  and wages, 294–295
Trade deficit, 33–35
Trade restrictions, 152
Training, 21–22, 48, 81–92, 125, 135, 312
  and external linkages, 127
  and flexibility, 89
  and organization, 89
  costs of, 88, 92
  in Germany, 87
  in Japan, 87–88
  learning at work versus learning in
    school, 83–89, 91

Union participation in decisions, 99

Videocassette recorders, 54, 56, 72, 74

Warehouse systems, automated, 95
Warner, Malcolm, 89
Westney, Eleanor, 90
White-collar workers, low productivity of,
  41
Work ethic, 81–82
Work force, new entrants to, 93

X-ray lithography, 107
Xerox, 9, 11, 52, 99, 117, 119, 121,
  123–124, 270–277

The industry reports are published in two volumes as

The Working Papers of the MIT Commission on Industrial Productivity
The MIT Commission on Industrial Productivity

Volume 1
The U.S. Automobile Industry in an Era of International Competition
The Transformation of the U.S. Chemicals Industry
The U.S. Commercial Aircraft Industry and Its Foreign Competitors
The Decline of U.S. Consumer Electronics Manufacturing

408 pages   ISBN 0-262-63126-1   MITWP1 $30.00

Volume 2
The U.S. Semiconductor, Computer, and Copier Industries
The U.S. Machine Tool Industry and Its Foreign Competitors
The Future of the U.S. Steel Industry in the International Marketplace
The U.S. Textile Industry
Education and Training in the United States

416 pages   ISBN 0-262-63127-X   MITWP2 $30.00

The two-volume set is available for $50.00.
ISBN 0-262-63128-8   MITWPS

For further information contact
The MIT Press
55 Hayward Street
Cambridge, MA 02142

Orders can be made by telephone at (617) 253-2884.